T.J. COLES was awarded a PhD from Pl 2017 for work on the aesthetic experie impaired people, with particular refer neuroscience and cognitive psychology. .. .. Logic, Coles is the author of *Britain's Secret Wars* and *The Great Brexit Swindle* (both 2016) and the editor of the forthcoming anthology *Voices for Peace* (2017). His articles have appeared in *Newsweek*, *The New Statesman*, teleSUR and *Z Magazine*, and in 2013 he was shortlisted for the Martha Gellhorn Prize for a series of articles about Libya.

Clairview Books Ltd.,
Russet, Sandy Lane,
West Hoathly,
W. Sussex RH19 4QQ

www.clairviewbooks.com

Published in Great Britain in 2017 by Clairview Books

A CIP catalogue record for this book is available from the British Library

Print book ISBN 978 1 905570 87 4
Ebook ISBN 978 1 905570 88 1

Cover by Morgan Creative (American dollar image © Dina design)
Typeset by DP Photosetting, Neath, West Glamorgan
Printed and bound by 4Edge Ltd, Essex

PRESIDENT TRUMP, INC.

HOW BIG BUSINESS AND NEOLIBERALISM EMPOWER POPULISM AND THE FAR-RIGHT

CLAIRVIEW

'Donald Trump's victory is an additional stone in the building of a new world.'

— Marine Le Pen, leader of the *Front National* (France)

Contents

Acronyms

ACA	Affordable Care Act (US, a.k.a. Obamacare)
AENM	Alliance of European National Movements
AFP	Americans for Prosperity
AN	National Alliance (Italy, Alleanza Nazionale)
BLM	Black Lives Matter (US)
BNP	British National Party
BZÖ	Alliance for the Future of Austria (Bündnis Zukunft Österreich)
CFR	Council on Foreign Relations (US)
CIA	Central Intelligence Agency (US)
DF	Danish People's Party (Dansk Folkeparti)
DHS	Department of Homeland Security (US)
DNC	Democratic National Committee and Democratic National Convention (US)
DVU	German People's Union (Deutsche Volksunion)
EO	Executive Order
EPI	Economic Policy Institute
EU	European Union
FBI	Federal Bureau of Investigation (US)
FN	Front National (France and Belgium)
FPÖ	Austrian Freedom Party (Freiheitliche Partei Österreichs)
FRP	Norwegian Progress Party (Fremskrittspartiet)
GATT	General Agreement on Tariffs and Trade
GDP	Gross Domestic Product
GNP	Gross National Product
HMO	Health Maintenance Organization
IMF	International Monetary Fund
Jobbik	Movement for a Better Hungary (Jobbik Magyarországért Mozgalom)
LGBT	Lesbian Gay Bisexual and Transgender (also Transsexual)

LN	Northern League (Italy, Lega Nord)
LPF	List Pim Fortuyn (Netherlands, Lijst Pim Fortuyn)
LPR	League of Polish Families (Liga Polskich Rodzin)
MI6	Military Intelligence Section Six (UK)
MIÉP	Justice and Life in Hungary (Magyar Igazság és Élet Pártja)
MS-FT	Tricolour Flame (Italy, Movimento Sociale Fiamma Tricolore)
MSI	Italian Social Movement (Movimento Sociale Italiano)
NAFTA	North American Free Trade Agreement
ND	National Democrats (Sweden, Nationaldemokraterna)
NF	National Front (UK)
NHS	National Health Service (UK)
NPD	National Democratic Party of Germany (Nationaldemokratische Partei Deutschlands)
NPT	Non-Proliferation Treaty
OECD	Organization for Economic Cooperation and Development
PAC	Political Action Committee
PEPs	Populist Extremist Parties
PRM	Greater Romania Party (Partidul România Mare)
PS	True Finns (Perussuomalaiset)
PVV	Party for Freedom (Netherlands, Partij voor de Vrijheid)
S&L	Savings and Loan
SD	Sweden Democrats (Sverigedemokraterna)
SME	Small-to-medium-sized enterprise
SNS	Slovak National Party (a.k.a. Slovenian National Party, Slovenská Národná Strana or Slovenska Nacionalna Stranka)
SOE	State-owned enterprise
SRP	Socialist Reich Party Germany (Sozialistische Reichspartei Deutschlands)
STEM	Science Technology Engineering Math
Super-PAC	Super-Political Action Committee
SVP	Swiss People's Party (Schweizerische Volkspartei)

TPP	Trans-Pacific Partnership
TTIP	Transatlantic Trade and Investment Partnership
UKIP	United Kingdom Independence Party
UN	United Nations
VAT	Value-added tax
VB	Flemish Interest/formerly Flemish Bloc (Vlaams Belang)
WTO	World Trade Organization

Propaganda Translator

Politicians and businesspeople use words to make us think they mean one thing (up) when in fact they mean something else, often the exact opposite (down). When ordinary people say 'free speech', they usually mean the right of individuals to speak freely without fear of reprisal or censorship. When politicians and their alt-right media supporters say 'free speech', they usually mean the right of wealthy white men to denigrate minorities.

The far-right and alt-right movements are full of semantic inversions. When they say 'nationalism' they don't mean nationalism in the sense of, say, protecting indigenous people's jobs and housing from economic migrants. They use the word 'nationalism' to mean the opposite: trading with and investing in foreign countries to profit corporations. Opposition to the EU is one example: former UKIP leader Nigel Farage opposes the European Union as a political entity but still wants to trade with it and with the rest of the world. When people in the alternative media say they are 'libertarian', they mean that they support the right of individuals and corporations to get rich at the expense of society.

To make clear what this book is about, here is our propaganda translator. It contains a word or a phrase and what people like Donald Trump, Nigel Farage and Marine Le Pen really mean when they use it.

Capitalism: A system in which a big government rescues and subsidizes otherwise failing corporations, often at the expense of workers and lower-middle class taxpayers. (Original meaning: A for-profit system of private enterprise free of state monopolies.)

Closed borders: Letting in and fast-tracking visas for high-skilled immigrants at the expense of low-skilled migrants and domestic high-skilled workers.

Corruption: Left, centrist and right-wing politicians who enact policies antithetical to the interests of the far-right/alt-right. The word usually invokes the failure of said parties to reduce taxes on the rich and instead adhere to the wishes of non-corporate constituents, like unions and voters.

Ending big government: Stopping tax money from going to the poor while keeping it flowing to the rich. (Original meaning: Stopping governments from interfering with individual freedoms.)

Free market: A highly subsidized economy in which protectionist barriers can be raised against superior foreign goods. Small-to-medium-sized businesses are allowed to fail and giant financial institutions and corporations are rescued by the state. (Original meaning: From the 19th century English system also known as *laissez-faire.*)

Level playing field: A global trade and investment system designed to favour US corporations. (Original meaning: A fair system in which each competitor has an equal chance of success.)

Liberal: Sense 1. A centrist politician (like Barack Obama or Hillary Clinton) who serves the interests of corporations, but not to the extent desired by right-wingers and far-righters. Sense 2. A member of the public who believes in taxing the rich and supporting the rights of vulnerable people (including migrants, people of colour, refugees and the poor). (Original meaning: From 18th century Enlightenment principles of fairness and tolerance.)

Libertarian: A person who advocates the freedom of individuals and corporations to make money at the expense of society. (Original meaning: From 18th century England and France, a person or group who or which advocates the rights of all men. With some exceptions, the rights of women was still anathema.)

Libertarianism: A political movement which supports cutting taxes for the wealthy.

Men's Rights: Opposition to gender equality.

Nationalism: Keeping out low-skilled migrants, supporting high-skilled migrants, letting foreign countries buy up domestic businesses (usually by offering them tax breaks) and negotiating trade and investment with foreign countries outside traditional apparatus and political unions.

Special interests: Usually unions, especially teachers' unions like the National Education Association of the United States.

White identity politics: White supremacy.

Preface

Mr Trump goes to Washington

'...*nonpoliticians represent the wave of the future*'.

— Donald J. Trump (with Dave Shiflett), *The America We Deserve*
(2000), p. 15

This book is about two things:

Part I concerns the dominant economic policy of our time: neo-liberalism. The book broadly defines neoliberalism as a combination of: making money from money, as opposed to making money from physical production and labour (financialization); rewriting rules to allow corporations to profit from risky transactions (deregulation); cutting back on social spending in order to balance national budgets (small government, a.k.a. structural adjustment); and insuring corporations against liquidation through taxation (big government, a.k.a. too big to fail).[1] It shows how neoliberalism empowers far-right politicians by making centrist parties less credible in that, by pursuing neoliberal policies, centrist parties fail to meet the needs of their voters.

The financial consequences of neoliberalism are: gross domestic product balloons; national debt balloons; profits for a tiny sector of the population balloon; a small number of individuals become mega-wealthy; wages for the middle classes stagnate; and wages for the poor decline. The root cause of the majority's misery is concealed by the corporate and even state-owned mainstream media. Phenomena like unemployment and high levels of welfare dependency are at best portrayed as the random workings of the world and at worst the fault of immigrants and scroungers.

The political consequences of neoliberalism are equally grim: centre-left and centre-right parties both pursue neoliberal policies and lose credibility and votes. A sizeable minority of voters made angry and hopeless by neoliberalism take to the extreme politics of people like Donald Trump, Nigel Farage and Marine Le Pen, who promised to take on the corrupt power elites by cracking down on easy targets.

Part II explodes the myths about Donald Trump, that he: 1) is a rebel; 2) is for the average working American; 3) is a protectionist; 4) is opposed to globalization; and 5) is acting of his own accord. The evidence presented here shows that although the majority of multibillionaires and corporations would have preferred a Hillary Clinton presidency (and indeed spent millions of dollars to get her elected), Trump is doing their bidding, not because Trump is a puppet, but because he shares their interests. Years before Trump came to office, big business (including the tech sector) lobbied Congress to bring factories, plants and jobs back to America (for reasons we explain later). Big business also lobbied to 'reform' immigration policy (meaning crack down on low-skilled immigrants).

The introduction defines neoliberalism. It explores what effect neoliberalism has had on mainstream politics in the US and Europe. It argues that neoliberalism is part of the overall trend of voter disengagement.

Chapters 1 & 2 trace the policy decisions in the US under the Democratic-controlled Congresses of Presidents Nixon and Reagan. The chapters demonstrate that privatization and deregulation are the major tenets of neoliberalism. The chapters also show that the same policy continued under the Democratic Clinton administration in the 1990s and how it led to low levels of union participation and political engagement. Rising unemployment and a weakened middle class were the main social consequences of this policy.

Chapters 3 & 4 are about the connection between neoliberalism and the rise of the far-right in Europe and the USA. In the US, it is actually the middle class (those earning $50–150K per annum) who are the biggest Trump and Tea Party supporters, not the poor. The so-called Alternative Right (the American term for the far-right) emerged as a fringe of the Tea Party and went on to hijack the Republican Party. In Europe, however, the far-right attracts mostly working class as opposed to middle class voters. We define the far-right in Chapter 4, as its emergence became more apparent after the global Finance Crisis of 2008. The Crisis was largely a result of neoliberal deregulation and financial speculation. Chapter 5 is about America's alt-right. Chapters 6 & 7 analyse Trump's cabinet and policies. Chapter 8 is about tax cuts and lobbying. Chapter 9 is about Trump's stand on foreign policy. It argues that we are being pushed closer to annihilation by America's reckless pursuit of nuclear-armed global hegemony, regardless of who is President.

The conclusion explores Trump's connections with the deep state, particularly the FBI. It compares Trump's behaviour toward the media with Obama's and demonstrates that although Trump is less superficially pleasant, he is merely following a trajectory. It also argues for a progressive politics and voter engagement at the local level.

Dodd–Frank: 'Death by a Thousand Cuts'

The Dodd–Frank Wall Street Reform and Consumer Protection Act is commonly known as Dodd–Frank after the representatives Barney Frank and Chris Dodd who introduced it. Retaining or repealing Dodd–Frank is a litmus test for how serious a President is about maintaining financial regulations and enhancing or ending the neoliberal project. Shockwaves from the global Financial Crisis are still being felt today. The Crisis resulted from the preceding decades of financial deregulation. Far from 'draining the swamp' as he promised to do on his campaign trail, Donald Trump is pursuing neoliberalism. His first step was weakening Dodd–Frank.[2]

In 2010, President Obama signed into law Dodd–Frank: the first step taken in 80 years to impose some control over the financial system and prevent another systemic crisis. Dodd–Frank amounted to the most stringent set of regulations on banks and financial institutions since the Great Depression of the 1930s. It went further than any preceding bill towards ending the institutionalized greed which caused the Financial Crisis of 2007–10.[3]

Obama's cabinet was a cabinet of bankers, so Dodd–Frank was far from perfect. The layers of regulation harmed small-to-medium-sized businesses, especially local banks. Media coverage of the Act inferred that it would hurt big business, which is hardly surprising given that the mass media are for-profit corporations which benefit from deregulation. The public had mixed feelings about Dodd–Frank, due in part to the limits it imposed on small-to-medium size businesses and the media's propaganda campaign against the Act.

An investigation into print media coverage of Dodd–Frank in the first couple of years of its enactment concludes that '[press] articles were more likely to say that the Dodd–Frank Act has or potentially may have a negative impact on the economic viability of U.S. banks or U.S.-based companies'. According to a Pew Research Center study undertaken in 2013, '49% of the public believed the government has not gone far enough in regulating financial institutions and the markets'. However, '[n]early as many (43%) believed the government had gone too far'.[4]

This is key to understanding the appeal of Trump among the minority of Americans who voted for him. As Arlie Russell Hochschild points out in her book on future Trump voters, many Americans, particularly small-to-medium-sized business owners, are now dependent on large financial institutions for several reasons: 1) large companies (which Dodd–Frank regulated) sub-contract to smaller ones (and defer the costs of Dodd–Frank to the smaller businesses); 2) many pensions are now tied to the stock market, so it is imperative for the market to boom in order to keep Americans' pensions valuable; and 3) many small-to-medium sized business owners have shares in larger companies. It is mainly this demographic of business-owning, pension-investing middle class Americans who voted for Trump.[5]

The data suggest that 79% of people who support the Republican Party's offshoot movement called the Tea Party agree that government regulation is excessive. This compares to 64% of Republicans and only 26% of Democrats. Part of Trump's appeal to the large minority who voted for him was his promise to dismantle regulation, supposedly to help the average working American. But Trump is merely advancing the neoliberal agenda: to give huge tax breaks to corporations and privatize social spending which will take a hit in the absence of federal tax revenues.

Trump's reaction to Dodd–Frank was a litmus test for his commitment to neoliberalism.[6]

Immediately after its enactment, US corporate lobbies attacked Dodd–Frank. Since it was passed, financial institutions spent hundreds of millions of dollars lobbying Congress to repeal it. Rather than full repeal, the strategy was 'death by a thousand cuts', in the words of Marcus Stanley of Americans for Financial Reform. The first cut was a bill passed by a majority of Republicans in 2014.[7]

It is alleged by *Forbes* that the liquidity firm Citigroup drafted a large part of the bill passed in 2014 which repealed a significant part of Dodd–Frank. Virtually every major financial institution lobbied to get the anti-Dodd–Frank bill passed: the American Bankers Association, the American Council of Life Insurers, Citigroup, the Credit Union National Association, Goldman Sachs, JPMorgan, the Securities Industry and Financial Markets Association, Wells Fargo and others. In 2015, the *New York Times* reported: 'In the span of a month, the nation's biggest banks and investment firms have twice won passage of measures to weaken regulations intended to help lessen the risk of another financial crisis'.[8]

The ultra-right elements of the Republican Party, notably the Tea Party, actively supported the anti-Dodd–Frank lobby. But as we shall see, certain individuals (including Trump's then-advisor Steve Bannon) believed that the Republican Party and the Tea Party movement was not fully committed to the neoliberal project. Giving total control over to Wall Street, big energy and so on, required a new far-right splinter group, known as the alternative-right (or alt-right). Trump rode to the White House in this alt-right Trojan Horse.

Trump was elected in part on a promise to repeal Dodd–Frank, which he claimed was harming American workers and tangling otherwise functioning businesses in red tape. In February 2017, Trump signed a law (H.J. Res. 41) repealing Dodd–Frank measures to force energy companies to disclose their foreign financial transactions. *USA Today* alleges that the repeal followed lobbying efforts from big oil, including ExxonMobil led by Rex Tillerson, Trump's Secretary of State.[9]

In the neoliberal system, the wealth of the mega-rich is accrued at the expense of the middle-class and poor majority. Neoliberalism has alienated millions of voters, who often see politicians as little more than puppets of big business. Many voters have simply given up on politics. Others have mobilized in unhealthy and destructive ways. Instead of organizing and putting pressure on the centre-left to adopt more progressive policies, many have turned to the far-right.[10]

In Europe, neoliberalism brought us Britain's exit from the EU (Brexit) and empowered France's far-right party, the *Front National* (FN). Now that an Islamophobic, racist misogynist is leading the world's most powerful nation, ugly, repressed tendencies are coming to the surface in a sizeable minority of people. The main champion of Brexit was Nigel Farage, then-leader of the UK Independence Party. Both he and the FN's leader, Marine Le Pen, attended exclusive meetings with the new US President in Trump Tower. Both have expressed their support for Trump.[11]

The Trump cabinet, the architects of Brexit and Le Pen herself are all advocates of neoliberalism. Le Pen has spoken of the need for a strong state to support business and growth. Farage has a background in banking and is keen to promote so-called 'free trade' with the US. Trump advocates bilateral free trade on US-centric terms. As this book will demonstrate, far-right parties support and want to accelerate the very pro-business policies that harmed many of their voters.

Big money and bigotry

'Do not have illusions; the world is a brutal place full of vicious people.'

— Donald J. Trump and Bill Zanker, *Think Big* (2007), p. 176

For over 40 years, British and American politicians have adopted neoliberal economic policies which have made a few individuals very wealthy at the expense of the majority. Over the last 25 years (particularly with the adoption of the Maastricht Treaty of 1992), European governments gradually signed up to the project. Money is the god of neoliberalism. It makes profit the centre of all human activity and concern. If something is not profitable, like social security or healthcare, it must be either eliminated or restructured. Neoliberalism sees everything as a business model. It involves tying the real economy of manufacturing, design and spending to the fake economy of liquidity, currency (de)valuations and bond trading. It involves privatizing all public services while using tax money to buoy failing financial institutions.[1]

What is Neoliberalism?

The term 'neoliberalism' is context-dependent and open to interpretation. Scholars agree on one thing: that critics of the policy tend to call it 'neoliberalism', while advocates use terms like *laissez-faire* and free market capitalism. Professor Bob Jessop's definition of neoliberalism is included as an entry in the *Wiley-Blackwell Encyclopedia of Globalization*. Citing Thatcherism and Reaganomics, Jessop defines 'neoliberal regime shifts' away from state control and public ownership as 'liberalization, deregulation, privatization, market proxies in the public sector, internationalization, and cuts in direct taxation'. This is the broad definition of neoliberalism that we use in this book. Let's look at some similar definitions used by established (and some establishment) institutions:[2]

Vice-President of the European Commission, Viviane Reding, describes neoliberalism as giving 'power to the markets rather than to politicians'. Democratic principles, including public ownership, would be reduced and eliminated by 'market discipline'. Regulation of 'economic or financial policy at [the] European level could only have caused harmful market distortions', according to the neo-liberal agenda. Concerning the European Union, Reding says: 'The fact that the Member States would continue to pursue their own, differing national economic, budgetary, tax, and social policies was not a weakness', according to neoliberals, 'but one of the great achievements of Maastricht' — a treaty led by Britain and signed by the Member States in 1992. Maastricht led to the single currency (the euro).[3]

Reding's point, that neoliberals find it easier to pursue their agenda by dismantling political unions like the EU and instead pursue so-called nationalist agendas, is key to understanding what is happening with the uneven rise of the so-called nationalist far-right. As this book documents, many supposed political nationalists (like Farage and Le Pen) are actually economic *internationalists* who believe in 'free trade'.

The World Bank was established by the US and Britain after World War II. It was designed to lend poor countries (re)con-struction money. It is responsible for death and misery in the third world, as it loaned corrupt dictators billions of dollars. Professor Grzegorz W. Kolodko is an economic reformer in Poland. In a World Bank paper, he defines neoliberalism as '[l]ow inflation, positive interest rates, balanced budget, fast privatisation, currency exchange rate either fixed or flouting, [and] taxes (low, of course)'. He concludes that the overall purpose of neoliberalism is '[t]o improve the financial standing of narrow groups of elites at the expense of the majority of society'. To achieve this end, 'neoliber-alism uses in politics and policies ... expressive liberal ideas ... [such] as liberty and democracy, private ownership and entrepre-neurship, competition and economic freedom'. This is the language that populists like Trump and his alt-right or libertarian-supporting internet media (like Alex Jones) employ to win votes. In reality, says

Kolodko, when these neo-'libertarians', including France's *Front National* leader Marine Le Pen, use words like 'individualism' and 'liberty', they are taking about *corporate* individuals and liberty for the rich.[4]

The International Monetary Fund (IMF) is a branch of the United Nations and, like the World Bank, was also established by the US and Britain after World War II. It acts as a credit enforcer for the World Bank. It is also responsible for massive levels of death and destruction in poor countries via so-called structural adjustment programmes. Nobel Prize-winning economist Joseph Stiglitz makes this case in his book *Globalization and Its Discontents*. (But he does so by exonerating his own institution, the World Bank.)

An article published by the IMF identifies ten characteristics of neoliberalism (also known as the Washington Consensus).[*] These originated in the USA in the 1970s and especially the 1980s, and were exported to the world, starting with Latin America. The characteristics are: 1) fiscal discipline (balancing budgets at the expense of social spending); 2) restructuring public spending away from health, education and social security; 3) cutting taxes for the rich; 4) liberalizing interest rates at the expense of utilities and housing; 5) liberalizing exchange rates, which cause fluctuation and speculation in international markets; 6) liberalizing trade by, for instance, making foreign countries privatize their national resources; 7) liberalizing foreign direct investment to allow foreign powers to take advantage of cheap labour; 8) privatizing domestic assets and services; 9) deregulating domestic financial institutions; and 10) protecting property rights (including intellectual property for technology and drugs) over human rights.[5]

The above IMF article talks about 'rebranding' neoliberalism, given its negative connotations. This is happening today (see Propaganda Translator), with politicians like Trump using protectionist language whilst arranging bilateral 'free trade' deals with

---

[*] To be clear, the author of the IMF paper defines what he naively thought to be neoliberal policies. As he continued implementing the programmes, he realized the opposite was true, as he says in the article. Hence we have adjusted the definition(s) accordingly.

foreign countries; closing the border to low-skilled migrants while championing those with high-skills; talking like a radical anti-corporatist while offering massive tax cuts to big business.

A paper published by the World Economic Forum defines neo-liberalism as 'an economic worldview that wrongly assumed that the benefits of economic growth would trickle down to those at the bottom'. (In the real world, it is questionable whether neoliberal advocates really believed in the trickle-down effect.) Neoliberalism also means 'government should embrace austerity and do little more than let markets work'. (Interestingly, the Harvard professor who wrote the article concludes: 'Until voters learn what to ask for from their governments, they are bound to dislike what they end up getting'. Kolodko – the Polish reformer – argues that the media's role is to ensure that the public doesn't even know what to ask for in the way of alternatives, hence the far-right's tendency to blame the vulnerable.)[6]

Finally, the Organization for Economic Cooperation and Development finds that governments tried to fix the negative consequences of neoliberalism by adopting more neoliberal policies. The author writes that the post-Washington Consensus came into being after the Financial Crisis of 2008. Rather than reversing the trends, the programme 'expands on earlier neo-liberal prescriptions, but with greater emphasis on the "neo", i.e. free market economics with a stronger policy environment and national equity rather than national wealth as the end goal of economic activity'. It did so by imposing crippling austerity, particularly in Europe.[7]

What is Populism?

Like 'neoliberalism' and 'far-right', populism is an elastic term covering a wide range of ideas and perceptions. The UN High Commissioner for Human Rights, Zeid Ra'ad Al Hussein, describes populism and the process as follows:

> Populists use half-truths and oversimplification – the two scalpels of the arch propagandist, and here the internet and social media are a

perfect rail for them, by reducing thought into the smallest packages: sound-bites; tweets. Paint half a picture in the mind of an anxious individual, exposed as they may be to economic hardship and through the media to the horrors of terrorism. Prop this picture up by some half-truth here and there and allow the natural prejudice of people to fill in the rest. Add drama, emphasizing it's all the fault of a clear-cut group, so the speakers lobbing this verbal artillery, and their followers, can feel somehow blameless.[8]

Two scholars at the Harvard Kennedy School — Inglehart and Norris — write that economic insecurity and cultural backlash are the two common themes underlying populism. 'There are many interpretations of [populism] and numerous attempts to identify the political parties and movements that fall into this category'. The three common features according to these authors are: anti-establishmentarianism, authoritarianism and nativism. However, as we shall see, some left-wing populists do not fit neatly into this category. Populists emphasize the needs of the 'silent majority' over 'corrupt elites'. The authors imply that this emphasis is made in order to win votes, not actually help the 'silent majority' to improve their lot.[9]

There are two kinds of populism: extreme right and progressive left. The broad majority fears right-wing populism because it usually consists of wealthy elite groups hijacking the concerns of working people in order to elevate those marginal elites to power by less than democratic means. Such means include intimidation of political opponents, the immediate passing of laws which consolidate the populists' power and the targeting of minority groups.

Progressive populists target the elites and the upper- and upper-middle classes. They come to power by bringing class consciousness to working people: that working and lower-middle class people are exploited by powerful elites. Progressive populists can use authoritarian means, such as ignoring constitutional procedures, in order to redistribute wealth, promote universal education and provide free healthcare. Similarly, right-wing populists use unconstitutional means but for right-wing ends: to privatize social resources and gain support for these actions among working people by blaming vulnerable minorities.

According to the Humanist Federation in a report for the European Union, populism 'rejects the political system'. Populists use 'simplistic and antagonistic images', including opposition to elites and national sovereignty. The report also claims that populists tend to rhetorically oppose globalization. The report is flawed, however, in that a left-wing populist government like that led by Hugo Chávez in Venezuela, welcomed globalization and the sharing of resources with other countries. Chávez used unconstitutional means to retain power (authoritarian) but supplied free fuel to freezing US citizens in the USA during winter, and arranged dentistry and doctor sharing programmes with neighbouring Cuba in exchange for oil.[10]

Chávez was also part of the so-called Pink Tide which sought to integrate Latin American countries into an economic system free of US domination. Chávez exemplifies the progressive populist who welcomed a people's globalization. After years of Chávez rule, Venezuela's social indicators rose considerably in terms of life expectancy, infant mortality and employment. But this was at the expense of wealthy business elites, whose share of wealth declined, as did parliamentary democracy as Chávez clung to power by ignoring constitutional procedures. The Chávez regime also failed to distribute wealth to the very poorest of Venezuela and poverty remained acute.[11]

Exploring Far-right & Alt-right

Definition. Dr Matthew Goodwin of the University of Nottingham is an Associate Fellow of the Royal Institute for International Affairs (Chatham House) in the UK. In a Chatham House report, Goodwin refers to far-right parties as populist extremist parties (PEPs). (Goodwin does not connect the dots between neoliberalism and support for the far-right.) PEPs, he says, share two characteristics: 1) they oppose immigration and ethnic/cultural diversity and 2) oppose establishment party politics. Since the 1980s, says Goodwin, Europe's PEPs have moved from fringe groups to joining coalitions in some countries (see Chapter 4), even in countries with a history of fascism: fascism being the logical outcome and extreme conclusion of PEPs.[12]

Dr Thomas Greven is Associate Professor at the Freie University Berlin. He wrote a paper on extremism for the Washington-based think tank Friedrich Ebert Foundation. In it, he correlates far-right tendencies with populism. Far-right parties are united by a common theme: 'Populism's central and permanent narrative is the juxtaposition of a (corrupt) "political class," "elite," or "establishment," and "the people," as whose sole authentic voice the populist party bills itself'. This is the platform on which Donald Trump ran for President in 2016.[13]

The dark twist is that the 'us versus them' dialectic is contingent on the 'us' being a homogenous cultural entity, of for instance white Europeans or white Americans. 'They' are coming to destroy our culture. 'They' are usually Muslims, but they can also be black people, immigrants and refugees of any religion or ethnicity, homosexuals, transgender persons, etc. According to this narrative, the corrupt elites (usually referred to as 'liberals') favour 'them' (immigrants, Muslims) over 'us', the exploited and forgotten ones. Greven concludes that the controversial message of the far-right is a marriage of convenience for the mainstream media because it is a profit-making, ratings-orientated institution. The more outlandish and vulgar the far-right, the more press coverage and airtime their leaders are afforded because they sell newspapers, generate online hits and boost TV ratings.[14]

America's Alternative-Right. The alt-right emphasizes 'patriotism'. Trump came to power for three reasons: 1) he and his circle of far-righters infiltrated the Republican Party and used it as a vehicle to mobilize America's angry middle class against the unpatriotic global establishment; 2) he succeeded because mainstream politics on the left and right failed to maintain the status quo; and 3) low voter turnout created a vacuum which Trump successfully filled. Because of points 2 and 3, Europe's far-right is also gaining ground. Europe's centre-right governments are turning ultra-right in pursuit of neoliberalism.[15]

America's alt-right mainly consists of well-off white men with a persecution complex who hate Islam and want to destroy anything humane about American society: the chance for universal healthcare, free education and social security. They believe, or some pretend, that their very existence is under threat by social progress.[16]

The American alt-right is an amorphous group which shares a basic philosophy: the duty of the American individual to make money. But usually (not always) the 'individual' means a white, Christian, male, corporate or entrepreneurial individual. They believe in small government for society and, by implication, a big government to rescue financial institutions. Some alt-righters believe in putting domestic manufacturing and production first.[17]

Other alt-righters believe in making trade deals with foreign entities. Their idea of 'nationalism' is nationalism which suits them and their businesses. In this respect, the alt-right — including Trump — has much in common with so-called libertarians and Republicans. Rather than explain this inconsistency, the contradiction is generally avoided in alt-right discussion forums and in alt-right media. The alt-right also draws heavily on Christian evangelical fundamentalism. Many of its supporters are Christian fundamentalists, as are many of its leaders. With these interests, the alt-right shares common ground with right-wing (as opposed to centrist) elements of the Republican Party.[18]

An alt-right precursor came to prominence in 2008–10, calling itself the Tea Party. It grew in popularity until circa 2012, when Obama was re-elected. The libertarian Tea Party movement was largely seen as a failure. Crucially, the Tea Party was financed by and in many ways was an offshoot of various institutes founded by wealthy Republicans (notably the Koch brothers), who have pushed for tax elimination and the destruction of social services, including public education and social security. Indeed, the anti-tax, anti-socialism agenda is another common characteristic of the alt-right and the broad right. Where they differ, however, is that the broad right is afraid of losing mainstream voters by pushing too hard for tax reform. The alt-right has no such fears.[19]

Where the alt-right differs from the Tea Party and the more centrist elements of the Republican Party, however, is in its blatant racism and xenophobia (now called white identity politics). The so-called liberal media is racist in that it tends to focus on crime committed by people of colour more than it does by crime committed by white people. It largely suppressed, for instance, cases of police shootings and therefore made the Black Lives Matter movement seem like a spontaneous uprising by angry black Americans, rather than the legitimate and mounting response to ongoing oppression. The mainstream has also largely ignored the fact that under the Democratic black President Barack Obama, America's prison population continued to grow as the largest in the world, with people of colour disproportionately targeted. The media also neglect to cover racial profiling in jobs, education and the electoral system. These factors combine to perpetuate the class struggle of many black Americans.[20]

The right-wing, libertarian alternative media is even more racist in that it exaggerates stereotypes and takes crime statistics out of context. Citing 'factoids', people like Rush Limbaugh and Alex Jones portray the struggle for equality by black Americans as a liberal plot by globalist communists to destroy white privilege. The same is true of Islam. The mainstream tends to imply that Muslims are dangerous by giving far more coverage to Islamic terrorists than it does to war crimes against Muslims committed by America, Britain and France. The alternative media, particularly the libertarian right, take it further and regularly refer to Muslims as a danger to the very survival of America.[21]

The political alt-right takes this kind of racism to its logical conclusion. It believes that whites are not only becoming a minority in the West, but that the white race is facing extinction. It believes that political correctness is a free-pass for Muslims to threaten democratic and, crucially, Christian values. It believes that feminism and social movements, like Black Lives Matter, seek to undermine the status of white (mainly Christian) men. The alt-right, right-wing and centrists in the Republican Party also share opposition to abortion and usually cite Christianity as a reason for preserving life, even at the expense of the mother. They forget their Christian values when it comes to supporting the death penalty: another thing that most alt-right, right and centrist Republicans have in common. In opposing abortion, they (including their female supporters) reinforce patriarchy.[22]

Trump's ex-chief strategist, Steve Bannon, is part of the alt-right. Bannon believes that Islam is a threat to the survival of America. He said in a speech in 2011 that the Republican Party hasn't the will to eliminate the burden of social security, which is a drain on his class of millionaires and billionaires. As a result, Bannon — with the backing of billionaire Robert Mercer — sponsored an insurgency, led by Trump, within the Republican Party to mobilize the millions of (mainly) white, middle class Americans who have been betrayed by left-wing politicians and their counterparts on the centre-right. Bannon worked for Goldman Sachs and, like Trump, is a free trade advocate. He made millions with online news and as a Hollywood producer.[23]

There is little doubt that Trump himself represents the alt-right.[24]

Europe's Far-Right. Every European far-right party and leader is opposed to the EU as a political organization, but nearly every single one of them advocates trading with and investing in European countries. Opposition to the EU as a political entity does not in itself make an individual or organization far-right, but each far-right party shares as a policy objective, abolition of the political union.[25]

Europe's far-right is slightly different to America's in that the *fundamentalist* religious element is largely missing. But religion plays a role in European political extremism where Islam, homosexuality and abortion are concerned. Most far-right parties in Europe are not reliant upon a strong Christian base, the way the Tea Party or alt-right is in the United States. In terms of religion, Europe's far-right has something in common with America's, namely its hatred of Islam. One of the common themes binding European political extremism is its citation of Islam as a mortal threat to European values.[26]

As we shall see in Chapter 4, what precisely constitutes the

European far-right is a difficult question because some parties believe in state-democratic control over national resources. Others (mainly Britain's UKIP and France's FN) believe in neoliberalism. One of the other commonalities is nationalism. Nearly all far-right parties in Europe are opposed in one way or another to the European Union. Contradictorily, they may wish to continue trading with the EU (i.e., to maintain neoliberal principles), but they evoke national sovereignty as a way of mobilizing support among disaffected voters.

One of the crucial distinctions between the European far-right and the American far-right is that, with some exceptions, the European far-right appeals to working class people. In America, the alt-right is a luxury of the middle class, again with some exceptions; the reason being that America's wealth, until the 1970s, was unprecedented. Even today, with all the economic hardship, most Americans are middle class but struggle to support themselves. In Europe, there are larger numbers of poor (measured by income) but much higher standards of social welfare, with the exception of Britain and many Eastern European, ex-Soviet countries.[27]

Both Britain and the US came early to the neoliberal programme and their poor and middle class populations watched their standards of living decline accordingly. In Europe, however, wealth was more equally distributed. Until the structural changes in the early-1990s, Europe's rich were and are generally less well off than America's rich. Now Europe and America are hotspots for billionaires. Countries like Austria, the Netherlands and Hungary retain superior pension, education, social security and health systems to those of the UK and the US. (Once, Britain's National Health Service was a world leader. But after decades of gradual destruction, that is no longer the case.)[28]

Europe's far-right appeals to the working classes who have been particularly affected, not only by the accelerated inequality wrought by neoliberalism but also by the loosening of social safety nets. In the USA, Trump tends to appeal to people over 35 years of age. In Europe, the far-right can appeal to people of all ages. In the US, the alt-right appeals to men and women (mostly men), whereas in

Europe the far-right tends to appeal more to men. European far-righters advocate closing borders to refugees, expelling migrants and welcoming specific groups of economic migrants. Both groups share a blanket distrust of Islam. Another common theme is the belief that the root cause of worker insecurity and broken social systems is refugees and immigrants, as well as the European Union as a political entity and its globalist agenda.[29]

Another way in which Europe's far-right voter base differs from America's is that most Europeans who vote for or support far-right parties tend to have less education than people who vote for centrist or left parties. In the US, many Trump voters and Tea Party supporters attended college and/or hold at least a college degree.[30]

Neoliberalism Empowers the Far-right

The social consequences of the neoliberal project have been devastating for working and middle class people. As this book will document in greater detail, the wealth and prosperity of most Americans was stunning by world standards. In any nation-state system, there are losers, and this is not to imply that a better system was impossible. After the Wall Street Crash of 1929 and the Great Depression that followed, America's economy was tightly regulated. The 1930s enjoyed a Wall Street-funded social programme called the New Deal. Particularly after World War II until the 1960s, most Americans gained a standard of living unique among nations. This 'golden age' was especially true for young white men and women. Union membership was strong compared to the early-1900s, when unions were brutally oppressed. Workers were politically engaged. But by the 1970s and '80s, the economists pushing neoliberalism had succeeded in finding political sponsors.[31]

Wealth started going into the pockets of the rich faster than it went to the working classes, many of whom had reached middle class status. As a result, a few middle class Americans became very wealthy, others became poor and the rest struggled to maintain their living standards. This all happened after the Civil Rights struggle had been won, at least technically. (For most black Americans, segregation was replaced by ghettoization and mass incarceration.) In the minds of many white Americans who grew up in this 'golden age' and gradually lost their status, black people and political liberals were to blame.[32]

The Democratic Bill Clinton administration made matters worse by further deregulating the economy in the 1990s. In Europe, particularly in the UK which followed the US model, the situation was equally desperate, except that most European countries never had a middle class as prosperous as America's. As the middle class weakened, a new generation of super-wealthy multimillionaires emerged from the state-sponsored financial and technology sectors. The sector is a big lobby today pressing for tax reform, job repatriation and migration reform (as we shall see). As the years went on – even after the Financial Crisis of 2008 – a growing number of people became mega-wealthy, reaching billionaire and multi-billionaire status. Their wealth was accrued from ownership of private assets, financial market manipulation (as enabled by Reagan, Clinton and others), real estate (like Trump) and the luxury goods market such as hotel services (like Trump).[33]

Europe has been suffering the neoliberal project since 1992, when the Maastricht Treaty brought the single currency (euro) to the majority of European Member States (excluding Britain) and imposed neoliberal principles across the continent, even during recession. As research in this book shows, the more neoliberalism was imposed on Europe, the faster people's standards declined, and the stronger the far-right became. This was especially true after impoverished Eastern European, ex-Soviet bloc countries (notably Poland) joined the EU in 2003. Hundreds of thousands of poor people looked forward to a new life in Western Europe. As Western Europeans' standard of living declined and a deceptive media protected the neoliberal agenda, many Europeans wrongly connected the dots and saw economic migrants as a threat.[34]

In predominately white nations like Austria and Belgium, the so-called 'war on terror' launched by the George W. Bush administration and supported by Britain gave the far-right a stronger anti-Muslim platform. As Muslims from North African and Middle Eastern states continued to seek refuge from both war and neoliberalism, and as terrorism hit Europe, Islam was demonized and a warped version of Christianity adopted by many European far-right parties. The use of religion to divide people is a form of identity politics. The most important form of identity politics, class, is missing from the debate, thanks to a media construction that portrays the wealthy as hard-working, lucky and paragons of virtue.[35]

There are more Christian Republicans than Christian Democrats. Donald Trump has successfully mobilized a large Christian-right voter base by using inflammatory anti-Muslim rhetoric and executive orders to try to ban many people from several Muslim countries from entering and working in the USA. But more than this, Trump has presented himself as a non-politician. Given the understandable hatred of politicians, Congress and the media by large numbers of Americans, Trump seized the opportunity to present himself as the nemesis of the corrupt establishment. Very wealthy people, including energy entrepreneurs the Koch Brothers, had already built up an alt-right political movement which gave Trump a voter base. It started as the Tea Party. It believes in making neoliberalism worse by cutting taxes for the rich and restricting migration. But it presents itself as being on the side of regular, hard-working Americans.[36]

Likewise in Europe, many far-right parties (including UKIP and the *Front National*) advocate neoliberalism but simultaneously present themselves as friends of the working class.

The Nationalism Hoax

To most people, especially poor and middle class voters, 'nationalism' means keeping immigrants out of the country, putting indigenous people first, producing and manufacturing domestically and buying and selling national and local goods.

This is demonstrably *not* the agenda of far-right leaders like Donald Trump, Nigel Farage and Marine Le Pen. They rant about Muslims and migrants in order to win votes. But they are not nationalists in any sense of the above definition. They are advocates of neoliberal globalization. The Orwellian propaganda system in which we live — both the mainstream and much of the for-profit 'alternative media' — tells us the opposite: that they are nationalists actively opposed to globalization. We regularly read headlines like 'the end of globalization', 'the age of protectionism', etc. It is easy to prove whose interests Trump et al. really represent.

The Republican Party. Now led by the far-right insurgent, Donald Trump, America's Republican Party is pursuing a global trade strategy and a domestic deregulation agenda. The global trade agenda is bilateralism. Instead of working out trade and investment deals with blocs (like the EU or the Asia Pacific region), the US will now work one-to-one with countries. This way America has the strategic advantage. In June 2016, candidate Trump told workers in a recycling plant: 'Globalization has made the financial elite, who donate to politicians, very, very wealthy. I used to be one of them'. But now he isn't? What caused Trump's miraculous transformation from billionaire globalist to billionaire nationalist? As we document in Chapter 8, big American businesses (including Apple and Goldman Sachs) lobbied hard to get the same immigration curbs and tax repatriation system that Trump delivered.[37]

'We need bilateral trade deals', candidate Trump told the recycling plant workers. 'We do not need to enter into another massive international agreement that ties us up and binds us down'. In his memo to the US Trade Rep., President Trump wrote: 'Trade with other nations is, and always will be, of paramount importance to my Administration'. Hence Trump's decision to withdraw from the multilateral Trans-Pacific Partnership (TPP) in favour of 'deal[ing] directly with individual countries on a one-on-one (or bilateral) basis in negotiating future trade deals'. With the usual hot air about protecting American workers, the White House states that Trump's decision to withdraw from the TPP, 'ushers in a new era of U.S. trade policy in which the Trump Administration will pursue bilateral free trade opportunities with allies around the world, wherever possible, to promote American industry'.[38]

The UK Independence Party. UKIP's ex-leader Nigel Farage has always advocated expanding free trade. In the real world, this is called neoliberal globalization. In the Orwellian inversion of reality it is called nationalism. Farage is a former banker and investor. 'We earn our way to national prosperity by free trade with the world', he says. That's a strange sort of nationalism and certainly not the kind his working class supporters want. In 2013, he highlighted the importance of the financial institutions which make up the neo-liberal economy. But he did not criticize them; he criticized the EU's power to regulate them. Farage is also a neoliberal in that he advocates deregulation: 'Financial services make up 10 per cent of the economy. It's ... insurance. Reinsurance. Stocks and shares. Futures. Commodities. Pension funds'. Farage said that the EU, 'is totally irrelevant to this industry whether we have a Labour or a Tory government because their livelihoods are now regulated by a [Commission which] is no friend of ours'. Farage said that by leaving the EU, '[w]e get back the ability to strike free trade deals. We can abolish tariffs on African produce'.[39]

After the Brexit result in 2016, Farage reiterated his commitment to global trade. He told the European Parliament: 'let's cut between us a sensible tariff-free deal, and thereafter recognise that the United Kingdom will be your friend, that we will trade with you, we will cooperate with you, we will be your best friends in the world'. Hardly the language of someone who wishes to see the end of the EU and concentrate on British farming, fishing, production and development.[40]

Le Front National, led by Marine Le Pen. Arguably for the first time, this party became a serious contender in the May 2017 French presidential election. Le Pen was beaten due in large part to low voter turnout. As in the US election 2016, most French voters liked neither candidate very much. When it comes to France's overseas territories (*outre-mer*) Le Pen's idea of economic nationalism is creating tax-free zones for foreign investors and employing local, low-paid labour. These will be known as French overseas 'priority investment zones'. Like Trump at home, Le Pen plans to cut civil service pay for overseas workers. Under such a scheme, teachers working in French territories will lose 30% of their salaries. So much for populism. 'I am attached to French public service', says Le Pen. 'I am attached to a form of social security for the most vul-nerable, I am obviously for a free economy, I am a big defender of entrepreneurs'. Le Pen says she advocates, 'a form of social security'. If it's anything like Trump's it will amount to privatization and financialization, meaning that social security is turned into a tradable commodity.[41]

Le Pen advocates a strong state to support big business. She praises France's 'association between the strategist state, which represents a defence of the interest of the entire population and the superior interests of the country, and the great entrepreneurs that created the power behind our Country'. She goes on to say that, '[i]n France, it's notably by the development of the public command and public research that all of our industrial giants were able to take part in a conquest of the world'. Conquest of the world? So much for nationalism. 'We have to help business and defend the markets. But the state has to be there to prevent drifts, to prevent excess, to enforce the rules of the game'. So much for small government.[42]

The Dutch Freedom Party. The Freedom Party is led by Geert Wilders, who was beaten in the March 2017 election by Liberal, Mark Rutte. In 2005 he wrote: '[The] Netherlands must, along with other countries that believe in free trade, as soon as possible [sic] open formal negotiations with the member states of NAFTA', the North American Free Trade Agreement (US, Mexico and Canada), 'to come to an Atlantic Free Trade Association'. This will be a version of the Transatlantic Trade and Investment Partnership, hated by socialists because of its privatization clauses and hated by EU corporations because of the exclusion of a financial chapter.[43]

Britain and the Netherlands have close financial ties. Several multinational corporations are Anglo–Dutch. These include Shell oil, Unilever foods and Elsevier publishing and arms. Wilders's economic position has softened (slightly) over the last decade. His 2004 manifesto was pro-market, anti-social welfare. Press reports indicate that he is still pro-market. In Trump language, Wilders said that for every new piece of legislation, two should be abolished (deregulation). Taxes should 'decrease annually'; state subsidies should be slashed; 'a ruthless downsizing' of the civil service implemented; and '[m]ore people [put into] work by abolishing the minimum wage'. Despite vocal opposition to immigration and Islam, Wilders is happy to trade and invest with foreign countries, implicitly at the expense of indigenous Dutch. He writes: 'In order to promote development in poor countries, abolish international trade barriers for these countries and their products'.[44]

Part One

BACKGROUND TO THE CRISIS

Chapter 1

Neoliberalism: Our common enemy

'The New York Stock Exchange happens to be the biggest casino in the world … If you allow people to gamble in the stock market … I see nothing terribly different about permitting people to bet on blackjack.'

— Donald J. Trump (with Tony Schwartz), *Trump: The Art of the Deal*
(1987), p. 197

Romance was part of Trump's appeal. He promised to resurrect the good ol' days, when white middle class Americans were not living in a false economy. When white people could actually spend on low-price, high-quality, American-made goods and still have enough left to save for a house and a car. Trump evoked a time when the majority of the poor were not desperately poor and people didn't have to work two or more jobs.

Compared to the Great Depression, post-war prosperity was staggering. But more than that, it was fairly equal. After the war, the rich earned as much relative wealth as the working classes earned from their relative salaries. Inequality declined from its 1930s' baseline. By 1950, wages had doubled or tripled.[1]

But after 1973, things changed. By the mid-1980s, average household *expenditure* tripled as wages remained stagnant. Between the years 1950 and 2000, the number of white Americans declined by 10%. The percentage of women in the workforce increased from over 30% in 1950 to over 45% by 2000. This added to the childcare burden. As the population aged, family sizes decreased.[2]

The good ol' days were over, and not by accident. A series of financial deregulations beginning with Nixon, continuing under Reagan and exploding under Clinton caused economic inequality to expand at the expense of the once-prosperous middle class. The economy also entered a regular boom−bust cycle. Poverty is highly stratified, with the southern states facing the highest levels of inequality, poor educational standards and bad health.

Despite their dislike of her and her party, the majority of poor Americans voted for Hillary Clinton in 2016. The poor – including people of colour[*] – usually vote Democrat because they perceive the Republicans as the party of the rich. At least with the Democrats, entitlements won't be reduced and taxes on the rich will remain high enough to fund social programmes; or so the theory goes.

It is important to pay attention to the decline of the American middle class – white, black and Latino/Hispanic – because Trump had stronger support among the middle class, including a small number of black and Latino/Hispanic middle class voters, than he did among the poor/working classes of all ethnicities.

After the War

In the first few years after World War II, the Truman government raised revenues by taxing the rich and allowing the poor to save and spend. After the War, the top tax rate was 94% of earnings. By 1949 it was 82.13%. The lowest rate of tax was 23% in 1945 and 16.6% in 1948. The figures show that economic stimulation can occur in periods of high taxation for the rich and low taxation for the poor. As taxes for the rich slightly declined, so too did taxes for the poor.[3]

Equally important was the willingness of banks to lend money to stimulate the 'real economy' of housing, cars and infrastructure. The percentage of private investment grew from a low of 13.6% in 1943 to a high of 48.4% in 1949. By the start of the 1950s, it had grown to 68.2%. Many of the products bought by the new American

---

[*] 'People of colour' as opposed to the now-unacceptable term 'coloured people' is a predominantly American expression. An article for National Public Radio's website states: 'In U.S. history, "person of color" has often been used to refer only to people of African heritage. Today, it usually covers all/any peoples of African, Latino/ Hispanic, Native American, Asian or Pacific Island descent, and its intent is to be inclusive'. (Kee Malesky, 'The Journey From "Colored" To "Minorities" To "People Of Color"', NPR, 30 March 2014, http://www.npr.org/sections/codeswitch/ 2014/03/30/295931070/the-journey-from-colored-to-minorities-to-people-of-color.)

consumer* — electric cookers, fridges, vacuum cleaners — were made in the USA.[4]

During this period US civil-sector labour grew from a population of 53.6 million to 57.8m as the military shrank from 12m to 2.7m. In peacetime about one-third of the war workforce was trained and put to work in private industry. The government subsidized many post-war industries, except steel and iron. The boom occurred in the retail and automobile sectors, whose workforces grew by a total of 4.6m. Federal and state government acquired nearly 600,000 employees. The Truman government balanced its huge public spending cuts (a drop of 35% of GNP) with the collection of tax revenues, which fell only a little (from $44.4bn in 1945 to $41.4bn by 1948). About 50% of the 4.9m women who entered the labour force during the war stayed there.[5]

Economists Friedman and Schwartz point out that the so-called index-number problem occurred when prices artificially lowered by the government (e.g., meat and gasoline) returned to their 'normal' price levels when the controls were lifted. Although this gave a false impression of consumer-goods inflation for a period in 1946, it did not amount to a crisis.[6]

What Went Wrong

By 1950, 89.5% of America's 150m-strong population was white. There were 1.4% more women than men. Of the 46m housing units, over half (51.3%) were owned by the occupants. Nearly 9 out of 10 families had both parents present. Close to 20% of women in a family were employed. The population was relatively young, thanks to the post-war baby boom and nearly 60% of families having children younger than 18 living at home.[7]

A paper in *Monthly Labor Review* notes that, '1973 marks a point

---

*Associate Professor David R. Henderson argues that freeing America from the strict World War II-era price controls is an example of deregulation. It is not. It is an example of the lifting of extreme War-era price controls. As far as peace-time controls are concerned, America's economy was well regulated. Leaving aside Henderson's ideological re-packaging of price control relief as an advocacy of free markets, we learn a lot from Henderson's article. See note 1.

of important change in trends in the rate of growth in productivity and in real GDP'. It wasn't just the embargo on Arab oil that caused financial shocks. Between 1950 and 1973, the annual rate of growth was 3.7% for GDP and 2.7% for labour productivity. Between 1973 and 1992, however, growth rates declined to 2.2% GDP and 0.9% productivity. During this period, savings declined as health expenditures increased.[8]

By 1980, the US population was older. The density of white people had declined to 83.1%. The size of the average family declined to 2.6 persons. 'Male participation in the labor market had continued its slow decline and stood at 76.4 percent in 1984', says the US Bureau of Labor Statistics. Female participation increased to 42.1% of the national workforce. Prices increased 'sharply': a product that cost $1 in 1972 cost $2.49 in 1984. Average household income increased by 105.5%, i.e., below price inflation. Average household expenses increased by 165.7%. Many people started losing out.[9]

Deregulation also has complicated effects on social trends and systems, including labour displacement.

One of the things that may have contributed to the inherent racism of some Trump voters is the decline in jobs for the over-55s. Listeners to the hate-filled alternative-right media, which includes Rush Limbaugh, the Alex Jones Show and some of the more extreme Fox News presenters, tend to be single, white old men. This demographic gave Trump his strongest support base. Between 1950 and 1960, over 86% of American men between 55–64 years were in work. By 1970, that had declined to 83%. The decline throughout the 1970s was rapid. By 1980, just 72.1% were in work. By 1992, the number had dropped to 67%. Instead of finding solace in left-wing political organizations, the majority of the 33% left out of the labour market either joined the poor class or stayed at home and vented their rage through Rush Limbaugh and the like.[10]

A paper in *Monthly Labor Review* finds that while some men sought retirement, others were laid off as a result of 'industrial restructuring'. For black men, the majority of layoffs occurred in factories. This led many to support the Democrats. As older white men saw their labour force participation decline between 1975 and 1992, they saw jobs for Asians double. Likewise, by 1992 the number of Hispanics in the workplace had grown to 8%. However irrational, it is easy to understand the resentment that many working- and laid-off white men feel against what they perceive to be pampered ethnic minorities. These dangerous delusions are explored in the context of far-right politics in Chapters 3 and 4.[11]

The Nixon Years

Nixon's era marks the neoliberal turning point. Trump ran on a platform of deregulation. But deregulation is what caused a lot of America's negative socioeconomic changes. Economists Campbell and Bakir identify 'five pillars' of a regulated (i.e., non-neoliberal) economy. They are:[12]

1) Federal deposit insurance. After the Crash of '29, America's Glass–Steagall Act 'laid down the ideas underlying the modern regulatory environment', write economists Diamond and Dybvig. The Act also established the Deposit Insurance Corporation which made all Federal Reserve System banks cooperate in getting 100% insurance in case of systemic failure. This basic underwriting was not challenged by Congress until the 1980s.[13]

2) Central bank-led regulations. America's central bank, the Federal Reserve (Fed), was established in 1913. Glass–Steagall and the Banking Act 1935 strengthened the regulatory power of the Fed over commercial banks, which were hitherto unregulated and thus contributed to the Crash of '29. The Securities and Exchange Commission was established by the Securities Exchange Act 1934 to limit reckless lending and investment practices on Wall Street.[14]

3) Increased transparency. The Securities Act 1933 covered stock and bond markets and gave the government some investigatory powers over transactions that were suspected of being harmful to the economy.[15]

4) Competition limitation. Glass–Steagall and the Banking Acts proscribed interstate and intrastate branching. Glass–Steagall also restricted interest payments on current accounts and savings accounts. Financial and non-financial investments were separated.

This prevented national production from becoming subordinated to financialization. Prior to the Crash of '29, 'the most powerful financial institutions were largely universal', write Campbell and Bakir. But after the Crash, i.e., after regulations were imposed, commercial, investment and insurance banking was separated in order to avoid a chain reaction in the event of systemic failure.[16]

5) Direct government intervention. The worst example of this is after a crisis, when the government uses tax money to rescue criminal banks. In the best case, however, the government can act as a lender of last resort to buoy the economy and manipulate interest rates to encourage consumer spending and prudential banking.[17]

The Democrat-controlled 93rd Congress (1973–75) was behind the Nixon administration. It pushed to eliminate 'needless barriers to competition' in the financial sector by lifting restrictions on local branches, prices for deposits (so-called regulation Q) and compartmentalization (i.e., allowing the interconnection of commercial, savings and insurance). Notice that the year of a pro-deregulation Congressional report, 1973, coincides with the studies quoted above which show that living expenses rose and standards declined.[18] Campbell and Bakir identify four 'pre-neoliberal attacks', which transformed the US economy into a neoliberal one:

1) Bank holding companies were established as a way of circumventing the McFadden Act 1927, which restricted the geographical competition of banks. Until the 1970s, the majority of America's 14,000 banks were single units.[19]

2) In 1973, the Fed suspended interest rate deposits on certificates of deposits over $100,000. Regulation Q meant that banks had to find creative ways of using money market instruments to finance businesses. New York banks in particular transformed into highly liquid markets to attract corporate customers. Negotiable Certificates of Deposit were issued to undermine regulation Q. The Money Market Mutual Funds, introduced in 1971, streamlined the process. They expanded the liquid secondary business markets from $3bn in 1976 to $80bn in 1980, then to $230bn in 1982.[20]

3) The credit contractions of 1966–70 describe a period in which European banks laundered US money to allow them to avoid Q-restrictions. By 1975, Euromarket loans had exploded from $25bn in 1968 to $130bn.[21]

4) Bank holding companies were also used to undermine financial regulations, particularly the rules on compartmentalization. A 1973 Congressional report found that bank holding companies were 'act[ing] as investment advisors to real estate investment trusts and mutual trusts' by leasing personal and real property, providing services (including bookkeeping and data processing) and 'operating insurance agencies'. Things were getting messy and more volatile.[22]

In 1978, the Supreme Court ruled that banks could export state usury laws. This led to the elimination of usury rate ceilings in several states and benefited bubble markets: liquidity firms and issuers of credit cards, especially Citibank. In 1980, President Carter signed the Depository Institutions Deregulation and Monetary Control Act, which increased deposit insurance from $40,000 to $100,000. The Act empowered savings and loan companies (S&Ls) and led to the crisis of the 1980s. (S&Ls are known in the UK as building societies). S&Ls specialize in mortgage and real estate lending. The Act also phased-out interest rate ceilings on deposit accounts.[23]

The Rising Cost of Healthcare

In addition to the mess being created in the financial sector, the foundations for the liberalization of health services were laid during the Nixon administration with the promotion of Health Maintenance Organizations (HMOs), the most prominent being Kaiser Permanente. Obama's Affordable Care Act, which Trump claimed to oppose, is criticized by Republicans as being far-left. But it is even less left-wing than Nixon's privatization reforms.

In 1971, Nixon's Assistant to the President for Domestic Affairs, John D. Ehrlichman, said to the President that negotiations had stalled on introducing a new system, the HMO. Ehrlichman approached Nixon for a final decision. 'I'm not too keen on any of these damn medical programs', said the President. 'This is a private enterprise', Ehrlichman assured him. 'Well, that appeals to me', Nixon replied. Ehrlichman explained: 'All the incentives are toward less medical care because the less care they give 'em [i.e., the public] the more money they make'. 'Fine', said Nixon. '[T]he incentives run the right way', Ehrlichman continued. This policy paved the way for the HMO Act 1973.[24]

In 1974, the Democratic Congress failed to approve Nixon's Comprehensive Health Insurance Plan. In the journal *Pediatrics Perspectives*, Freed and Das compare the much maligned Affordable Care Act (or 'Obamacare') with Nixon's 1971 and 1974 proposals. They conclude that Nixon's 1974 proposal was fairly liberal, within the narrow context of what constitutes liberalism in the American free market system. Nixon's plan 'offer[ed] insurance at reasonable group rates to people who did not meet income requirements to qualify for other programs'. Specifically, this would have helped 'self-employed or high-risk individuals'.[25]

Since the 1970s, thanks to Nixon-type shenanigans, the quality and quantity of American healthcare has declined. Specialist Evan M. Melhado writes that post-1960s' reforms, 'increasingly left behind public-interest ideals and their underlying extramarket values in favor of organizing and improving health care markets'.[26]

An analysis by the Commonwealth Fund concludes that '[t]he U.S. spent 5 percent of gross domestic product (GDP) on health care in 1960; health care now consumes 17 percent of the nation's budget'. However, the high-cost, poor-performance structure of American healthcare means that, '[w]hile investment in health care has contributed to improved health and productivity, other countries have devoted a far lower share of GDP to health care and achieved comparable or better health outcomes'. Most of the middle class (about 50% of Americans) have insurance. The poor (about 50 million Americans) do not.[27]

A study by the Economic Policy Institute finds that college graduates are increasingly unable to get jobs which provide health insurance. Employer-sponsored health insurance coverage for college graduates declined from 61% in 1989 to 31% by 2012. The major decline occurred after the year 2000, when little over half of recent college graduates received employer-provided health coverage. The authors go on to note that for high-school graduates, employer-provided coverage fell from 24% in 1989 to 7% by 2012.[28]

Trump has criticized the great waste of public health expenditures but blames it on regulation, not on privatization, as we shall see.

The Reagan Years: Finance

'Under Ronald Reagan we had the best corporate tax rate in the industrialized world', writes Donald Trump in his book, *Great Again* (2015, p. 155). The Democrat-controlled Congress of Ronald Reagan also oversaw major deregulations of the financial sector. Economists Diamond and Dybvig write: 'In the 1950s and 1960s the banking industry was a symbol of stability. By contrast, recent years have seen the greatest frequency of bank failures since the Great Depression'.[29]

In 1979, the Fed doubled interest rates to reduce inflation. As a result, savings and loan (S&L) associations issued their customers fixed-interest loans at lower rates than the borrowing rate. This led to mass insolvency among S&L companies, which failed to attract capital. In 1981, the Federal Home Loan Bank Board decided to allow S&Ls to get away with lax accounting procedures. This led to major fraud. The Board was then decentralized to oversee banks and S&Ls at the regional level, which weakened its regulatory power. The Federal Deposit Insurance Corporation noted that the Board was so influenced by financial lobbyists that it was essentially a 'doormat[...] of financial regulation'.[30]

The Garn-St. Germain Depository Institutions Act 1982 reduced the Federal Deposit Insurance Corporation's oversight and introduced restrictions on minimum stock ownership. Deregulation also allowed S&Ls to adjust mortgage rates and expand lending practices. In a move that essentially provided S&Ls with taxpayer coverage, S&Ls switched from state to federal charters.[31]

New accounts were opened to allow companies to compete with

Money Market Mutual Funds, which are short-term bond holders. 'Nearly every state ... still had strict usury laws on their books, but banks were able to charge any interest they wanted nationwide', writes Matthew Sherman of the Center for Economic and Policy Research. Under Garn-St. Germain, S&Ls were allowed to act more like banks and less like specialized mortgage lenders.[32]

By 1983, the Federal Savings and Loan Insurance Corporation held only $6.3bn in reserves to rescue institutions like S&Ls, yet S&Ls were already $25bn in debt. S&L portfolios shifted away from home mortgage loans to risky real estate ventures, like condominiums; the kind of things built by Trump.* By 1986, S&L home mortgage assets had shrunk from 78% to 56%.[33]

A bubble was blown by S&Ls issuing credit cards, lending up to 20% of their assets, investing up to another 20% in real estate and writing limitless cheques in a process called negotiable order of withdrawal accounts. Congress then passed the Economic Recovery Tax Act 1981, which allowed S&Ls to sell mortgage loans and offset losses against tax for a decade. Wall Street bought a load of bad S&L loans, some up to 60% of their value, and bundled them as taxpayer-backed loans through guarantees by the banks Fannie Mae, Ginnie Mae and Freddie Mac. By 1986, the bonds were bought by S&Ls for $150bn.[34]

In three years (1982–85), S&L assets grew by 56%, signalling a crash. S&Ls started making riskier and riskier investments as deregulation allowed them to hold certificates of deposit (i.e., federally-insured savings) at high interest rates. In addition, individual bankers were responsible for a large number of frauds and scams. Between 1986 and 1995, nearly a third of America's 3,234 savings and loan associations crumbled. By 1989, the Federal Savings and Loan Insurance Corporation closed or resolved 296 organizations, when it was replaced by the Resolution Trust Corporation (RTC). Up to 1995, the RTC closed or resolved 747 institutions. The taxpayer forked out $100bn.[35]

That was finance. What about Reagan's industrial policy?

---

* There is no suggestion that Trump profited from the S&L crisis.

The Reagan Years: Industry

In his first two years in office, Reagan subsidized the economy with 265 interventions known as aids. These amounted to $44bn in so-called supply-side interventions in agriculture and construction – something akin to Trump's vision to Make America Great Again®.[36]

Direct and loan guarantee credit provisions were the main tools of Reagan's supply-side policies, which amounted to a huge federal redistribution of resources. Reagan's reforms in 1981 favoured the real estate and utilities sectors. Financial institutions started taking risks in the real estate sector instead of investing in industry.[37]

Part of the hopelessness among American workers emanates from the deindustrialized areas. Deindustrialization accelerated under Clinton, but was underway with Reagan. 'We have ... an industrial policy through our tax code', said Reagan in 1984. 'I do not favor that'. Otis L. Graham's scholarly study of Reagan-era neoliberalism concludes that '[t]he official doctrine was the promotion of free trade: the practice was selective protectionism and export promotion'.[38]

Reagan failed to protect textiles, for instance, because the Asian economies were opening up and American apparel-makers could do better exploiting cheaper labour abroad. Conversely, the steel and automotive industries pushed for more protection against superior Japanese products. Congress was 'forced ... to advance toward ever-greater protectionism' as America faced a trade deficit over its 'growing import vulnerability'.[39]

At the same time, the Democrat-led Congress published lengthy reports extolling the virtues of privatization. When unions complained that services were being badly managed and getting into debt as a result of government restructuring, Reagan had them fired. As Trump writes in his book, *Great Again* (2015): 'We've had presidents ... who have managed to build consensus and get things done. When President Reagan fired the air traffic controllers during his seventh month in office, he sent a signal to the unions that they heard loud and clear' (p. 79). (Trump continues his anti-union propaganda in *Time to Get Tough*, 2016: 'guess who the big winners [in healthcare reform] have been? President Obama's backers who backed Obamacare! More than 50 percent of the waivers have gone to union members', p. 124.)

But how did Reagan internationalize the US economy?

The General Agreement on Tariffs and Trade (GATT) was set up by the US and Britain as a way to negotiate and integrate international trade. There is some ongoing debate among economists about whether GATT actually contributed to trade. One thing is certain, however: GATT was shaped in ways that benefitted Anglo–American corporations in the post-World War II recovery era. America's 'free trade' crusade weakened GATT's systems of capital regulation. Before Reagan became President, America spent $334bn on imported goods and services. By the end of Reagan's term, America was spending $663bn. 'Our trade policy rests firmly on the foundation of free and open markets', said Reagan's speechwriters in 1986.[40]

In that year, Reagan launched GATT's Uruguay Round, which eventually led to the creation of the second major international trading body, the World Trade Organization (WTO). Two years later, Reagan approved the US–Canada Free Trade Agreement 1988, which morphed into NAFTA (more below).

Another pillar of neoliberalism is immigration: of the right kind. Governments don't want immigrants who haven't skills for certain jobs and who may end up relying on social security. But they do want immigrants to fill the shoes of American workers in the case of a domestic skills shortage or to take part in highly exploitative labour, such as fruit picking. Any complaints about long hours and low pay can be met with threats to send them home. Reagan signed the Immigration Reform and Control Act 1986, which penalized bosses who hired illegal workers. It also beefed up border security. Yet the Act legalized nearly 3 million undocumented labourers. In this respect, Trump is also like Reagan. Despite the rhetoric against 'illegals', Trump's books make clear his intention to fill skills shortages with migrants (more in Chapter 3).[41]

Chapter 2

Class divisions and union decline

'Hungry people work harder and are much more motivated to make great strides forward in life. If you are satisfied with your current financial situation, what is going to motivate you to do all the things you need to do to become rich and successful?'

Donald J. Trump and Bill Zanker, *Think Big* (2007), p. 24

The deregulations of the '70s through to the '90s were wonderful times for the wealthy. The Economic Policy Institute (EPI)'s study on wage stagnation finds that in 1965 the CEOs of America's 350 biggest companies made 20 times more than the average worker. By 2012 they were making nearly 300 times more. The wealth did not trickle down. It went into three pockets: the banks (as savings), the speculative economy (as investment) and the luxury goods economy of yachts, jewellery, jet-setting, etc. (the 'plutonomy' economy). Whereas the average worker was working harder by 2013 than they had in 1973, the average CEO was not. Other data suggest that CEO pay grew twice as fast as corporate profits.[1]

Where Did All the Money Go?
Neoliberalism is also harmful because it rewards creative destruction. The bigger the crisis, the higher the dividends for those who helped cause it. The biggest financial institutions, as well as energy companies, posted record profits after the Financial Crisis of 2008. By 2015, there was a record 10.4 million individuals worth over a million dollars in the US. Their wealth totals $11.6 trillion. By 2016, there were 540 billionaires in America. Their wealth totals nearly $2.4 trillion.[2]

The lack of political participation on behalf of working and middle class Americans, coupled with the decline in union participation, has added to the lowering of wages and benefits.

The EPI study notes that '[w]age stagnation for the vast majority was not created by abstract economic trends. Rather, wages were suppressed by policy choices made on behalf of those with the most income, wealth, and power'. The middle class would not have shrunk and the working classes' standards declined were it not for successive governments, especially Reagan's, denying 'a higher minimum wage' and 'rights to overtime pay'. Other factors include 'providing paid sick leave, protecting the labor rights of undocumented workers, and restoring the right to collective bargaining'. All of which were suppressed or weakened by Reagan et al.[3]

Until the early-1970s, the hourly wage-to-expense ratio (compensation) for the majority of American workers rose by 91%. Productivity rose by 97%. Between 1973 and 2013, however, hourly compensation increased by only 9% and productivity by 74%. In other words, most people are working much harder for less pay and fewer benefits. Because of the economic restructuring outlined in the previous chapter, the wages of the top 1% grew by 138% while the bottom 90%'s wages grew by only 15%. Some of the bottom 90% actually saw wages decline. Between 1979 and 2013, low-wage earners saw their incomes decline by an average of 5%. In a more equal system, the bottom 90%'s wages would have grown by 32%.[4]

Middle-wage earners saw an average growth of only 0.2%, and that was only because of a short period of wage growth in the 1990s when unemployment fell. High-wage workers on the other hand enjoyed an average 41% rise.[5]

The weakening of the unions started in 1960 and continued steadily until 1980, when it really speeded up. The Economic Policy Institute study shows a direct causal correlation – almost a mirror – between union membership decline and the percentage of income share going to the top 10%.[6]

David Jacobs writes for the London School of Economics: 'the differences in U.S. family incomes accelerated sharply after 1980'. Jacobs analyses the political influence of the Reagan era over the economy and income inequality. He concludes: 'Stronger unions decrease the differences in earnings within firms', meaning that with strong unions, labourers can earn more and CEOs and managers less. '[B]efore the politically induced steep decline in union strength that began in 1981, unions probably were the most effective pressure group that lobbied for policies helpful to less economically fortunate U.S. citizens'. In the Carter years (mid-late-1970s), there were over 2,000 union election recognitions and victories. By 1981, the number had fallen off a cliff to below 1,000, where it remained.[7]

The Decline of the Middle Class

In *Great Again* (2015) Trump tries to appeal to America's 50 million poor people by pretending that they constitute 'the middle class'. He describes them as 'the bedrock of this country' (p. x). Actually, the middle class is the middle, not the bottom 45–50 million who tend to vote Democrat.

Post-war prosperity was such that by 1971, 61% of Americans were middle class. These days only 50% of Americans are middle class. Just 4% of Americans enjoyed higher-incomes in the post-war years. Now the figure is 9%. In 1970, 62% of America's aggregate income was distributed among the middle class and 29% went to the upper class. By 2014, however, 43% went to the middle class and 49% went to the upper class, even though upper class earners were and remain in the minority. Today, 29% of Americans are lower class (or working class) and 20% are upper class.[8]

Determining who is 'middle class' is a difficult task. Pew Research says that 120.8m American adults are middle class. Most of the remaining American adults are working class. A one-person household earning $24,000 to $73,000 per annum is middle class, according to Pew's standard. But a five-person household needs to earn $54,000 to $162,000 to qualify. To complicate matters further, *Business Insider* calculates the value of income across states. The article excludes the number of persons per household from its analysis. Still, it demonstrates that households need to earn above $40k per annum to qualify as middle class in Alaska, California, Connecticut, the District of Columbia, Hawaii, Maryland, Massachusetts, Minnesota, New Hampshire, New Jersey and Virginia.

Money goes further in Arkansas, Alabama, Kentucky, Louisiana, Mississippi, New Mexico, South Carolina, Tennessee and West Virginia. In these states, people need to earn $25k–29k per annum to qualify as middle class. The other states require workers to earn $30–40k to qualify – hence the popularity of Trump in rural areas among middle class Americans who might seem 'poor' by city measures.[9]

Harvard sociologist Dr William Julius Wilson notes that '[r]ising inequality is beginning to produce a two-tiered society in America. The more affluent citizens live lives fundamentally different from the middle- and lower-income groups. This divide decreases a sense of community'. As we shall see in the next chapters, the 'divided sense of community' is empowering the far-right. A Pew Research Center survey finds that '85% of self-described middle class adults say it is more difficult now than it was a decade ago for middle class people to maintain their standard of living'.[10]

A Stanford University study finds 'a steady decline in the proportion of families living in middle class neighborhoods from 1970–2007, and a corresponding increase in the number of families in neighborhoods at the extremes of the neighborhood income distribution', i.e. very rich and very poor. 'The residential isolation of the both poor and affluent families has grown over the last four decades', the Stanford study continues. This has damaging effects on social cohesion, as wealthier families seek to literally fence themselves off from their poorer, supposedly more crime-prone neighbours. '[O]nly 15 percent of families in 1970 lived in one of the two extreme types of neighbourhoods [i.e., rich and poor], but by 2007 that number had more than doubled to 31 percent of families'.[11]

The Financial Crisis and Great Recession made things worse. America's income distribution (2015 figures) is as follows: 11.6% of the population earns less than $15,000 per year; 10.5% earns between $14–25,000; 10% earns between $24–35,000; and 12.7% earns $34–50,000. By far the biggest bracket is the $50,000 to $74,999 group, which consists of 16.7% of the population. 12.1% earns $74–100,000 per annum, 6.2% earns $150,000 to $199,999 and 6.1% earns over $200,000. Yet, as we have seen, the upper brackets get a bigger share of the pie.[12]

When it comes to black Americans: 1.2% are upper class, 46.5% are middle class, 28.8% are working class, and 23.5% are in poverty. By 1984, the median net worth of the average black American adult was $6,679 (in savings, assets, interest on earnings, etc.) compared to the average white's $76,951. Like white people, black people saw their median net worth decline. By 2009, it had dropped to $5,677.[13]

The Continuation of Poverty

'Consumption patterns' is an inefficient measure of poverty because it proves little beyond the fact that the price of certain goods – not all goods – has declined and poor people can buy more cheap things. It doesn't mean that buyers have real, material wealth, such as savings, decent health insurance and the ability to pay rents and mortgages without worrying where the next cheque is coming from.

Consumption patterns don't prove that people have more money. It is also a bad sign because the quality of very affordable goods is often low. If poor, stressed families and single persons buy processed, ready-to-eat meals, they may become undernourished and develop obesity, require medical treatment and incur extra costs. Likewise, if they smoke and drink to relieve anxiety, they also incur more health problems.

Despite this flawed methodology, a report by the US National Bureau of Economic Research concludes that absolute poverty in the US has increased since 1970. The so-called official poverty rate is 'an absolute measure intended to capture the fraction of people below a threshold that is constant in real terms'. This measure indicates 'that deprivation has become more widespread over the past four decades'. By 2010, the poverty rate was 2.5% higher than in 1970 even though GDP per capita had doubled. The authors note that conservatives, including Ronald Reagan himself, used this measure as an excuse to try to limit and use propaganda against welfare measures, including tax credits, unemployment insurance and income support programmes.[14]

Economic deregulation meant that financial institutions could wreak havoc on the real economy by blowing speculative bubbles. To offset the most dreadful consequences and prevent a peasants' revolt, tax exemptions, deductions and credits were introduced in the mid-1980s by Democrats in Congress during the Republican Reagan administration. These so-called noncash measures had no long-term effect, say the authors, but did alleviate persons in immediate need. They act as a kind of buoy to prevent total impoverishment, such as homelessness.[15]

Based on the 'official measure', which includes consumption-based statistics, Pew Research finds that since Lyndon B. Johnson's 'war on poverty', 'the demographics of America's poor have shifted'. Fewer black Americans live in poverty compared to the 1960s, but far more Hispanic Americans live in poverty. It's also worth noting that due to racist social control policies, hundreds of thousands of black and Hispanic Americans are in jail or on parole.[16]

One of the few benefits of the neoliberal period has been inflation-adjusted Social Security, which has contributed to the reduction of poverty among the elderly: 28.5% of older Americans were poor in 1966 and 9.1% were poor in 2012. Childhood poverty, however, has fluctuated at around the 14% mark. (In particular, the children of middle class black Americans today can expect to grow up poor.) According to Pew, 'the wealth of the lower-income tier plunged by 45%' in the 2000s.[17]

It is no accident that Trump had a big southern constituency. We have already seen dramatic differences in the levels of modern income needed to qualify as middle class across states. In 1969, 31% of Americans lived in the south. Yet 45.9% of them were poor. The southern poverty rate (17.9%) was higher than in other regions. Taking into account population growth, southern poverty rates have hardly changed. By 2012, the region was home to 37.3% of America's population and 41.1% of its poor.[18]

The Clinton Years

The final nail in the regulatory coffin was the Bill Clinton administration (1993–2001). Clinton repealed laws and prevented government intervention in speculative markets, until they collapsed. These deregulations built upon the Nixon–Reagan era and ultimately contributed to the Crash of 2007, the Crisis of 2008 and the ongoing Recession.

Clinton's government approved NAFTA. NAFTA is the North American Free Trade Agreement. It is a lengthy legal text between the governments of America, Canada and Mexico. It was drafted in secret and in opposition to the labour unions, who didn't even get to see a draft copy until it was too late. NAFTA is the very symbol of 'free trade' and neoliberal globalization. It created a customs union between the three signatories and eliminated barriers to trade. This was good for consumers because prices went down. It was bad for American factory workers because US companies not only relocated to Mexico, where they enjoyed cheaper labour and lower health and safety standards, but could also threaten to offshore as a way of intimidating unions.

NAFTA was devastating for Mexican farmers who could not compete with huge imports of mechanized American products. NAFTA is in part why so many Mexicans are seeking work in the US. NAFTA is also bad for Canada's environment. NAFTA provisions allowed signatories to be sued for interfering with corporate profits. Under Chapter 11, Canada became the world's most sued nation by corporations (mostly American) who challenged various environmental laws introduced by the Canadian government as threats to their profits.[19]

Donald Trump has been very critical of NAFTA, threatening to renegotiate to get a better deal for America – meaning its corporations – or else withdraw from the treaty. Yet NAFTA has its origins in the Reagan administration. A North American Accord was proposed in 1979 by the Republican Ronald Reagan shortly before his taking office as President. The Democrats in Congress voted against the Accord until 1992, when Bill Clinton was elected. Under Bush I in the 1980s and early 1990s, the US had already liberalized the Mexico peso in exchange for providing Mexico with loans. Mexico was in no position to argue.[20]

A report by Cornell University notes that in the US, union

membership had declined from over 50% in the 1950s to 12% by the 1990s, due in large measure to aggressive anti-union laws, policies, and practices. 'U.S. workers, trade unions and their allies ... mounted a strong campaign of opposition to NAFTA'. This was due in part to Clinton's refusal to include a strong Social Charter. The Citizens Trade Campaign (sic) and Alliance for Responsible Trade were formed by concerned citizens. Despite their efforts, NAFTA was approved by Congress on a vote of 234 to 200.[21] Unions were given almost no time to read the huge document. Despite this, they managed to write a critical report which was largely ignored by Congress.

According to a report by the US Economic Policy Institute, NAFTA cost American workers 700,000 jobs, many of which were moved to Mexico. California, Michigan and Texas were the hardest hit. Surviving sectors saw a decrease in wages and benefits, with bosses using the threat of off-shoring to Mexico as a way of driving down labour costs and unionization. NAFTA was a big contributor to Mexican migration to the US. The EPI report goes on to note that 'several million Mexican workers and families' were adversely affected in the agricultural and small business sectors by imports of cheaper US goods. '[T]he dramatic increase in undocumented workers flowing into the U.S. labor market ... put further downward pressure on U.S. wages'. The report concludes that NAFTA was a 'template' for a world trading order 'in which the benefits would flow to capital and costs to labor'.[22]

In 1994, Clinton signed the Riegle–Neal Interstate Banking and Branching Efficiency Act, which eliminated restrictions on interstate banking and branching. Mergers increased by 27% in an eight-year period. In 1996, the Supreme Court eliminated some of the limits on late fees for credit card payments (*Smiley vs. Citibank*). The Court overruled state regulations and late fees jumped from $5 to $40.[23]

The biggest merger took place in 1998, when the Fed approved the Citicorp–Travelers merger, which allowed the liquidity firm Citicorp and the insurance giant Travelers to create the biggest financial institution to date. This put America well on the way to having an economy monopolized by a few financial institutions.[24]

In 1999, Clinton signed the Gramm–Leach–Bliley Act which repealed Glass–Steagall, the benchmark of financial regulation. The repeal of Glass–Steagall was supported by Fed chairman Alan Greenspan and Treasury secretaries Robert Rubin (ex-Citigroup and later Goldman Sachs) and Lawrence Summers. The Act allowed the actions of banks, securities and insurance companies to merge for the first time since the 1930s.[25]

In 2000, Clinton signed the Commodity Futures Modernization Act, which prevented the Commodity Futures Trading Commission from regulating most of the financial transactions known as derivatives. Derivatives can become so complicated and cause so many financial institutions – asset firms, banks, insurers, mutuals, trusts – to suffer, that multibillionaire hedge fund CEO Warren Buffett famously describes them as 'financial weapons of mass destruction'. The head of the Commodity Futures Trading Commission, Brooksley Born, warned about the risks of unregulated derivative markets. It has been alleged by various economists that Lawrence Summers personally intervened to prevent Born from acting on her concerns. The Act was passed by Congress without objection because it was sneaked through as an attachment to an 11,000-page spending bill. The derivatives market exploded from $106tr in 2001 to $531tr by 2008, when the market – triggered by rising oil prices and the housing collapse – finally imploded.[26]

Chapter 3

America's far-right:
Disappointment gets angry

'This country is a magnet for many of the smartest, hardest-working people born in other countries, yet we make it difficult for these bright people who follow the laws to settle here . . . Let me state this clearly: I am not against immigration . . . I love immigration . . . What I don't love is the concept of illegal immigration . . . I don't mind putting a big, beautiful door in that [US–Mexico] wall so people can come in and out LEGALLY.'[*]

– Donald J. Trump, *Great Again* (2015), pp. 19–29.
(emphases in original)

Trump claims to be anti-establishment. But establishment means different things to different people. For many poor black people, it means the police and judicial system which exploits their social vulnerability. For the poor it means the rich who take the biggest share of the pie. For them, Republicans and Democrats are the same, though they have a slight preference for Democrats. For the rich, it means the government which overregulates their businesses and overtaxes them. They prefer so-called libertarian Republicans, who claim to speak for businesses. For the middle class it means a government which gives their jobs to ethnic minorities and spends their hard earned money on welfare scroungers.

When Donald Trump and the Tea Party speak of 'freedom' it means freedom from taxes. For the racist, it means freedom from blacks and Mexicans. For some Christians, it means freedom from Muslims. When former UK Independence Party leader Nigel Farage expresses opposition to the 'establishment', the establishment means the British government, which has stuck to a slow-growth

---

[*] In the original text, there is an ellipsis between 'out' and 'LEGALLY' (p. 25). I have removed it for ease of reading.

European Union instead of relaxing regulations and looking abroad for profits. But for UKIP's supporters, the establishment means the politicians who have allowed immigrants to flood the country. When Marine Le Pen talks about '*liberté*', she invokes the ancient glory of *La République* among older, white voters. To them, it means *liberté* from immigrants.

The Tea Party: When the Rich Mobilize

The historical Boston Tea Party was a crucial turning point in the history of Anglo–American relations. The brutal British colonial government shipped tea to Boston, Massachusetts, from India, where it was committing crimes on a genocidal scale. British corporations were losing out to illegal tea smuggling and in 1773 Parliament passed the Tea Act to undercut the illegal trade. Effectively seen as a tea tax, members of the original Thirteen Colonies organized against the Act. Tea Act resistance peaked on 16 December when a secret society of anti-Tory Whigs, calling themselves the Sons of Liberty, dumped tea cargo into the Boston harbour. The British government responded with force, appointing a Royal Governor of Massachusetts and passing laws against so-called Coercive Acts.[1]

The Boston Tea Party is an important symbol of resistance in the minds of millionaire American libertarians. It was a trigger for the War of Independence. Today, the Tea Party symbolizes freedom from oppression. The thinking behind the modern Tea Party movement taps into the deep paranoia among the middle and upper middle classes, that their wealth and freedom from taxation is being undermined by Democrats, poor people, blacks, Mexicans, etc.

The majority of Tea Party (TP) supporters differ ideologically from the wealthy patrons of the organization. Where they agree, however, is in the size and role of government. Sixty per cent of Americans say that it is the responsibility of government (i.e., the taxpayer) to look after those who haven't the means of looking after themselves. By contrast, only 40% of Tea Partiers share this view. The figure is slightly higher among white evangelical Tea Partiers, probably because of the in-group (solidarity) ethos that comes with organized religion.[2]

The TP website was set up in 2004. The TP movement came to prominence in 2009/10, when a number of Republicans opposed Obama's tax-funded economic stimulus package. It was not a separate political party, but a movement within the Republican party. It also appealed to certain right-wing ideologues as an alternative to the left-wing Occupy Wall Street movement, which targeted some of the real culprits of everyone's economic misery: the financial sector. Trump has succeeded in mobilizing Tea Party members who became dissatisfied with the way the organization was run.[3]

The media tended to imply that the TP was the right-wing working class answer to Occupy. It turns out that most of its non-political funders and its political members (i.e., people from Congress) are themselves members of the so-called 1%. They are millionaires and multimillionaires who fear taxation and regulation. They can't be so blatant as to say that, so they package their ideology in terms vague enough to appeal to people's personal ideas about what patriotism and liberty mean.

In reality, the TP tends to appeal mainly to hardworking, white middle class, rural Americans who have seen their economic status decline and their hard work fail to match their expectations and entitlements. Some, particularly small business owners, have legitimate grievances against heavy taxation on small- to medium-size businesses and heavy regulation. The Dodd–Frank Act 2010, for example, regulated the mega-rich corporations but also added to the overregulation of small-to-medium size businesses and hurt small-time bosses.

Most Tea Party members, however, simply want less government involvement in business, meaning cutbacks on social security, medical insurance and education.

SourceWatch writes: 'While promoted as a spontaneous "grassroots" movement, many of the activities of Tea Party groups were organized by corporate lobbying groups like FreedomWorks and Americans for Prosperity'.[4]

Created in 2004 from the merger of two similar groups, FreedomWorks has spent hundreds of thousands of dollars backing Republican candidates in Kentucky, Mississippi and North Carolina. Its board of directors have included Steve Forbes of *Forbes* magazine, Frank Sands of Sands Capital Management and former Chamber of Commerce budget policy director, Matt Kibbe. FreedomWorks sponsored fake grassroots (or astroturf) websites which opposed Obama's bailouts to save some homeowners. The website claimed to speak for renters and generated false anger to divide renters from homeowners and landlords.[5]

A leaked memo from the Tea Party Patriots' website planned the infiltration and disruption of Democratic Party town hall meetings. The given Democratic representative should be subject to crowd behaviours designed to 'rattle him', says the memo. Between 2011 and 2013, the TP organized a self-described 'push back against domineering unions'. It organized a petition to support Michigan Governor Rick Snyder's anti-union politics and published numerous anti-union blogs.[6]

Americans for Prosperity (AFP) is another group backing the TP. It was founded by the billionaire brothers Charles and David of Koch Industries. AFP is committed to 'cutting taxes and government spending'. It also sponsors pro-Constitution propaganda to 'educat[e] citizens' about the supposed limits of government over individual (i.e. corporate) freedoms. After the 2012 Republican defeat, the AFP wrote a study concluding that the Republicans have to re-evaluate their media strategy. The best solution, they said, is to sell the free market as a tool of prosperity. 'Americans place a great importance on taking care of those in need and avoiding harm to the weak. We consistently see that Americans in general are concerned that free-market policy – and its advocates – benefit the rich and powerful more than the most vulnerable of society', says the AFP analysis. The AFP decided that this perception has to be countered.[7]

In 2016, it donated $225m to the US election cycle. This included $1.5m on propaganda for Ohio governor Ted Strickland. Ohio was a swing state which went to Trump in the shock Electoral College victory.[8]

Who Joins the Party?

Tea Party supporters and especially members and key funders tend to be in the higher income bracket. This would suggest that the Tea Party as a movement is really the rich trying to mobilize a core sector of Republican and potential Republican voters.

An example of this is Tea Partier Sarah Palin (Alaska Gov.) whom, during the McCain–Palin campaign, regularly referred to the self-employed labourer, Joe the Plumber: and by implication to the average hard-working Joe. In reality, there is no record of Joe (real name Samuel Joseph Wurzelbacher) ever working as a plumber or being a member of a plumber union. Wurzelbacher actually told Obama that he was looking to buy a small plumbing business. Somehow he became 'Joe the Plumber'.[9]

The Republican House Tea Party Caucus was founded by the Republican for Minnesota, Michele Bachmann. It consisted of 60 members, 33 of whom were millionaires. Six of the millionaires were worth over $20m. A Tea Party Caucus member is more likely to be a millionaire than the average non-Tea Party Republican. By 2010, the median average net worth of the average House Tea Party Caucus member was $1.8m. Other House members have a net average worth of $755,000. The average non-Tea Party Caucus House Republican has less net worth: $774,280. The median net worth of House Democrats, by contrast, is $635,000.[10]

In 2010, the *New York Times* and CBS commissioned a poll to find out who supports the Tea Party. The majority of its backers are 'more affluent and better educated than the general public. They tend to be white, male and married. They are loyal Republicans'. According to the poll, Tea Partiers are 'ideologically' opposed to Democrats because they have 'conservative' views on religion, marriage and migration. According to the polls, only 25% of Americans believe that the Tea Party's views are shared by most Americans. By contrast, 84% of Tea Partiers believe this.[11]

Forty-seven per cent of Tea Partiers get their information about the TP from the television, 24% from the internet, 8% from newspapers and 4% from emails. 11% get their info about the TP from other sources. 80% of Tea Partiers think there is either 'some' or a 'lot' of difference between the TP and the Republican Party. When asked, 'What should be the goal of the Tea Party movement?', 45% of Tea Partiers said it should be to '[r]educe federal government', 9% said '[c]reating jobs', 6% said 'cutting the budget', 6% said 'lowering taxes', 7% said electing their own candidates and 7% said some other issue was important.[12]

Tea Partiers tend be more religious than the average American, though less religious than the Christian right. By 2010, 33% of Americans took the Bible literally, compared to 47% of Tea Partiers. 36% of Americans attend Church on a weekly basis, compared to 46% of Tea Partiers. 20% of Americans consider religion to be the most important thing in their lives, compared with 29% of Tea Partiers. A 2011 study by the Public Religion Research Institute found that, '[d]espite conventional wisdom, only about a quarter (27 percent) of [Tea Partiers] consider themselves libertarians'.[13]

Seventy per cent of Americans support increasing taxes on millionaires, compared to 40% of Tea Partiers. Eighty per cent of Tea Partiers favour a smaller government providing fewer services, compared with 50% of Americans. Here, the Tea Partiers share the same interests as the Party's wealthy donors and managers: fewer resources for the poor and needy. By implication, this also means less money for bailing out Wall Street and subsidizing big corporations. But in practice, the same wealthy people behind the Tea Party are the same people who lobby for government intervention on their behalf. Sixty-seven per cent of Americans support raising the minimum wage to $10 per hour. Only 41% of Tea Partiers support the raise. Less than one-third of white Tea Partiers support legalized abortion, compared to 53% of Americans. Twenty-five per cent support same-sex marriage (47% of Americans support it).[14]

Political scientists Street and Dimaggio note that 91% of Tea Party supporters live in rural and suburban areas and 89% are white. Williamson et al. note that Tea Partiers tend to oppose 'the social safety net' for working people because they oppose the notion than their hard work should fund layabouts. Trump understands his constituency. In his book *Time To Get Tough* (2016), he writes, 'it is counterproductive and cruel to allow America's safety net to morph into a hammock' (p. 107). By implication, many Tea Partiers are against racial minorities because racial minorities tend to have a higher percentage, per capita, of welfare dependence than whites. Tea Partiers might not even realize they are being racist because they appear to be unaware of the fact that social structures are inherently racist. 'Tea Partiers are more likely than other conservatives to agree with statements such as "If blacks would only try harder they could be just as well off as whites",' say Williamson et al., who also note that Tea Partiers 'are more likely to disagree with statements like "Generations of slavery and discrimination have created conditions that make it difficult for blacks to work their way out of the lower class".'[15]

The End of the Party?

The previous chapters document the decline of the middle class as a result of domestic neoliberal policies. Heather Boushey analysed the data and concludes that 'Tea Party supporters are in the group of Americans adversely affected by the hollowing out of the middle class in the last few decades'. Boushey goes on to note that '[t]he education data alone are impressive: 37 percent of Tea Party supporters have at least a college degree, compared with 25 percent in the sample overall. It makes sense for these folks to be among the higher earners in our economy'. But many aren't. They are angry that their standards have declined, their hard work isn't paying off as it should, given their status; and the demographic factor, i.e., that most of them are white.[16]

Boushey also points out that the average Tea Partier is aged 45 to 64 – the highest earning age group. '[W]e would expect them to be at their highest for lifetime earnings', but again thanks to neoliberalism they are not. These are exactly the kinds of people that Trump tries to motivate with slogans that appeal to giving everyone a fair shot at living the American Dream.[17]

Support for the TP dropped, even among Republicans, between 2010 and 2013. In 2010, an NBC/*Wall Street Journal* poll found that 30% of Americas had a favourable view of the TP. 54% of Republicans identified with the TP and 58% agreed with its policies, according to a study by Cornell University's Roper Center. A CBS study found that 19% of Republicans thought the TP was 'too extreme'. By 2013, more than double thought the TP was too extreme. Only 28% of Americans had a favourable view of the Tea Party, according to a CNN/ORC poll, whilst 56% had an unfavourable view. An NBC News/WSJ poll found that 70% of Americans claimed not to be members. Interestingly, in the Republican primaries only 36% of Republicans identified with the TP. According to Pew, less than half (40%) of Republicans said they agree with the TP.[18]

Defining the Far-right

For the purposes of this book, 'far right' describes political organizations that mobilize electoral support by implying that minority groups (foreign, ethnic, religious and/or cultural) are endangering Western 'values'. Such political organizations threaten to ban immigrants from entering their countries and suggest directly or indirectly that large numbers of immigrants or all immigrants should be deported. Far-right parties will usually – but not always – run on this single issue. They will often claim that the economic system in their country is facing an untenable strain because of immigrants.

For the purposes of this book, raising concerns about migration levels does not automatically make an individual or group far-right. Nor does being an isolationist and/or nationalist. Nor does being opposed to economic neoliberal globalization ('free trade'). Yet, often these sentiments – anti-immigration, nationalism and rhetorical opposition to 'globalization' – are shared by far-right political parties across Europe.

Far-right parties differ from typical fascists of the Hitler–Mussolini variety in that they do not openly espouse violence in their own countries. They are much like centrist and left-wing parties, however, in that they may advocate a violent foreign policy, usually in the name of defeating terrorism and preserving domestic 'freedoms'. However, such advocacy may contradict their professed isolationism. Unlike the Nazis, they do not openly espouse the extermination of a particular ethnic or religious group. Unlike the Nazis, they have no formal commitment to racial, national, religious or ideological superiority.

They do, however, imply and sometimes openly state that 'Europeans' or 'Americans', which predominantly and implicitly means white people, are under threat. Their main targets are Muslims or individuals from Muslim countries, usually the Middle East, North Africa and sometimes other parts of Africa. In most cases, this means that far-right groups indirectly refer to Arabs and black people (or Turks in the case of Germany and Austria, and Pakistanis and Bangladeshis in the UK) as threatening white secular or Christian conventions.

'Far-left', for the sake of this book, refers to political groups that have the opposite view of the far-right, except when it comes to neoliberalism. Both the far-left and far-right oppose neoliberalism, but for different reasons. The far-left opposes it because it hurts people. The far-right rhetorically opposes it in order to win votes, but in practice due to the fact that international structures (like the EU and the WTO) constrain the freedoms of large corporations. The far-left considers privatization and economic neoliberal globalization as the root cause of poverty, inequality and declining social services. It welcomes immigrants and often believes in relaxing national borders. It is a grassroots type of globalization which puts people of flesh and blood above corporate persons. The far-left believes in taxing the rich, redistributing wealth to society as a whole, nationalizing industry and protecting the environment by limiting fossil fuel use and switching to low-carbon economies.

The far-left and far-right share two broad ideas: that 'elites' have far too much wealth and that 'globalization' – corporate globalization, that is – is doing more harm than good. Unlike the far-right, however, far-left groups tend to be grassroots, financed by working people and the middle class. Far-right groups, conversely, attempt to fool their constituents because they are formed and led by wealthy corporatists who actually believe in neoliberalism ('free trade') while pretending to be against it. The United Kingdom Independence Party is a prime example of this, as is Donald Trump in the USA; hence Trump's pro-immigration passages in his books and anti-immigration campaign rhetoric.

In *Time to Get Tough* (2016), he writes: 'America doesn't need freeloaders who come here to live off our welfare system. We need legal immigrants who bring skills, prosperity and intellectual capital'. Instead of allowing criminals to stay, it would 'be better if we invited foreign students graduating from our colleges to stay to build American companies, instead of foreign companies that will wreak havoc against Boeing, Caterpillar, and many other of our great American companies' (pp. 144, 145).

Chapter 4

Europe's far-right: Poverty gets angry

'In 1981, we got a sudden wave of buyers from France ... François Mitterrand had been elected president, and anyone smart and wealthy realized immediately that Mitterrand was going to hurt the French economy ... [H]e was a socialist, and ... began nationalizing companies.'[*]

— Donald J. Trump (with Tony Schwartz), *Trump: The Art of the Deal* (1987), pp. 184–85

After the signing of the Maastricht Treaty 1992, European Union member states imposed on their citizens the kind of neoliberal deregulations outlined in Chapters 1 and 2. European neoliberalism had the same effects across Europe as it did in the USA: stagnating wages, increasing migration, outsourcing, riskier behaviour by financial institutions and a weakening of the social safety net. These factors combined to weaken centrist governments, make the left lose all credibility (except as an alternative to centre-right governments) and empower the far-right.

The EU is a customs union comprised of 28 member states. They are Austria, Belgium, Bulgaria, Croatia, Cyprus, Czech Republic, Denmark, Estonia, Finland, France, Germany, Greece, Hungary, Ireland, Italy, Latvia, Lithuania, Luxembourg, Malta, Netherlands, Poland, Portugal, Romania, Slovakia, Slovenia, Spain, Sweden and the UK (at present). Many of these countries have one or more far-right representatives in their parliaments. In general, the success of far-right parties has been growing over the last 20 or so years. Working people in Eastern European countries are torn between

---

[*] In the same paragraph, Trump also points out that Mitterrand sold nuclear technologies and was thus a 'dangerous man', like Trump's political idol, Ronald Reagan.

wanting to avoid the pitfalls of the 'free market', including losing jobs to immigrants, but also avoid falling back into Soviet-style dictatorship. After World War II and until the recent present, Greece, Spain and Portugal suffered under military juntas or associations with juntas, and now want to avoid a repetition of the past. (Greece's far-right Golden Dawn mostly runs on a left-wing nationalization platform, with an uncomfortable mix of anti-immigrant extremism.)

In this chapter, Austria is cited as a case-study to demonstrate that, in some countries, there is a battle between the progressive left and the far-right. The two most important far-right groups, Britain's UKIP and France's *Front National*, are explored in greater detail below. They are the most important because Britain, France and Germany are the most powerful EU states. Germany's far-right party hasn't had much electoral success. Donald Trump has close ideological connections with UKIP and the *Front National*.

We find that while the Tea Party had support among the middle class, UKIP and the *Front National* appeal more to working class voters. The common points between the Tea Party and Europe's far-right parties is that older white males are disproportionately represented. UKIP is one of the more extreme far-right parties in Europe because, unlike many far-right groups, it opposes social welfare, nationalization and promotes economic neoliberalism. It supports both the 'free market' and cutbacks to social security. Like the Tea Party, the *Front National* also supports the 'free market', but acknowledges the need for heavy state intervention.

Europe's Free Market Experiment

Between World War II and the liberalizations of the 1970s, there was a 'consensus' between governments and the public 'over the solidification of welfare state guarantees leading to governments increasingly taking responsibility for the security of their citizens', say political scientists Bohrer et al. However, with the adoption of neoliberal policies, 'competition led to constraints on domestic political agendas, particularly with regard to social expenditures'. Governments found themselves increasingly constrained by integration into a so-called free market global economy. The Maastricht Treaty of 1992, which led to the creation of the euro, 'formalized these constraints'.[1]

By the year 2000, 14 out of 15 EU member state governments were 'left-wing', including the 'big four': France, Germany, Italy and the UK. With the exception of the UK, which never adopted the euro, the Maastricht Treaty required governments, left and right, to impose fiscal austerity (i.e., social cutbacks) on their populations, even during the recession of the early-1990s. At first, publics responded rationally and progressively by voting for left-wing governments. But as conditions deteriorated, the publics lost faith in left governments. Instead of mobilizing and demanding action from their representatives, many people gave up. Low voter turnout and failure to engage in union activities ensured that the centre-right and far-right gained significant ground.[2]

The first major success of the far-right in modern Europe was the propulsion of the Austria Freedom Party (discussed below), which came second in the 1999 elections. The EU-wide policy of slow growth, high unemployment and welfare cutbacks, 'create[s] a large pool of disenchanted citizens amenable to radical appeals'. Perhaps of equal importance, this has also created 'a crisis of perception' among working and former middle class white Europeans: that their jobs are going to immigrants. The authors conclude: 'since migration rates vary substantially, we can infer ... that changes in rates of migration into European countries cannot adequately explain increases in votes for the far-right'.[3]

Europe's Far-right[*]
At the time of writing, Belgium's Vlaams Belang (Flemish Interest) holds one out of 17 seats in the Brussels Parliament and 6 out of 124 in the Flemish parliament. The party considers itself pro-Israeli in the fight against Islam. The party professes broad opposition to migration, yet backs economic neoliberalism.

---

[*] Information in this subchapter is found at http://www.europarl.europa.eu/ and http://www.demsoc.org/.

Bulgaria's Attack Party is one of the most difficult to place on the left–right spectrum. It is linked to the Bulgarian Orthodox Church. It has 11 out of 240 National Assembly seats. It believes in Bulgarian national superiority and is anti-Semitic, anti-Muslim and anti-Roma. Its left-wing aspects, however, include investing in health and education and renationalizing the country's assets. Its nationalistic tendencies – some positive, some negative – tend to make it anti-EU.

Croatia's Patriotic Coalition consists of eight different parties, including the Croatian Christian Democratic Party, the Pensioners Together Bloc, the nationalist Croatian Party of Rights and the Conservative Croatian Democratic Union, which holds 49 of the country's 151 parliamentary seats. The latter party left the coalition in July 2016, as did over a thousand members of the Croatian Party of Rights and the Croatian Peasant Party. This left the more right-wing elements in charge. Some of the coalition members are associated with the World War II Nazi puppets, the Ustashe, which killed hundreds of thousands of Gypsies/Roma and Jews in concentration camps.

Cyprus is under joint Greek–Turkish governance. The National Popular Front (ELAM) recently won two seats in the 56-seat parliament. It opposes Turkish Cypriots and immigrants. It is closely associated with the Golden Dawn party of Greece.

The Danish People's Party is explicitly nationalist, anti-Muslim and monarchic. It holds 37 out of 179 seats in the Folketing (parliament).

Estonia's Conservative People's Party holds 7 out the Riigikogu (parliament's) 101 seats. It is an ethno-nationalist, anti-EU party. It opposes social cutbacks on health and education and advocates fluency in Estonian among educators and health professionals. It opposes abortion and same-sex relationships.

The Finns Party holds 37 out of 200 seats in the parliament. It supports the welfare state but opposes the EU. At the European Parliament, it works with the UK Tory Party and Poland's Law and Justice Party to weaken the institution. The party is far-right in the sense that it opposes same-sex marriage and seeks to put national identity on the school curriculum. It also opposes the reduction of fossil fuels in favour of industrial investment. It supports working migrants only.

The Alternative for Germany holds no seats in the Bundestag but holds 145 out of 1,857 in the state parliaments. It has allied with Austria's far-right FPÖ, denies anthropogenic climate change, seeks to conscript men over 18, opposes the EU and is broadly against immigration.

Greece's Golden Dawn holds 26 out of 725 regional seats and 18 out of 300 in parliament. Some of the Golden Dawn's policies are progressive. They include: nationalizing natural resources and state banks, offering tax breaks to young parents, increasing domestic production, demanding World War II-era reparations from Germany, cancelling the illegal national debt and integrating economically with China, Iran and Russia. Other policies are regressive: using nationalized resources to extract fossil fuels, expanding 'free trade' and expelling illegal immigrants.

Jobbik (the Movement for a Better Hungary) is a Christian nationalist party which came third in the 2014 election. It has 24 out of 199 representatives in the National Assembly and 81 out of 419 seats in the County Assemblies. In a blow to freedom of speech, the Supreme Court of Hungary ruled that radio and television cannot refer to Jobbik as far-right, but rather 'radical right', as the party describes itself. Its policies include opposition to EU integration and migration and advocacy of a police state and the death penalty. One of its policies is divestment from Israel but for negative reasons, namely anti-Semitism.

Italy's Northern League for the Independence of Padania is a regionalist party. It has 2 out of 20 seats in the regional government assembly and 12 out of 315 in the Senate. The party has been mopping up votes from disenfranchised socialist, communist and Christian voters who feel that the central government has too much power.

Latvia's National Alliance is a coalition formed by the far-right All for Latvia and the conservative TB/LNNK. It holds 17 out of 100 seats in the Saeima (parliament). The party's main platform is opposition to migration. It is anti-Russian and has mobilized demonstrations against immigrants.

The Netherlands' Party for Freedom opposes government spending on the public, supports the 'free market', opposes the EU and is hostile to immigration and Muslims. The Party opposes dual citizenship. Some of its policies are progressive but for regressive reasons, such as wanting to ban kosher and halal slaughter, not for the sake of animal welfare but to weaken non-Christian religions. The Party holds 12 of the 150 House of Representative seats and 9 of the 75 Senate seats.

Poland's ruling Law and Justice Party is rhetorically Eurosceptic, broadly 'free market' and pro-US. The Party is anti-abortion, anti-homosexuality and anti-immigration. In 2014, it joined Britain's Tory government to work on 'reforms' within the European Parliament.

Slovakia's Kotleba (People's Party–Our Slovakia) won 14 seats out of 150 in the National Council. The Party's progressive policies include opposition to American hegemony and NATO. It is, however, anti-Roma and anti-Muslim and runs on an ethno-nationalist platform.

Sweden's Democrats hold 49 out of 349 Riksdag (parliament) seats. It is a politically conservative, culturally far-right party which opposes immigration, particularly Muslim immigration, and the regional sovereignty of Sweden's ethnic Samis who live in the north.

UKIP: Party of the Paranoid

Tory Prime Minister Theresa May said that Britain and the US have an 'enduring and special relationship', which is why Trump telephoned nine heads of state before speaking to her. The first British politician to meet President-Elect Trump was UKIP leader Nigel Farage, who is not part of the Tory government. Trump suggested that Farage should become Britain's ambassador to America. May and the Foreign Office killed the proposal, unsurprisingly.[4] By May 2017, UKIP had zero MPs (after their only MP quit) and was crushed in the local council elections earlier that month.

The so-called anti-establishment success of Trump and Brexit, which UKIP championed, has empowered Europe's nationalist far-right. The strong political alliance between Trump and Farage, and the fact that Farage has received a warm welcome on pro-Trump shows like Fox and the Alex Jones Show, suggests that traditional politics, where politicians are the middlemen/women of big business, is weakening and big business is coming directly to the fore.[5]

UKIP is the United Kingdom Independence Party. Its two main platforms are anti-immigration and opposition to Britain's involvement in the European Union. It was formed as the Anti-Federalist Alliance in 1991 by historian and former Liberal candidate, Alan Sked. It became UKIP in 1993. Sked appears to have backed away from UKIP because it moved too far right and, according to Sked, had too much in common with the far-right British National Party (BNP). In terms of success and popularity, at the European Parliament elections of 2004 UKIP took second place to the Referendum Party, founded by millionaire James Goldsmith, whose members include Priti Patel, who is now a Tory MP and a member of Theresa May's cabinet. UKIP came third (securing 2.6m votes).[6]

After a key member defected in 2005, UKIP found itself competing with the BNP. In opposition to Nigel Farage, several core members suggested forming a pact with the BNP. In 2006, Farage, an ex-banker and ex-Tory, was elected leader. In 2009, UKIP won 13 seats in the European Parliament. In 2013, it got 22% of the local election vote share. It 2014, it won 24 seats in the European Parliament. In the 2015 general election, UKIP won two seats in the British Parliament and gained 3.8m votes (or 16% of the vote share).[7]

Like America's Tea Party, UKIP is financed by the wealthy. In a 2012 report, Farage said: 'The key to money for us will be the hedge fund industry'. UKIP's donors from 2014 (for example) included £1.3m from the real estate developers the Highstone Group, £199,500 from hedge fund CEO Stuart Wheeler, £85,000 from management consultants Growth Financial Services Ltd, and £65,000 from property developer, Mura Estates.[8]

So, who actually votes for UKIP? The typical UKIP voter is older, poorer and has fewer qualifications than the average British voter.

UKIP has managed to mobilize support on an anti-EU basis by claiming that Brussels has power over the British economy. With few exceptions, such as the fishing and farming sectors, this is factually incorrect. Britain has opted out of more EU legislation than any other country. Older voters tended to vote for Britain's exit from the EU (Brexit) in 2016. 46% of all voters in the UK are over 50 years old. By comparison, 71% of UKIP voters are over 50. Only 13% of UKIP voters hold a university degree. We point this out not to insult people but to show that UKIP voters have had fewer life choices and fewer rewards for their hard work.[9]

UKIP has been absorbing the Labour Party's votes since circa 2004. This happened because Poland and Romania acceded to the European Union and hundreds of thousands of Poles and Romanians settled in Britain. This became a particular sore point after the Financial Crisis. The 'centre-right' Tories came to power in 2010 in a coalition with the Liberals, who betrayed their 'liberal' platform by agreeing to Tory austerity. In 2010, 60% of UKIP supporters voted Tory. By the 2013 by-election, however, just 12% of UKIP supporters voted Tory.[10]

The YouGov polling agency finds that many UKIP voters are to the left on domestic issues in that most favour the (re)nationaliza-tion of domestic industries and services. But at the same time, more UKIP voters than Tories read the right-wing, racist, anti-immigrant tabloids.[11]

Interestingly, 40% of Tory voters place themselves right-of-centre on the political spectrum, but less than half of UKIP voters self-identify as right-of-centre (46%). Just 25% of Tories self-identify as centre or left-of-centre. But 36% of UKIP voters self-identify as centre or left-of-centre. This means that progressive activists and intellectuals should be reaching out more to UKIP voters, many of whom have left-leaning tendencies on issues other than immi-gration.[12]

UKIP constituents are a hotchpotch of political ideologies. Their main concerns are that Britain accepts too many immigrants and that Brussels has too much power over Westminster. UKIP voters include people who support or supported the racist English

Defence League and the BNP. But they also include ex-Labour voters who believe in working class values but who feel sold out by Labour's unwillingness to discuss immigration. Three million people who voted Labour in 1997 had abstained or switched to the far-right by 2010. Seventy-eight per cent of these defectors cite immigration as their motivation. When Tony Blair took office as leader of the self-styled New Labour Party, net immigration was 55,000 a year. By the time Blair left in 2009, it was 250,000 a year.[13]

Most UKIP voters, however, are ex-Tory supporters.

It is also interesting to note that *fear* of change and *fear* of immigration is more important to UKIP voters and *Front National* voters in France than actual immigration.

According to the British think-tank Demos, 80% of the British public generally opposes immigration. Most opponents are white. They constitute a '[d]isproportionate ethnic English opposition to immigration', caused in part by the declining number of white English people. In Chapter 1, we noted the decline of white America and some of the ugly politics that result from this demographic shift. The ethnic bases for opposition to immigration in the UK are not universal. Many white British people are opposed to white Polish and white Romanian immigrants. Nevertheless, the authors point out that the share of so-called visible minorities (e.g., people of African, Bangladeshi, Chinese etc. descent.) doubled in England and Wales between 2001 and 2011.[14]

The authors made the very important discovery that integration is the key to overcoming prejudice and attraction to far-right politics. '[W]hite British opposition to immigration, and far-right voting, is lower in locales with more minorities and immigrants'. So-called white wards, where white people are isolated in high-density migrant and ethnic minority areas, do however tend to have higher levels of support for far-right parties more than in areas where whites are integrated.[15]

A map of UKIP voters and potential UKIP voters by the *Telegraph* shows that UKIP is more popular in regions of low migration than in regions of high migration. The map illustrates the importance of perception over reality in the minds of UKIP voters.[16]

Le Front National: *Party of the Poor*

France's *Front National* (FN) is a republican party vehemently opposed to the European Union and the euro. It runs on an anti-Islam, anti-immigration platform. Its *de facto* leader, Marine Le Pen, advocates state intervention in the economy to prop up businesses until businesses can succeed without subsidies.

The FN was founded in 1972 by ex-paratrooper Jean-Marie Le Pen, who led the party until 2011 when his daughter, Marine, took over. Le Pen the elder was born in Brittany (northern France) in 1928. Ironically, or perhaps not so ironically, Le Pen studied law and had a reputation for beating up communists. At that time, the French Empire was trying to hold on to Vietnam in opposition to 'communist' nationalists. Le Pen joined the Foreign Legion and fought in the battle of Dien Bien Phu, Indochina.[17]

This biographical sketch shows Le Pen's ideological opposition to communism and a willingness to use violence to advance nationalist goals. At 28, Le Pen was the youngest member of the French parliament, the National Assembly, having served in the populist UDCA party. Le Pen supported a Muslim politician, Ahmed Djebbour, who opposed the FLN – Algeria's national liberation group which used terrorism to defeat the much greater terror of the French occupation. Le Pen presumably supported the Muslim candidate for tactical reasons, namely that in Algeria proper the FLN was a socialist organization which attacked Muslims. Le Pen served as an intelligence officer in Algeria in the late-1950s. (Soraya Djebbour, Ahmed's daughter, took office in local council elections in 1986. But Soraya disassociated herself from the FN, citing racism and Islamophobia.)[18]

Le Pen retired from the military and went on to produce music associated with the Nazis. The FN attracted neo-Nazis and traditionalist Catholics. The FN won its first seat in the European Parliament in 1984. In 2002, bolstered by the 9/11 attacks, Le Pen secured 10% of the national presidential election vote. In terms of money, Le Pen inherited wealth from a supporter named Hubert Lambert, who provided Le Pen's mansion in Saint-Cloud.[19]

The polls show that as France became more neoliberal after it signed the Maastricht Treaty, support for the far-right increased.

In the 1995 elections, the FN won five of France's 22 metropolitan regions and 18 out of the 96 metropolitan departments. The FN's success in cities and towns, especially in industrial and urban areas in the north, north-east and central east, stemmed from increased support, 'from workers and unemployed voters and from those defining themselves as disadvantaged'. Like Labour losing votes to UKIP in Britain, traditional left voters switched to Le Pen, where the blue-collar vote leapt from 16% in 1988 to 27% in 1995. Support from white-collar workers also rose from 14% to 19% in the same period.[20]

Eleven per cent of the self-described 'privileged' voted for Le Pen, as did 8% of the 'well-off'. Ten per cent of the upper-middle class voted for him, as did 15% of the lower-middle class. But 19% of the *classes populaires* (working classes) voted Le Pen. Interestingly, support was highest among shopkeepers and artisans. Le Pen's success came from uniting voters traditionally 'on separate sides of the right/left divide'.[21]

James Shields of Aston University writes that by 2007, the FN had received nearly 4m votes and agreement with its policies was at an all-time high. 'In three presidential elections, Le Pen had seen his support grow from 0.7 per cent (fewer than 200,000 votes) in 1974 to 14.4 per cent (4.4 million) in 1988, then 15 per cent (4.6 million) in 1995'. In 2002, Le Pen got 16.9% of the popular vote. According to Shields, Le Pen's voter-base was 'strongest among blue-collar workers, small self-employed and unemployed in economically run-down areas of the north, north-east and south-east – typically areas most affected by industrial restructuring, high crime and immigration, with voters receptive to Le Pen's economically protectionist, anti-immigration, strong-arm law-and-order, "French first" policies'.[22]

In this respect, Le Pen voters are different from Tea Party supporters in the US in that they tend to be working class, not middle class. By the 2017 general election, the rise of Le Pen had weakened the already unpopular Socialist Party and strengthened the right-wing Republican party led by the Thatcherite François Fillon; until, that is, scandals damaged Fillon's credibility and Emmanuel Macron (ex-Rothschild & Cie Banque) emerged from the shadows of the Socialist Party to defeat Le Pen, running as an alleged independent.

Austria as a Case-study: When the Left Triumphs, Just

Austria, France and the Netherlands symbolize the battle against the far-right. France's status quo 'socialist' Emmanuel Macron snatched victory from the jaws of Le Pen at the last minute. The Liberals of Holland beat Geert Wilders, with enough room however for a possible coalition with the far-righter. Austria's President-elect, Alexander van der Bellen, is a member of The Greens–The Green Alternative party of Austria, which started out as two parties. Van der Bellen entered the race as an independent. In May 2016, he narrowly beat the far-right Austria Freedom Party (FPÖ) leader, Heinz-Christian Strache. Strache challenged the decision at the Constitutional Court and won. The Court ruled that Austria must hold a second election. The FPÖ's candidate Nobert Hofer was defeated by van der Bellen in the December election.[23]

In 1984, Austria's two main 'green' parties coalesced and attracted young, middle class urban voters. The coalition sells itself as anti-establishment and has garnered a reputation for members arriving in parliament donning jeans and trainers in place of suits. The party flaunted its anti-hierarchy credentials by electing a mannequin (they built a figure literally made of straw and nominated it leader).[24]

By the 1990s, '50 percent of Green voters had close ties' to either of Austria's two main 'green' parties. '[R]oughly 35 percent of Green votes came from floating voters who had abandoned the two major parties' (US Library of Congress). The party also shifted to a pro-European Union policy. Some members considered forming an alliance with the Austrian People's Party, a centre-right Catholic–democratic organization. By 2014, the Greens had succeeded in getting ministers elected in several states. The Greens now have a near-100% loyalty base among their voters.[25]

At the other end of the spectrum is the far-right Freedom Party of Austria (FPÖ), founded in 1955. In 1983, the FPÖ formed a coalition with the left-of-centre Social Democratic Party. When Jörg Haider became influential in the party, it lost a number of liberal members and ran on a solid platform of anti-establishment, anti-Islam and xenophobia. The FPÖ gained 26.9% of the vote in 1999, up from 5% in 1983. It formed a coalition with the Austrian People's Party but by 2005 had faltered, gaining only 10% of the popular vote. Haider quit to form the Alliance for the Future of Austria. Strache took over the party with a strong constituency of young males (32% of support from the under-29s compared with 10% of women under 29).[26]

The 2014 election saw the FPÖ winning 40 seats and coming 7th. By 2016, all that changed. Nobert Hofer ran for President in 2016 against the Greens' van der Bellen. Dubbed the 'Donald Trump of Europe', Hofer represents the FPÖ and has served on the boards of the following businesses: Eurosolar Austria, Mapjet AG, International Sky Services AG and the PAF private trust. He is a self-professed Thatcherite.[27]

The far-left van der Bellen's voters are broken down as follows. Among those who voted for either candidate: women under 30 years who voted for van der Bellen, 67%; women age 30–59, 59%; women over 60, 56%. Men under 29, 42%; men between 30–59, 37%; men over 60, 45%. Hofer's vote share is as follows: Women under 30, 33%; women between 30–59, 41%; women over 60, 44%. Men under 29, 58%; men between 30–59, 63%; men over 60, 55%.[28]

Hofer's voters are as follows: working class, 86%; public servants, 45%; private sector workers, 40%; self-employed, 53%; pensioners, 49%. Van der Bellen's are as follows: working class, 14%; private sector workers, 60%; public sector workers, 55%; self-employed, 47%; and pensioners, 51%. These polls suggest a relatively equal split of the vote share, except among the working classes who seem to favour the Thatcherite Hofer.[29]

Inequality is at the heart of the far-right/far-left split.

A report by GINI finds that Austria's inequality, labour flexibility and unemployment are low by European standards but have increased markedly since the 1970s, after which the Greens and the FPÖ started gaining ground. 'As in many other Western societies, the starting point was a transformation in the economy at the end of the 1970s and the beginning of the 1980s, wrought primarily by two oil shocks and the liberalization of trade and capital markets'. The authors point to 'a slight but continuous rise in income inequality among Austrian households between 1983 and 2010'.[30]

The report also notes that, 'income tax data show a nearly continuous rise in the inequality of wage distribution since the mid-1990s' (sic). By 2004, '[t]he least wealth was found, as expected, among low earners, young adults, workers and low-skilled', that is people who were more likely to vote for Hofer's FPÖ. The GINI report notes that, 'the bottom 40 per cent of households own no housing whatsoever'.[31]

Very important, and a common theme in the rise of extreme politics, is the decline in union membership. In Austria, union membership declined from 60% in the 1970s to 30% by 2010. Although at the high end of the OECD[*] average, voter turnout has been declining since the 1970s. As in most countries, the Financial Crisis and austerity-aftermath saw declining levels of trust in government. Austria is unique among European countries in its perception of inequality: 'The vast majority of Austrians perceive inequality ... to be excessive'. Neoliberalism has damaged the historic perception of the social partnership, which, in the mythology, balanced employer and employee interests. Austria spends more on pensions, social protection and education than the OECD average, but Austrians see the rewards of their hard work going to the richest 10%.[32]

Between 1980 and 2010, debt-to-GNP more than doubled. The consolidation of welfare over employment and the mounting national debt were bolstered by Austria's accession to the EU in 1995 and its adherence to the Maastricht Treaty, which effectively ended the social contract by privatizing services, laying off public

---

[*] Organization for Economic Cooperation and Development.

sector workers and reducing benefits. Poverty grew by 17% in 20 years. The report also goes on to mention that fewer Austrians returned to education in the 1980s–90s, a trend which has remained stable, due in part to the devaluation of college degrees. Social mobility is a problem and remains largely class-based. There is a shortage of day-care facilities. These factors are partly responsible for women giving birth at the average age of 28.5 years, which is high compared to the rest of the world. Marriage rates have declined and divorce rates have risen to nearly 45%. This is due in large part to money-related stress.[33]

Youth unemployment in Austria averages 8.2% compared with general unemployment at just over 5%. According to the European Monitoring Centre on Change, 'Austrian [youth] have above average unemployment rates'. The organization says that of particular concern is the use of temporary contracts in the form of apprenticeships and traineeships. Many young people are insecure and, thanks to cutbacks and privatization which began in the 1980s and became more apparent after the Financial Crisis, are not fully supported by the state. In addition, many see migrants and second generation migrants taking 'their' jobs. Between 2007 and 2012, the government initiated a programme to train potential migrant school dropouts, free of charge, and get them into work or higher education.[34]

Despite the large base of disaffected young Austrians, the far-right was unable to gain a majority in the contested 2016 Presidential election. Trump has empowered Europe's far-right, but grassroots progressive leftism is not dead yet.

Chapter 5

Alt-right now: Billionaire populism

'It is better to live one day as a lion than 100 years as a sheep.'

— Benito Mussolini. Quoted by Donald J. Trump, *Twitter*,
28 February 2016

The financial deregulations outlined in the preceding chapters created a new class of billionaires and multibillionaires in the hedge fund industry. Until the 1970s, financial institutions (banks being the most profitable) made most of their money by supporting industry and private consumers, typically through issuing loans. Deregulation shifted profit-making from the 'real economy' of production and consumption to the financial economy of debt, services, liquidity and derivatives.[1]

The last 40 years have seen the growth of non-banking financial institutions: advisors, asset firms, clearing houses, creditors, hedge funds, insurers, liquidity lenders, pension companies and ratings agencies. They claim that the Financial Crisis was caused by *over-regulation*. Worried about Trump's anti-hedge fund rhetoric and promises to protect America against foreign competition, Wall Street poured record donations into the coffers of the Clinton campaign. But a core of hedge fund managers saw through the hot air and backed the Republicans. Only the Republicans, and especially the extremist ones like Trump and his advisor Steve Bannon, would repeal the Democrats' post-Crisis regulations, like Dodd–Frank discussed in the Introduction.[2]

In November 2016, CNBC reported that '[j]ust 12 percent' of hedge fund managers polled by Preqin 'think Trump will have negative effects on the nearly $3 trillion [hedge fund] industry'. The report also notes that '57 percent believe the likelihood for repatriation of at least some of the $2.5 trillion in corporate cash sitting overseas will benefit the industry'. It turns out that hedge fund

CEOs, particularly Robert Mercer of Renaissance Technologies, are quietly funding a loose ideological movement known in America as the 'alt-right' (alternative right). The alt-right is a broad spectrum which includes everything from white supremacy to anti-feminism, from rejection of traditional Republicanism to advocacy of outright migration and refugee prohibition. As well as general opposition to Islam, which the alt-right regards as a backward culture, the alt-right shares one common goal: ending taxes at the expense of social spending. The hedge fund class of billionaires can't admit their aims publicly through television and radio appearances, so they have set up alternative media platforms on the internet which utilize the worst aspects of populism, including racism and xeno-phobia.[3]

The Billionaires Backing Trump

Trump claims to be so rich that he didn't need the money of 'special interest' groups. The aim of this propaganda was to show that he's so pure as a billionaire he didn't need to become corrupted by taking the money of people who were funding his political rivals in the Democratic Party and even in the Republican Party. The logic, if you can call it that, was: vote for a billionaire because he can't be bought by billionaires.[4]

Although Trump received far less funding from Wall Street than Clinton, Trump did receive sizeable donations from fellow billion-aires, particularly from hedge fund CEOs. Many backed the Republican Party because they wanted an end to the kind of Dodd–Frank regulation which cripples their profit-making potential. The financial community overwhelmingly backed Hillary Clinton for President in 2016. However, hedge funds were split over Trump, with the biggest, Warren Buffett's Berkshire Hathaway (which some argue isn't a hedge fund) and George Soros's Soros Fund Man-agement backing Clinton. Others backed Trump. The *Wall Street Journal* published a false story that most hedge funds were backing Clinton. But as *Fortune* points out, most of the so-called hedge funds mentioned by the *WSJ* article are not hedge funds, but include asset firms and liquidity companies.[5]

Hedge funds 'embraced Trump more than he's letting on', says *Fortune* magazine. By August 2016, Trump claimed to have raised a mere $19,000 from hedge funds compared to the 'tens of millions' given to the Clinton campaign. *Fortune* notes: 'Trump's head of fundraising, his national campaign finance director Steven Mnuchin is in fact a hedge fund manager. So is Carl Icahn, the businessman Trump regularly [cites] as top supporter. Another Trump backer is Stephen Feinberg, who is the head of Cerberus Capital Management'. The article goes on: 'Robert Mercer, too, the hedge fund manager who once supported Ted Cruz, is now reportedly backing Trump'. About 20% of Trump's funding came from the hedge fund sector.[6]

Mercer is the hedge fund billionaire CEO of Renaissance Technologies. He indirectly funded Clinton's rival, Cruz, with $11m. Reuters describes Mercer as 'a powerful financial force in conservative politics'. (Cruz's wife Heidi is a Goldman Sachs executive.) Paul Singer of Elliott Management donated $2.5m — as did Kenneth Griffin of the Citadel Investment Group — to an organization helping Republican candidate Marco Rubio. Other hedge funds backing Republicans include Steve Cohen's Point72 Asset Management, David Tepper's Appaloosa Management and Larry Robbins's Glenview Capital Management.[7]

Tom Barrack of Colony Capital and Wilbur Ross of WL Ross & Co. also backed Trump.[8]

Although many did not back Trump, they welcomed his presidency. David Tawil of Maglan Capital said: 'I would expect that the easing-up on Wall Street will occur more around the edges' with Trump as President. After Trump won, money manager Anthony Scaramucci spoke of the anti-Wall Street and anti-K Street rhetoric coming from politicians. Scaramucci said: 'That nonsense is ending: the anti-banking cabal and the screed of hatred for people that live on Wall Street'. Ray Dalio of Bridgewater Associates said of Trump: 'there are pluses and minuses. I don't think he is necessarily protectionist, and he is very pro-business with his policies ... Money chases hospitable environments, and if you create an environment where the taxes are lower, for example, it can attract money from all over the place. Money moves very quickly'.[9]

John Paulson (worth $9.8bn) founded Paulson & Co. He made his money using credit default swaps, one of the money instruments responsible for the Crisis. Bill Ackman (worth over $1bn) of Pershing Square said of Trump: 'He's going to launch an infrastructure program. He's going to take corporate taxes down to sensible levels. He's going to get things done ... And that's extremely bullish for growth in the United States'. After Trump won, Dan Loeb of Third Point LLC said: 'This environment is undoubtedly better for active investing – just as active investing was considered to be on its deathbed'. Loeb is particularly keen on higher interest rates, tax cuts (or non-government monetary stimulus in the nomenclature) and lower correlations between securities and stock dispersion.[10]

Alt-right Ideologues

The alt-right is a loose movement of would-be politicians, internet and radio pundits and think tanks. We might first ask, to what is the alt-right an alternative? The Obama years were glory days for the financial institutions which posted record profits, thanks in no small part to bailouts. But there were a few problems: overwhelmingly, it was the tax money of the middle classes and upper classes, not the lower classes, which bailed out the banks. The alt-right wants a balance between lowering taxes for the rich and ensuring that risky financial transactions will receive bailouts. The alt-right is also an alternative to the status quo media which is not, on the whole, pushing for tax reform.[11]

Under the banners of patriotism and libertarianism, the alt-right's common theme is eliminating taxation and dismantling social spending (on education, healthcare, state pensions and welfare). Because of the establishment left's (i.e., Obama and candidate Clinton's) bare-minimum commitments to social spending, the alt-right smears the establishment left as 'socialism'. Another ideology shared by alt-righters is Islamophobia. The movement considers Islam un-American, inherently backward and a threat to national security. The messages of the alt-right are often mixed because at one end of the spectrum lies white supremacism; at the other lies opposition to illegal immigration.[12]

The amorphous alt-right has succeeded in employing women, minorities and homosexuals to attack feminism, people of colour and LGBT rights. This apparent paradox (e.g. of gay alt-right men denouncing homosexuals and homosexuality) can be explained by class. Most alt-right followers are middle to upper class (i.e., they or their parents earn over $50K a year. This question is connected to the broader one concerning the popularity of the alt-right in America, a point to which we shall return). The majority of alt-right supporters are middle class white men. Let's look at some of their propagandists.[13]

Andrew Breitbart

In his book *Righteous Indignation* (2012), the late journalist Breitbart (worth over $9m) describes a 'New Media war against the Progressive movement and its standard-bearer, President Obama, as well as the vast left-wing media apparatus that rigs the national narrative'. The so-called national narrative is rigged against wealthy white men, Breitbart infers. The libertarian alt-righters are on a crusade to liberate hardworking Americans from taxation and scroungers, as well as the corrupt left-wing establishment. 'America is in a media war', says Breitbart. 'It is an extension of the Cold War that never ended but shifted to an electronic front. The war between freedom and statism ended geographically when the Berlin Wall fell. But the existential battle never ceased'. The so-called weapons of the 'left' are schools, newspapers, network news, art, music, film and television, which indoctrinate children with subversive notions, like equality, racial and religious tolerance and solidarity. (As if that's true.)[14]

The radio host Rush Limbaugh, 'shot the first shot of the New Media war over twenty years ago', Breitbart continues. 'The constellation of AM talk radio, the Internet (*Drudge Report*, plus countless bloggers), and Fox News represent the successful, better-late-than-never counterattack against the left's unchallenged control of a center-right nation'. Notice Breitbart's false assumption that the nation is 'center-right'. As we shall see, public opinion polls suggest that on most issues, most Americans are left of the government: both left-wing and right-wing governments. Worse, some of the alt-right appear to be genuine ideologues. On writing his book, Breitbart writes: 'I feel it is a moral imperative and a patriotic duty'. Some of the many aspects of the 'left' (i.e., the government) opposed by Breitbart include 'taxing, overtaxing, ... redistribut[ion]'. He describes himself as 'a reluctant cultural warrior'.[15]

Stephen K. Bannon

Breitbart News co-founder Bannon holds a Master's Degree in national security studies and is an ex-Naval Officer. Worth $10m, he also worked for Goldman Sachs before making a career in the alternative media. He is very much influenced by a book called *The Fourth Turning* (1997), in which the authors suggest that history can be neatly divided into periods of decline and fall. America is in a period of inevitable decline. Above, we note that some alt-righters might actually be committed ideologues. Bannon could be one of them. He believes that his mission is to save America in this dark period, lest it goes the way of all former great powers.

Speaking at the right-wing Liberty Restoration Foundation in Florida in 2011, Bannon complained: 'we've built in a welfare state that is completely and totally unsustainable ... The scale of federal spending ... sucks dollars out of everywhere else ... The system lacks the political courage to actually take it on'. Hence the need for a splinter movement, hence the birth of the alt-right. '[T]he Republican establishment did not support [the Tea Party] ... They were mocking the Tea Party', says Bannon. He lays out more alt-right objectives: 'Why is the budget not being cut? It's not cut because it's not easy to cut. Everybody's gonna have to take a hit here. And if we draw a line – and it has to be a tough [one] – no more taxes, no more tax increases'.[16]

When government robs even more from the poor, the poor (many of whom are black and Latino–Hispanic) tend to get politically active. If they can be portrayed as pampered socialists living easy off the sweat of the hardworking, white American middle-class, it is easier to not only deny them, but make them look like an alienated fringe. By denigrating both directly and by association politically and socially oppressed people, the alt-right pre-empts the inevitable social upheaval caused by massive welfare reductions.[17]

Bannon continues. Part of the problem has been the 'apathy of the middle', meaning the unwillingness of the Republicans to free taxes and slash more public spending, and apathy from the 'apparatus on the left'. Some far-righters think of themselves as centrists. They consider Republicans left-wing and Democrats socialists. (To them, people like Sanders are off the spectrum.) Like Breitbart, Bannon believes 'we're a center-right nation ... But there's only a small core ... prepared to throw their being ... into trying to change this'. Enter Trump the populist with his anti-establishmentarianism.

Bannon sought to mobilize the disaffected middle class, which was easy to do given how low their status had fallen thanks to the very neoliberal policies (like tax cuts) advocated by Bannon: 'The anger of the Tea Party is not racism. They're not homophobes. They're not nativists. What they are is common sense, practical, middle-class people [who] understand that they're paying for their own and for their children's destruction'. Criticizing the Occupy Wall Street movement, Bannon lamented: 'those kids ... have no idea about the fundamentals of our liberty, the fundamentals of free market capitalism'. If they were educated, said Bannon, they would realize that the real enemy is big government (see Propaganda Translator), not big money. Big money is the solution.[18]

Ann Coulter

Ann Coulter is the millionaire history-graduate lawyer daughter of FBI agent, John Vincent Coulter. As a teenager, she was indoctrinated with neoliberal tracts written by Milton Friedman and Nixon's Treasury Secretary, William E. Simon. Coulter seems genuinely worried that 'America' (however one defines it) is disappearing. Coulter indirectly shares Bannon's end-time philosophy and moral crusade to save the country. 'We allow everyone else in the world to have a home, even though theirs are far less successful than ours', writes Coulter in her book, *In Trump We Trust* (2016). '[O]nce a species is gone, it's gone ... the same is true of countries. If Trump loses, at least we'll finally know: it was too late'.[19]

Coulter complains that '[t]he left had too much time to bring in ringers and change the country's demographics'. Here Coulter shares the ideology of the extreme alt-righters like Richard Spencer, head of the National Policy Institute, who famously exclaimed, 'Heil Trump!'. Coulter is worried that blacks and Mexicans are ending white America and that Muslims are threatening the country's Judeo–Christian foundations. (Bannon also mentions 'Judeo–Christian values'.) For Coulter, the alt-right is a vehicle in which to appeal to a core of middle class Americans who feel cheated by the establishment. The Republicans have lost votes because even when they are in power, the average North Carolinian, for instance, 'still loses his job to a foreign worker or a closed manufacturing plant, his kids are still boxed out of college by affirmative action for immigrants, his community is still plagued with high taxes and high crime brought in with all that cheap foreign labor'. Trump is the first Republican candidate not to self-censor over these issues, says Coulter.[20]

Trump can say these things because he's rich enough not to 'need the party and the donors'. By failing to mention these important issues (which we argue in Part II of this book are not so important to most Americans), the Republican Party is 'suicidal'. Unlike Trump, the core of globalists funding the Republicans have prevented candidates from talking about 'immigration, trade, and wars to remake the Middle East'.[21]

Lauren Southern

Ezra Levant is a Canadian ex-tobacco and big energy lobbyist who launched the alt-right internet show *The Rebel Media*. One of its reporters is Libertarian Party of Canada candidate, Lauren Southern. Southern has appeared on America's *The Alex Jones Show* (a popular mouthpiece for Trump) and is the author of the book, *Barbarians: How Baby Boomers, Immigrants, and Islam Screwed My*

Generation (2016). The book has been praised by Coulter and 'anarcho-capitalist' alt-righter, Stefan Molyneux.[22]

The Southern brand of alt-rightism is an unapologetic opposition to solidarity and compassion. Southern writes: '[i]t is . . . a recklessly naïve, utopian view of the world holding hands, loving each other, and singing Kumbaya, even though all of history, social science, and common sense militate against that actually happening'. Southern's brand of socioeconomic individualism has been present in one form or another throughout history, but in our time it is formulated as economic policy in the form of neoliberalism.[23]

Southern cites Milton Friedman who 'famously said that you can't have open borders and a welfare state'. But Republicans don't go far enough, she says. 'The problem is that they think you can get rid of the welfare state by having open borders'. This approach failed in Europe, says Southern: not that any western European state ever tried to destroy its welfare system, except the UK whose government is trying to, but for reasons other than migration. (As we shall see, it is actually the left-voting, liberals Bill Gates and Mark Zuckerberg pushing a hard-line on borders.) Immigrants are to blame for an expanding welfare state, says Southern, in large part due to voter 'fraud'. This meal ticket 'causes the entire government to go broke'.[24]

Southern's hatred of migrants extends to her belief that they 'ask for . . . deliberately low wages'. Migrants 'also depress wages and take much-needed work in the most vulnerable native communities'. Of course, Southern is not referring to First Nations when she says 'natives'. (They could tell her a thing or two about immigrants stealing jobs: and land and life.) Mainstream conservatism has failed in its refusal to act against immigration. '[B]oth liberals and conservatives in the West are constantly pushing for more immigration, even when that immigration occurs against the wishes of their people, or against the letter of their own laws'. Following Coulter's theme that America is at risk of extinction at the hands of liberals, Southern writes that low-skilled immigrants (notice her opposition to low-skilled, not high-skilled migrants) 'siphon money out of our domestic economy and send it back to their own countries, which boosts those countries at our expense'.[25]

The Billionaires Behind the Alt-right

The alt-right media, especially *Breitbart News* and its infamous affiliates like Milo Yiannopoulos, appear to have popped up out of nowhere. The success of the alt-right media is commonly attributed to the large number of people in America and across the world who share their views. But the reality is that the alt-right is a fringe movement. Its success can be largely attributed to secretive billionaire donors.

Robert Mercer

Above we noted hedge fund billionaire Robert Mercer. Mercer and his daughter Rebekah not only financed the Trump campaign and *Breitbart News* (to the tune of $10m in 2011 alone), but the Mercers reportedly arranged for Steve Bannon to work in Trump's cabinet. *Vanity Fair* reports that Robert and Rebekah Mercer spent $13.5m in donations to organizations supporting Republican Ted Cruz. After Cruz dropped out, their funding went to Trump. *Bloomberg* alleges that Rebekah met Trump's daughter Ivanka and her husband, Jared Kushner. Rebekah reportedly suggested that Trump employ *Breitbart* editor Steve Bannon as his chief strategist.[26]

Peter Thiel

Reddit was founded in 2005 as a news aggregation/sharing/rating and community forum site. In 2014, a pool including Peter Thiel invested millions of dollars in the website. Thiel (worth over $2bn) is the founder of PayPal and a major Facebook investor. He is a staunch Trump supporter whose book on technology start-ups, *Zero to One* (2014), inspired the Trump team's use of social media in the election campaign.[27]

After Thiel invested in Reddit, users established a subreddit called /r/The_Donald. KnowYourMeme.com analyses the Trump–Reddit pages. The About section reads: '/r/The_Donald is a subreddit for supporters of United States president-elect [now President] Donald Trump. Members of the online community often refer to themselves as "centipedes" and have been associated with the loose conservative group known as the "alt-right"'. The page also says: 'While the subreddit has a rule against "racism/anti-Semitism," posts and comments expressing "Islamophobia" are not restricted. On February 10th, 2016, a /r/The_Donald moderator stickied a post announcing to "stop reporting Islamophobia" '. The moderator wrote in full: 'Jesus Christ people, stop reporting Islamophobia. We don't fucking care about our "Islamophobia problem" AT ALL!' (emphasis in original).[28]

In 2015, author, journalist, webmaster and troll Chuck C. Johnson was banned from Twitter following requests for donations to murder Black Lives Matter activist, Deray McKesson. Johnson was later photographed at a dinner with white supremacists held in Washington, DC. In 2017, *Forbes* reported that Johnson 'is working behind the scenes with members of the transition team's executive committee, including billionaire Trump donor Peter Thiel, to recommend, vet and give something of a seal of approval to potential nominees from the so-called "alt-right" '.[29]

Palmer Luckey
Luckey is an entrepreneur worth $700m. In 2014, he sold his Oculus virtual reality start-up to Facebook for $2bn. Luckey started posting on Reddit's /r/The_Donald in an effort to raise funds for a non-profit entity called Nimble America. Under the username NimbleRichMan, Luckey wrote: 'I am a member of the 0.0001% ... I have supported Donald's presidential ambitions for years. I encouraged him to run in the last election ... I have already donated significant funds to Nimble America ... I will match your donations dollar for dollar'.[30]

'Shitposting' is a term used to describe forum posts and threads that take a subject off-topic and include generic abuse. It has been used by Trump supporters as a propaganda weapon against Hillary Clinton. KnowYourMeme.com notes that one of its Trump-supporting moderators allowed Palmer Luckey's Nimble America to get some free advertising, noting the success in shitposting. The site confirms that in September 2016, 'moderator TehDonald [sic] of the /r/the_donald subreddit submitted a post promoting ... Nimble America, remarking that the community had "proven that shitposting is powerful and meme magic is real." Meanwhile, Redditor NimbleRichMan [i.e., Luckey] submitted a /r/the_donald post asking for help defeating Hillary Clinton by donating to Nimble America'.[31]

Systemic Racism: Alt-right Distraction

The American system is inherently racist, as are most state systems (including Britain's). We should not allow the rise of the alt-right to distract us from the fact that centrist governments, including those thought of as progressive and liberal, are not much better in practice. Here are some examples:

In Chapter 6, we expand on the fact that the Electoral College, which allowed the losing candidate Trump to become President, has its roots in slavery. Under numerous US Presidents, including so-called Democratic progressives like Andrew Jackson, Native Americans were almost exterminated. Today, Native Americans have some of the lowest levels of income, savings and life expectancies in the US, as well as some of the highest levels of drug and alcohol dependence. They are disproportionately killed by the police. Where Black Lives Matter succeeded in putting police brutality against blacks on the agenda, state-killings of Native Americans go largely unnoticed.[32]

Continuing under its first black President, America imprisoned more people than China and Russia, making it number one in prison population statistics. Prison labour is also a feature of the state-funded, privately run system. A disproportionate number of inmates are people of colour: Native Americans, African–Americans, Hispanics and Latinos. Proportionally, more black Americans are killed by the police than white Americans. Proportionally, more black Americans are stopped and searched and imprisoned for minor offences than whites. As noted in this book, black Americans have fewer savings, job prospects and educational opportunities than whites.[33]

When it comes to Arabs (and by association Islam), America is one of the most racist countries. Mainstream media constantly associate 'Arab' with 'terrorist' and a threat to national security.

Although Arab–Americans are generally wealthier than African–Americans, they are subjected to equal amounts of racial profiling. Worse still, this prejudice makes it easier for Presidents like Obama and Trump to kill hundreds of thousands of people in the Middle East and North Africa, and to target individuals for death via the drone programme and special forces assassination missions on the ground. Obama personally authorized the murder of many of the 2,500 Arabs killed in his drone programme between 2009 and 2017. Obama's team planned and Trump authorized an operation in Yemen in violation of international law, which led to the deaths of 25 civilians, including 9 children in January 2017, making it arguably Trump's first war crime. This is not uncommon.[34]

Former Marxist-turned-alt-righter, David Horowtiz, denies that any of the above is evidence of systematic racism in the USA.

In his pro-Trump book *Big Agenda* (2017), Horowitz concludes: 'there is no systematic racism in America's institutions, and if there is, it is already illegal and easily remedied'. Horowitz offers no solution to the racism he says doesn't exit. Horowtiz's contention, that 'underrepresentation' is a liberal 'myth', comes from the fact that '[n]inety percent of the multimillionaires in the National Basketball Association are black'. Horowitz asks, Is there is a single person 'denied university admission on the basis of their collective group identity'? He answers, no. But in 2015, *The Atlantic* reported that from 1994 to 2013, black enrolment in colleges 'skyrocketed'. The success in beating discrimination is 'due to the hard work of black families, college admissions officers, and education advocates'. The magazine concludes, however: 'at top-tier universities in the United States', such as Harvard and Yale, 'it's a different story. There, the share of students who are black has actually *dropped* since 1994' (emphasis added).[35]

As noted above, most black people have fewer opportunities than most whites. But Horowitz suggests that blacks are inferior, hence white people rule by default: 'they failed as individuals to meet other – nonracial, nongender – standards'. As Arlie Russell Hochschild notes, middle- and lower-class Trump supporters in the south share this misunderstanding of what constitutes racism. (For many, racism simply means using words like 'nigger'.) Feeding the white-male-is-persecuted narrative, Horowitz chides so-called oppression studies 'in which white male Americans are the villains'. He even goes on to invert reality and say that now all-black zones in colleges are causing a new segregation in America, one in which whites are the victims.[36]

Who's Heard of the Alt-right?

As disturbing as the trend is, it is worth remembering that the alt-right is a fringe that appeals to a narrow demographic including college-educated wealthy people: it does not represent America any more than UKIP and Le Pen represent Britain and France.

By December 2016, 54% of Americans had never heard of the alt-right. Only 17% had heard 'a lot' about it (28% heard 'a little'). Knowledge is split along party lines. Liberal Democrats and left-leaning independents are more likely to have heard of the alt-right (66%). Conservative or moderate Democrats are least likely to have heard of it (39%), as are Republicans and right-leaning independents (40%). Of those who have heard of the alt-right, one third associate it with white nationalism and/or white supremacy (34%). Others associate it with racism/prejudice (14%) and the extreme right (12%). Again, the results are split along party lines. Democrats (47%) are likely to associate it with white racism compared to Republicans (17%). Only 1% of Democrats describe it as a conservative movement, as do just 8% of Republicans.[37]

Part Two

THE TRUMP DECEPTION

Chapter 6

President Trump: Soul of a rebel

'The reason my hair looks so neat all the time is because I don't have to deal with the elements very often. I live in the building where I work. I take an elevator from my bedroom to my office. The rest of the time, I'm either in my stretch limousine, my private jet, my helicopter, or my private club in Palm Beach, Florida ... If I happen to be outside, I'm probably on one of my golf courses.'

Donald J. Trump (with Meredith McIver), *How to Get Rich* (2004), p. 152

That an openly racist, xenophobic misogynist won the presidential race put a record one in five Americans in a 'bad mood'. It left many liberal voters, pundits and activists concerned that the far-right are gaining ground in the USA.[1]

This is the mass media's presentation of the 2016 election.

But the real world is more positive. Trump was the most unpopular candidate in history (the 'centrist' Clinton followed a close second). Clinton's percentage victory was a victory for young voters, women and people of colour. Trump's percentage defeat was a defeat for older, white males. Trump only 'won' because the Electoral College stole the vote for him, the way it did for George W. Bush in 2000. Even more positive is the fact that had the self-professed socialist Sanders not been defeated by Clinton, he stood a good chance of winning. This means that mobilized voters and potential voters must now get involved in politics and force candidates like Sanders to follow through on their campaign pledges.

Myths #1 & #2: Trump Won & the Polls Were Wrong
The mainstream media claimed that Trump's so-called win was 'one of the most astonishing victories in American political his-

tory' and that Trump won because of his ability to 'capture[...]' both pessimism and optimism' with slogans recycled from the Reagan era (David Smith in the *Guardian*). According to this perspective, Trump 't[ook] advantage of ... an opening' in the Midwest, where the Democrats had failed (Michael Barone in *National Review*).

But the truth is that Trump actually lost the popular vote to Hillary Clinton by 2.6m votes. This means that the majority of Americans who voted are not racist, xenophobic and misogynistic. According to National Popular Vote Tracker, Clinton got 65,259,681 votes and Trump got 62,692,056 votes. This also means that the polls were right after all: the majority of Americans did vote Clinton.[2]

Trump's victory is the fourth time that the Electoral College process stole an election for a candidate who lost the popular vote. This is known by political philosophers and sociologists as the voter paradox. It has happened three times before in American electoral history. The third time was in 2000, when the election was stolen for Republican George W. Bush from Democrat Al Gore. It reminds Americans and the world once more that America is a democracy for elites. Article II of the Constitution states: 'each State shall appoint ... a Number of Electors, equal to the whole Number of Senators and Representatives to which the State may be entitled in the Congress'. Notice that it does not give the public the right to elect the President.[3]

The Twelfth Amendment states: 'The Electors ... shall name in their ballots the person voted for as President' by the state. This process is called the Electoral College. According to the government archives, the College was established by the Founding Fathers, 'as a compromise between election of the President by a vote in Congress and ... by a popular vote of qualified citizens'. Notice that in either case it is not a direct vote (hence the caveat 'qualified' citizens). The College consists of 538 electors, so a majority of 270 electoral votes is required for the given candidate to win. Each candidate has their own group of electors who are usually chosen by the candidate's party.[4]

Complicating things further, 'state laws vary on how the electors are selected'. The archive states: 'when you vote for your [presidential candidate] you are actually voting for your candidate's electors'. So American 'democracy' is based on trust: that the elector is trusted to vote for the President of the represented citizen's choice.[5]

The mockery of American democracy is spelled out in the US government archive: 'There is no Constitutional provision or Federal law that requires [the] Electors' of the Electoral College 'to vote according to the results of the popular vote in their states'. Let it sink in. The government webpage continues: 'Some states, however, require Electors to cast their votes according to the popular vote'. Some, but not all. And those that don't, face only fines: they are not required by law to follow the wishes of the public. 'These pledges fall into two categories – Electors bound by state law and those bound by pledges to political parties'. Ergo, if a given state pledges allegiance to the Republican Party and the Democrats get a majority, the Electoral College can still vote Republican.[6]

Not surprisingly, public opinion polls have consistently shown that Americans would prefer to elect their presidents directly rather than have them elected by the Electoral College. But the archive states: 'Many different proposals to alter the Presidential election process have been offered over the years, such as direct nation-wide election by the People, but none have been passed by Congress'.[7]

The Founding Fathers made compromises which affected the Electoral College. At the Philadelphia Constitutional Convention 1787, the Connecticut or Great Compromise reassured small states that they would have equal Congressional Representation. This led to the creation of the Electoral College. '[N]umbers alone' guarantee smaller states 'a greater proportion of electoral power than they should enjoy', says Associate Professor Todd Estes of Oakland University. If we take the case of Delaware, which has comparatively few citizens, we find that it was allotted three representatives at the Electoral College. Virginia, the most populous state at the time, had twelve.* This meant that a greater proportion was allotted to Delaware.[8]

An electoral map by the *Washington Post* shows that Trump won the smaller states, including Arkansas, Montana, North and South Dakota, Utah and Wyoming.[9] Of these small state wins, only Iowa and Ohio switched from Democrat to Republican since 2008 and 2012. Another *Washington Post* study finds that many small states that Trump won had lost jobs to China and Mexico, due in large part to the neoliberal policies discussed in Chapters 1 and 2, and their political effects discussed in Chapter 2. Researchers Ator et al. found that Chinese imports harmed US manufacturing jobs in vulnerable industrial areas, particularly after 2001. In addition, Jensen et al. argue that incumbent parties (in this case the Democrats) are likely to lose votes when imports from China and Mexico increase, particularly where low-skilled manufacturers face direct competition, i.e., in swing states.[10]

Cerrato et al. found that since China joined the World Trade Organization in 2001 and America signed the much-hated NAFTA in 1994, imports of Mexican oil and Chinese steel have harmed domestic producers and manufacturers. For every one point increase in Chinese imports in 2016, Trump gained a 2.9% increase in popular support among those harmed by so-called free trade. Geographically, this was more pronounced in the Midwest and southeast.[11]

Trump, TV & the Alt-right
As soon as media mogul Rupert Murdoch announced he was backing Trump, we should have known who would win. Murdoch

---

*The second compromise was called Three-Fifths. Slave-owners were appointed additional three-fifths representation because their slaves were three-fifths human, according to the compromise. This meant that slave owners, particularly in the South, had greater numbers in the House of Representatives and Presidential vote share. Estes writes that the three-fifths compromise, 'inflated the electoral influence of slave-holding states by as many as twelve votes'. This apparently cost Federalist John Adams the election of 1800 to the salve-owning Thomas Jefferson. (See endnote 8) has consistently backed winners in Britain and the US: Margaret Thatcher (Tory), John Major (Tory), Tony Blair (New Labour), David Cameron (Tory) and George W. Bush (Republican), Barack Obama (Democrat) and Donald J. Trump (Republican).

Murdoch owns the far-right Fox News. A Fox producer explained that whereas Murdoch had previously opposed Trump, he and Fox founder the late Roger Ailes changed their tune. They were telling the anchors: 'Make sure we don't go after Trump ... We've thrown in the towel'. *New York Magazine* also reports that Fox's 'ratings dip whenever an anti-Trump segment airs'. Trump's super-PACs* spent only $8.2m on Trump ads up to August 2016, compared to Clinton's which spent $37m. But Trump got free air-time. According to media analysts Tyndall, Trump's 2015 coverage on the three major news channels ABC, CBS and NBC, amounted to one-third of all campaign coverage – 327 minutes, more than the 16 Republican challengers combined. Clinton got 121 minutes of air time.[12]

A *Christian Science Monitor* analysis finds that the Democratic party sabotaged its own media campaign in order to promote Hillary Clinton over the more genuine socialist, Bernie Sanders. This backfired (or not) because Trump ended up getting more views than either Clinton or Sanders, who would have probably beaten Trump had he been given the chance. Trump knew how to handle the media. By making the most outrageous comments he could, Trump achieved two objectives: free advertising and stoking the flames of populist, anti-government anger. Between May 2015 and May 2016, Trump got $2.8bn-worth of free TV advertising, says media statistics firm mediaQuant. By comparison, Clinton got $1.1bn-worth of free advertising.[13]

Let's turn to the alternative media:

When we look at who listens to the show, we shouldn't be surprised that alt-right radio, TV and internet superstar Alex Jones

---

*Super-Political Action Committees. These are organizations which pay for propaganda to promote their favourite presidential candidate.

followed the wind of popular opinion — among his show's demographics, at least — and became an unashamed Trump supporter.

Jones started out in the early-1990s as a young libertarian journalist with the Genesis Communications Network. His films opposed the federal government and exposed many of their crimes, including the murderous breaking of the siege at Waco and complicity in the 9/11 atrocities. Although he was always anti-immigration, over the years Jones and his British sidekick Paul Joseph Watson have drifted further to the right, denigrating minorities and women. Jones was fodder for Clinton's anti-Trump campaign propaganda. It culminated with Trump giving Jones a full-length interview.

At the time of writing, Jones's internet platform Infowars.com gets about 7.7 million unique hits per month, 6.5 million of which are from the US. By a large margin, the majority of listeners are men above the lower and lower-middle income brackets, but under the upper income bracket ($100k+). Over 55s are the biggest demographic. Most graduated from high school and hold a college degree, like Tea Party voters. A slight majority is childless and the overwhelming majority is white. They are likely to watch typically 'manly' programmes, including 'Bear' Grylls (who is certainly no bear) and Hannity (Sean Hannity being the raving right-wing Fox presenter). People who serve(d) in the military and work in government, construction and business are also more likely to listen to Alex Jones. They also tend to watch more hockey than other sports, including football. The average Alex Jones listener fits the angry middle class, white American male stereotype.[14]

Rush Limbaugh is another Jones-type figure. Older than Jones, Limbaugh constantly rails against feminism, black people, criminals, migrants, the federal government, public schools, social security and other threats to wealthy white American men. For Limbaugh, the former amount to a 'left–liberal' assault against deserving white men.[15]

Limbaugh's website reaches 2.5m people a month, 95% of whom are American. Like Alex Jones's listeners, the majority of Limbaugh enthusiasts are white men over the age of 55 (especially over the age of 65), who have a college degree. Unlike Jones's listeners, Limbaugh's fans are upper-middle class, earning over $150k. A small majority are childless. They also tend to watch Hannity and enjoy hockey. They tend to work in or have retired from the military, government or business administration more than other professions.[16]

The far-right Foxnews.com reaches 29 million Americans per month. As far as the TV show is concerned, ratings nosedived until 2015, when Trump came on the scene, promising to ban Muslims, expel immigrants and make America great again. Fox and Trump had a mutually beneficial relationship: Trump boosted its ratings and Fox provided him with free advertising. The *Atlantic Monthly* reports: 'The median age of Americans watching CNN, MSNBC and Fox News is over 60. Half of Fox News viewers are over the age of 68'. The magazine points out that retired persons watch more than 50 hours of TV per week and Fox does particularly well among people who never went to college and are aged 70 and over, i.e., a typical Republican voter.[17]

Myth #3: Americans are Right-wing
Since myth #1 is debunked above, myth #3 — that Trump's victory proves most Americans are right-wing — dissolves. As the progressive left gain some traction in Britain (with the Corbyn-led Labour Party) and in the US (with the huge amount of popular support for Bernie Sanders), the propaganda machine churns out distorted facts that most voters self-identify as right-wing or centrist.

One of the functions of mass media is to isolate individuals, geographically and intellectually. Traditionally, unions were the place to discuss and participate in politics. As we saw in Chapters 1 and 2, union membership has declined steadily in the US since the 1980s. Concentration of ownership by wealthy shareholders and high revenues from advertising mean that mass media are not the people's media, but rather a media structured in ways that reflect narrow interests.

Despite this constraint on the intellect, Americans' views (and those of people around the world more generally) are usually progressive.

On a number of issues, the general public is left of the government. A CNN/ORC poll finds that 60% of Americans oppose Trump's proposal to build a wall along the US–Mexico border. (In fact, one already exists care of Bill Clinton's Operation Gatekeeper.) Two-thirds say that mass deportation is undesirable and they support citizenship applications for so-called 'illegals'. Even a majority of Trump supporters oppose mass deportation. In terms of immigration priorities, 51% say that developing a plan to allow 'illegals' to become legals should be number one. Only 36% say that stopping migrants should be a priority. Just 11% say that deportation should be a priority, whilst 88% say that if immigrants speak English, pay taxes and work they should be allowed to stay.[18]

On health, 58% of Americans support replacing the Affordable Care Act (ACA) with a tax-funded system (37% oppose). According to Gallup, the joint proposal of either keeping the ACA or replacing it with a tax-funded universal system gains majority support by 2 to 1 (the minority supports private healthcare).[19]

Sixty-two per cent of Americans believe that the government spends too little on the poor. Only 12% say there's too much money spent on the poor. (Contradictory evidence from the same agency, that half think the government spends too much on welfare, may be explained by the relentless anti-welfare propaganda in the media.) Forty-six per cent of Americans support, compared to 37% who oppose, government intervention to lessen inequality, says an AP–NORC poll.[20]

In addition to the above, it is likely that Bernie Sanders would have beaten Trump had Sanders beaten Clinton in the Democratic nomination.

Sanders is the Democratic representative from Vermont. He voted to enable America's (and Britain's) illegal wars against Serbia in 1999 and Afghanistan in 2001. He did, however, oppose the invasion of Iraq in 2003 and spoke out against bombing Iran, unlike Hillary Clinton who voted for all of the wars and suggested that 'all options are on the table' when it comes to Iran. Sanders also voted for Bill Clinton's Crime Bill 1994, which led to further incarcerations and deaths by police of black and Hispanic Americans. Despite these serious flaws for which he should be held accountable, Sanders represented the only chance to bring some truly socialist policies into the heart of American politics.[21]

By May 2016, Sanders would have beaten Trump by 15 percentage points (NBC–WSJ poll). A second, CBS–NYT poll reckoned that Sanders would win by 15 percentage points. They put Clinton's lead at 3 points and 6 points respectively. Clearly Sanders had a major advantage. By June, Sanders had a 49.7% lead over Trump, according RealClearPolitics. The poll extrapolates from dozens of other agencies, including Fox, CNN, *Bloomberg*, the *Wall Street Journal*, IBD/TIPP investors and the academic Quinnipiac. At that time, Clinton was trailing Trump in several polls, which the mainstream media wanted to ignore.[22]

According to a November survey of 1,638 registered voters conducted by Garvis Marketing, Sanders had a 12 point lead over Trump (56% to 44%), and 60% of women would have voted Sanders had they had a choice between him and Trump, as would 52% of men. The poll showed that Clinton had a two percentage point lead over Trump, which was reflected in reality by the fact that Clinton won the popular vote (but lost the Electoral College). Ninety-one per cent of Democrats preferred Sanders over Trump, as did 55% of Independents and 16% of Republicans, whilst 69% of self-described moderates preferred Sanders to Trump, 93% of 'somewhat liberal[s]' and 94% of 'very liberal[s]'. Seventy-five per cent of self-described 'somewhat conservative[s]' preferred Trump, as did 77% of 'very conservative[s]'.[23]

Sanders would have smashed Trump among people of colour: black 88%, Asian 97%, Hispanic 53% and 57% 'other'. The white vote would have been split 50–50. Sanders would have also won on religious grounds, except among evangelical Christians (39%). Jews 66%, Muslims 68%, 'other'/none 78%, Protestant 52% and Roman Catholic 51% would have voted Sanders.[24]

Sanders would have beaten Trump among educated voters and by age. In the end, a majority of Christians and older whites voted Trump because the hated Clinton was their only other choice. Had

Sanders been there (according to Garvis), the following percentages of persons with educational attainment would have voted Sanders: bachelors 56%, high school 50%, post-grad 63%, 'some college' 49% (the only minority) and 'some high school' 69%. By age: 18–29, 67%; 30–49, 55%; 50–64, 54%; and 65+, 53%.[25]

In two Trump states, Michigan and Wisconsin, Sanders beat Clinton in the pre-election primaries.[26]

Stabbing Bernie in the Back

So, why didn't Sanders beat Clinton and go on to destroy Trump?

The ruling body of the Democratic Party, the Democratic National Committee, played many dirty tricks to make sure that the corporate-backed Hillary Clinton did better than the union and single donor-backed Bernie Sanders. In other words, the elites within the Democratic Party would rather see a Republican victory than a Democrat victory led by a socialist. The same is true in the UK, where centrists and right-wingers in the Labour Party would rather see the party implode and hand victory to the Tories than have a socialist lead the country.

The DNC scheduled the first round of its debates at the worst possible times, when TV shows were broadcasting more popular programmes, such as sports and crime shows. Political analyst Doug Mataconis comments: 'the debate schedule, both in the way it limits the number of debates and has scheduled most of them on weekends, seem to be part of a strategy' by the DNC 'to protect the presumptive front-runner for the nomination', i.e., Hillary Clinton, 'by limiting the amount of free media time'.[27]

On the eve of the crucial California election, which Clinton won, Clinton said she was not going to debate with Sanders. The debate would have been particularly important as it would have been covered by the right-wing Fox News and may have seen many likely Trump voters shift to Sanders.[28]

Deborah Wasserman Schultz is the Democratic representative for Florida's 23rd congressional district. Until Obama forced her resignation, she was chair of the Democratic National Committee. A lawyer for the Sanders campaign wrote a letter to Schultz accusing the Hillary Clinton Fund of violating campaign finance regulations by taking 99% of donation monies for itself instead of helping smaller candidates, particularly via its Hillary for America campaign account. It was alleged that 99% of Hillary Clinton's Victory Fund did not go to smaller candidates as intended, but was effectively stolen by the Clinton campaign. A lawsuit citing six potential violations was filed against Schultz, then-head of the DNC, by Sanders supporters. But Schultz moved to reject the lawsuit, claiming it had been improperly filed. But process server Shawn Lucas was filmed serving the suit. Lucas was later found dead of a prescription drug overdose.[29]

In 2015, *The Intercept* revealed that a pro-Clinton CNN op-ed by Atlanta's mayor Kasim Reed was actually written by a Clinton lobbyist and edited by a Clinton super-PAC. It was sent to CNN via the super-PAC. Also in 2015, the Clinton campaign had gathered information on voters and potential voters and had kept it from the Sanders campaign. Due to a technological error, Sanders did gain access to the database. In response, the Schultz-led DNC revoked Sanders's access to the database.[30]

Chapter 7

Privatization as policy

'[W]e are incredibly blessed to live in a nation where 97 percent of those considered poor own a color television and have the electricity to power it.'

Donald J. Trump, *Time to Get Tough* (2016), pp. 109–110

Let's continue debunking the Trump myths:

Myth #4: Trump Won the Working Class Vote

Clinton won the popular vote. Polls show that Sanders would have beaten Clinton.

Since 2010, Congressional approval has never gone above 20%. It was at a low of 18% by August 2016, up from 13% in July. Crucially, when the data are stratified, we find that 13% of Republicans approve Congress, compared with 19% of Democrats (and 20% of independents). This suggests that any Presidential candidate railing against the state, especially 'corruption' and 'incompetence' in Congress, would do well among voters; particularly a Republican candidate. Edison Research found that three-fifths of American voters said the country had gone 'seriously off on the wrong track'. Among those three-fifths, 69% voted Trump and only 25% Clinton. Nearly 25% are 'angry' with the government and make up 'the core of Trump's support'.[1]

So when Trump made way-out statements which further alienated him from his own Republican party, it fed into the public's hatred of Congress and, among a small core of voters, made Trump look like a real anti-establishment figure.[2]

In 2016, voter turnout was at a 20-year low. In 1996, 26.3% of American voters voted for Bill Clinton compared to 21.8% who voted for Bob Dole. In 2008, 33.7% of American voters voted for Obama compared to the 29.1% who voted for McCain. In 2016,

26.5% voted for Hillary Clinton compared to 26.3% who voted Trump. In total, 55.4% of eligible voters came out to vote – the only time in recent history that the percentage was lower was in 1996, when 53.5% turned out. Low voter turnout is indicative of the dissatisfaction that most Americans feel about the electoral system.[3]

Looking at the data more closely, Trump swing states bucked the national trend and actually had higher voter turnouts in 2016 than in 2012. In short, Trump voters got motivated and organized. In Florida, 9.4m people voted (8.5m in 2012); in Michigan, 4.8m (4.7m in 2012); and in North Carolina, 4.7m (138,000 fewer in 2012).[4]

One of the persistent media myths about Trump is that economically marginalized voters swept him into office. In fact, more middle class Americans voted for Trump than working class Americans. According to the exit polls, 52% of voters making less than $50k a year voted Clinton. 41% of voters making under $50k a year voted Trump. In other words, Clinton had an eleven-point lead over Trump with working class Americans. A slight majority of those making over $50k a year voted Trump, 49%, with 47% voting for Clinton. John Hudak of the Brookings Institution writes about the theory that Trump won over economically marginalized voters. This only 'seems to make sense for white voters', says Hudak because whites – many, but not all – tend to be less economically marginalized than people of colour.[5]

Trump also captured a disproportionate share of the Christian vote. Most American Christians who vote, vote Republican in Presidential elections. Between 54% and 59% of Protestant/other Christian Americans (excluding Catholics) voted for Bush, McCain, Romney and Trump in the electoral years between 2000 and 2016. Atheists vote overwhelmingly for the Democrats: between 23% and 31% voted Republican between 2000 and 2016.[6]

So, how did Trump do? He got 58% of the Protestant/other votes, compared to Clinton's 39%. He got 52% of the Catholic vote (Clinton 45%); 60% of the white Catholic vote (Clinton 37%); 26% of the Hispanic Catholic vote (Clinton 67%); 24% of the Jewish vote

(Clinton 71%); 29% of the vote from 'other faiths' (Clinton 62%); 81% of the white 'born again'/evangelical vote (Clinton 16%); and 61% of the Mormon vote (Clinton 25%).[7]

Higher church attendance increases the likelihood of a Trump vote. 56% of those who are religious and voted Trump are likely to attend services at least once a week, compared to 40% of religious Clinton voters.[8]

Trump also had a disproportionate share of the male vote: 54% of female voters picked Clinton, compared to the 42% who picked Trump; 53% of men voted Trump compared to 41% who picked Clinton; 52% of voters with a college degree picked Clinton (43% picked Trump), compared to the 52% without a degree who backed Trump (44% voted Clinton).[9]

Race and education are another factor. Interestingly, white college graduates voted Trump by four points over Clinton. And Trump's mobilization of non-graduate whites was the most politically successful since 1980: 67% of non-graduate white voters voted Trump, compared to the pitiful 28% who backed Clinton.[10]

Clinton succeeded in mobilizing young voters (18–29). They voted for Clinton 55%–37%. But this was down from those who voted Obama in 2012: 60%–36% (the 36% voted for the Mormon Republican, Mitt Romney). Voters aged 65+ voted Trump 53%–45%.[11]

Returning to race: In 2008, 67% of Latinos voted Obama. In 2012, 71% of Latinos voted Obama. In 2016, 66% voted Clinton, 28% voted Trump (27% voted Romney in 2012, but 31% voted McCain in 2008). Sixty-eight per cent of Hispanic voters oppose the construction of a wall along the US–Mexico border whilst 46% of whites and 82% of blacks oppose it. Seventy-eight per cent of Hispanic voters said illegal immigrants should be given the chance to apply for legal status, whilst 67% of whites and 82% of blacks support this.[12]

Myth #5: Trump is Anti-establishment

Anti-establishment means different things to different people. If you hate immigrants, 'anti-establishment' could mean a Republican candidate who is 'tough' on migration, even though more immigrants were deported under Obama than under any other President. 'Anti-establishment' could be opposition to the billionaires who have enriched themselves at everyone else's expense. Or it could mean opposition to government regulation which constrains the freedoms of the rich.

There is so much hatred of government and big business – at all levels – among ordinary Americans, that someone who appears to share their anger, even if they are part of the ruling class, will resonate with a solid – if small – core of voters. But Trump is the very definition of the establishment. He is worth $3.1bn, according to *Forbes*. There are 319 million Americans. According to *Forbes*, there are 540 billionaires in the USA. Ergo, Trump is not a member of the upper 1%: he's in the upper 0.00016%.[13]

'Outside of his eponymous real-estate focused Trump Organization, the New York billionaire also holds liquid investments worth as much as $170 million – including shares in the big banks and multinational companies he railed against on the campaign trail'. *Forbes* alleges that Trump owns or until recently owned at least $2.5m in Citigroup, Goldman Sachs, JP Morgan, Morgan Stanley and Wells Fargo. As he chided Ford for its outsourcing of American jobs, he continued to hold $1m in the companies. He also holds millions of shares in Apple, Bank of Nova Scotia, Berkshire Hathaway (Warren Buffett's hedge fund (which some argue isn't a hedge fund)), Celgene (pharma), Chevron, ExxonMobil, GlaxoSmithKline, Google, Johnson & Johnson, Kinder Morgan (pipeline company), Merck, Phillips 66 (which has a stake in the Dakota Access pipeline), Procter and Gamble, Royal Bank of Canada, Shell, Toronto Dominion Bank and Walmart.[14]

As one would expect, Trump's political views reflect his business interests. In his own books, Trump has constantly championed the very deregulation which enriches his class, to which we will now turn.

Trump's socioeconomic philosophy is summed up on page 62 of *The America We Deserve*, published in 2000. In it, Trump writes:

'The business of America is truly business, because business is the task of linking private ambitions to social needs'. Despite his opposition to free trade in his campaign rhetoric, he also writes: 'what's worked beautifully throughout American history is the free-market economy. What has brought us low is government bureaucracy and corruption' (p. 37). Trump believes in 'systematically doing away with red tape' (p. 29) because 'I have a lot of trouble with the way government collects and handles our money. Hidden taxes make me mad as hell' (p. 30).

Chapter 1 of this book shows how regulation and higher taxes on the rich enabled tens of millions of working Americans to become middle class and live the American Dream. Trump by contrast writes of an 'American Dream unencumbered by bureaucratic ineptitude [and] government regulation [and] confiscatory tax policies'. Trump then writes in opposition to racism, sexism and homophobia: a position about which he forgot when running for President (p. 36).

As we also saw in Chapter 1, debt can be a stimulus for growth if the loan is spent on the real economy: of mortgages, vehicles, infrastructure, training, education, etc. Debt is bad when it is internationalized by financial institutions who make money by repackaging debts and trading them on the stock market. But Trump writes: 'Both debt reduction and tax reduction are necessary'. Tax reduction means tax reduction for the rich and debt reduction means cutting government spending on social services (p. 39). As he writes on p. 193: 'Social Security has a liability that's almost $20 trillion ... Ink just doesn't get any redder than that'. Trump backs up his welfare cut plans by citing right-wing economists, including Daniel J. Mitchell (Heritage Foundation) and Milton Friedman (an architect of neoliberalism). For Trump, Social Security is a means of making money. 'Fortunately, the system is running surpluses invested in Treasury notes and can tap the interest earned off these revenues' (p. 196). Trump's solution is to use welfare money to invest in mutual funds (p. 197) and raise the retirement age to 70 (p. 202).

Although Trump talks about helping needy families, he then goes on to champion cutbacks on social security, or '[w]elfare reform' which 'encouraged more than 300,000 welfare recipients to leave the public assistance rolls [between 1997 and 2000 in New York]' (p. 58). Encouraged means *forced*. Trump appears to believe in survival of the fittest. If you're able to work hard, you'll survive. He champions the 'economic development and welfare policy' in Los Angeles. In LA, regulators 'have stepped back and let human ingenuity and ambition take its course' (p. 59). Between the time that Clinton passed the Personal Responsibility and Work Opportunity Reconciliation Act 1996 and the year 2000, 'welfare caseloads dropped by 2.2 million' in LA (pp. 59–60). The Social Security that cannot be cut, 'could be invested in REITS — real estate professionals run by professionals' (p. 198). Or taking from the poor to give to the rich.

At the very least, Trump cannot be accused of inconsistency in his hatred of social security. In the updated version of *Time to Get Tough*, sixteen years after *The America We Deserve*, he writes: 'The next president America elects must be committed to serious welfare reforms that overhaul the system and roll back Obama's disastrous public assistance policies' (p. 115). But Trump also understands the political economy of retaining some kind of privatized welfare system: 'the bigger you grow the welfare state, the bigger you grow your electoral army' (p. 114). Trump implies that he will promote religion as a way of advocating marriage, because children born in wedlock are less likely to need social security (p. 110).

Team Trump: Filling the Swamp[*]

Trump promised to 'drain the swamp' in Washington. But he's

---

[*] The information in this subchapter is taken from
https://assets.donaldjtrump.com/TRUMP_ECONOMIC_ADVISORY_
COUNCIL_FINAL.pdf, http://money.cnn.com/2016/08/07/news/economy/
donald-trump-economic-advisers-diversity/, http://www.thetimes.co.uk/article/
billionaires-plan-to-repair-the-rust-belt-556kbdwz5 and
https://www.theguardian.com/us-news/2016/dec/02/trumps-rich-pickings-
president-elects-team-could-be-wealthiest-ever.

filled it with millionaires and billionaires. Trump's economic team of 13 individuals consists of 13 white men aged between 50 and 74 who are worth a combined $14bn.

Tom Barrack is founder of the property investment firm, Colony Capital, worth $25bn. (Until 2014, Barrack himself was a billionaire.) He served as Deputy Undersecretary of the US Department of the Interior under Reagan. The business press notes that Barrack made a fortune buying up cheap property in the wake of the '80s savings and loan scandal.

Worth $10.5bn, Andy Beal is the founder of Beal Bank and Beal Bank USA, which bought power and infrastructure bonds after the Enron energy crisis of 2001, aircraft industry-backed debt instruments after 9/11 and real estate loans after the Financial Crisis of 2008. His other businesses include the CLG Hedge Fund, CSG Investments and the Loan Acquisition Corporation.

Stephen Calk founded the Federal Savings Bank and National Bancorp Holdings. He has advised JPMorgan Chase, the Ohio Savings Bank, CitiMortgage and the General Electric Mortgage Insurance Company.

Dan DiMicco, Trump's trade advisor, is the former CEO of Nucor steel.

Steve Fienberg is co-founder of Cerberus Capital Management, a hedge fund worth $40bn. Fienberg has a personal wealth of $1.25bn.

Harold Hamm is worth $9.3bn. He made his money from shale oil and was also picked by former Republican presidential runner Mitt Romney as energy advisor.

Dan Kowalski was Deputy Staff Director of the Republican Budget Committee for 20 years.

Millionaire Howard Lorber runs Douglas Elliman, the largest residential real estate brokerage in the wealthy metropolitan area of New York. The firm is part of a bigger group, Vector, owned by Lorber.

David Malpass was Reagan's Deputy Assistant Treasury Secretary and Deputy Assistant Secretary of State under Bush I. Malpass was also chief economist at Bear Stearns during the six years prior to its collapse.

Following in his father's footsteps, Steve Mnuchin worked at Goldman Sachs between 1985 and 2002, where he made $46m. Mnuchin went into the hedge fund industry, working for Sears Holdings before founding Dune Capital Management, which invested in two Trump projects. The Federal Deposit Insurance Corporation bought the failing housing lender IndyMac and sold it to Mnuchin, hedge fund billionaire George Soros and hedge fund manager John Paulson for $1.6bn. The bank was renamed One-West and sold to the CIT Group for $3.4bn after a series of allegedly unethical foreclosures.

Stephen Moore is an economist at the Heritage Foundation and an advocate of Reagan-era supply-side economics; a policy which contributed to the decline of real wealth in America. Moore co-founded the pro-Tea Party Committee to Unleash American Prosperity.

Professor Peter Navarro is fanatically anti-China and the only academic in Trump's cabinet.

Worth $8.6bn, John Paulson is alleged by several authors to be one of the players who brought down the US financial market in 2008. Paulson made his money in hedge funds by betting against the subprime mortgage lending market in the run-up to the Financial Crisis of 2007/08. He was also critical of the Treasury's financial stability mechanisms.

Former Rothschild Inc. bankruptcy advisor Wilbur Ross specializes in buying and restructuring failing coal, steel, textiles and telecoms companies. He is worth $2.9bn.

Billionaire Steve Roth is a real estate investor and chairman of Vornado Realty Trust.

A couple of women were on the sidelines: Diane Hendricks is worth $5.3bn and is co-founder and chair of ABC Supply. She also owns the Hendricks Holding Company. Hendricks is a major Republican donor, including to the Koch Brothers' Freedom Partners Action Fund. Another is Liz Uihlein, wife of millionaire Republican donor, Richard.

Trump's Cabinet*

Vice President Mike Pence, Governor of Indiana: Pence has voted for every free trade deal and favoured NAFTA, CAFTA and the WTO. Pence is a Tea Party supporter whom as Governor pushed for school vouchers, a policy which benefited private schools. A Roman Catholic Democrat, Pence converted to evangelicalism and Republicanism early in life. He supports the death penalty, supports the privatization of social security and rejects evolution in favour of creationism. Despite being part of a government actively involved in the wholesale destruction of Syria, Governor Pence unsuccessfully moved to block Syrian refugees from settling in Indiana. Pence also backed the Iraq War 2003.

Pence has pledged to help Trump repeal the Johnson Amendment to the Constitution which taxes churches that endorse political candidates. Pence denies anthropogenic climate change and rejected Indiana's participation in the Environmental Protection Agency's Clean Power Plan to limit emissions. He has also signed laws prejudiced against LGBT people and laws that oppose abortion. In the case of the former (Indiana Senate Bill 101), so-called religious freedoms would have been protected over the rights of minorities, had sections of the law not been redrafted following pressure from activists. Pence also signed HB 1337, which banned certain abortion procedures and limited the practices of abortion providers. The Supreme Court issued an injunction against the bill, citing its unconstitutionality. Pence also voted against the Patient Protection and Affordable Care Act.

Millionaire Gary Cohn of Goldman Sachs will lead the National Economic Council. Having worked for US Steel, Cohn was recruited by Goldman Sachs after dealing options on the NY Stock Exchange.

ExxonMobil CEO Rex Tillerson is Secretary of State. One thing that might have eased nuclear tensions between Russia and

---

*The information in this section is taken from http://www.amny.com/news/elections/trump-s-cabinet-top-appointments-vincent-viola-mick-mulvaney-other-final-picks-1.12625129, http://www.rollingstone.com/politics/features/meet-president-trumps-cabinet-of-horrors-w454596 and
http://uk.businessinsider.com/carls-jr-wants-open-automated-location-2016-3.

America is Tillerson's appointment to office. In 2011, his Exxon-Mobil firm signed a deal worth $300bn with Russia to drill in the Artic. In 2013, Putin awarded him an Order of Friendship. However, what we may have gained as a species in the easing of international tensions, we will lose in the Artic melting that occurs when more oil is drilled and burned. 'The global free market for energy provides the most effective means of achieving U.S. energy security', says Tillerson, who is one of the few climate change believers in the Trump cabinet. Not only did Exxon fund anti-climate science propaganda, but Tillerson has been reticent about acknowledging the full extent of human impacts on the climate.

Steven Mnuchin is Treasury Secretary, the Goldman Sachs billionaire mentioned above.

Chief of Staff Reince Priebus is a lawyer and chair of the Republican National Committee. Priebus helped organize the Tea Party in Wisconsin.

Trump's original National Security Advisor was Lt. Gen. Mike Flynn, a registered Democrat and Director of the Defense Intelligence Agency between July 2012 and August 2014. The private Flynn Intel Group provides intelligence to governments and businesses, including to Turkey's leader, Erdoğan. Flynn has made peace overtures toward Russia (which is a good thing) but has done so at the expense of Islam by claiming, for instance, that Sharia law is taking over in America. Flynn once tweeted: 'Fear of Muslims is RATIONAL' (his emphasis), and that Russia and the US should work together to attack Muslims.

Secretary of Defence is General James Mattis, who, during his time as head of operations in Afghanistan, once said: 'It's fun to shoot some people'. Mattis also led the US assault on Fallujah, Iraq, in 2004. Under the now-debunked pretext that al-Qaeda was based in the city, British and American troops destroyed Iraq's major centre of resistance by putting fences around the town, preventing civilians from fleeing (according to Oxfam), and subjecting the town to massive bombardments, including (in November of that year) a new form of nuclear or radiological weapon which raised radiation levels in the city above that of Hiroshima. Infants are still being born with the most horrific disfigurements ever recorded.

Attorney General Jeff Sessions is junior Senator from Alabama, having served as Attorney General in the state at different points between 1994 and 2014. In these roles, he supported the illegal invasion of Iraq 2003, President Bush's tax cuts, and proposed an amendment to ban same-sex marriage. Like Mike Pence, he opposed the Patient Protection and Affordable Care Act. Sessions has also voted against at least four major immigration bills.

The attempted appointment of Andy Puzder to Secretary of Labour was a real kick in the teeth to unions. Puzder is the CEO of CKE Restaurants, giving him a $4m salary. Before getting into the food industry – and saying that 'attractive' models were used in his commercials because 'ugly' women don't sell burgers – Puzder was a Missouri lawyer who drafted the Missouri House Bill 1596, which prohibited state money being used for abortions. In 1989, the Supreme Court upheld the law. An opponent of Fight for $15, a movement which seeks to raise the minimum wage, particularly for fast-food workers, Puzder also supports replacing workers with automata because machines are, in his words, 'always polite, they always upsell, they never take a vacation, they never show up late, there's never a slip-and-fall or an age, sex, or race discrimination case'. Puzder's rationale is that government social security incentives and tax disincentives prevent him from raising working wages.

Dr Tom Price is Health and Human Services Secretary, a Republican Representative from Georgia who is also a climate change-denying physician. A Rotarian, Price also served on the boards of the North Fulton Chamber of Commerce. Price voted to extend the rights-stripping USA Patriot Act 2001, oppose the Emergency Mortgage Relief Program and repeal parts of the Health Care and Education Reconciliation Act 2010. Like most of the rest of the cabinet, Price opposes abortion. Price has also supported deregulating the farming industry, including weakening the Environmental Protection Agency's oversight.

Transportation Secretary Elaine Chao was Labor Secretary under Bush II. Chao was vice president of syndications at the Bank of

America's Capital Markets Group, as well as a banker for Citicorp. Via the latter's White House Fellowship scheme, she joined Reagan's government in 1983 and worked as an administrator for the Department of Transportation. Under Bush I, she worked at the Peace Corps, a voluntary organization which promotes America to the outside world.

Through her upbringing, Education Secretary Betsy DeVos is linked to modern-day Calvinism. A billionaire, DeVos promotes school privatization through her position as chair of the American Federation for Children. She advocates the expansion of 'school choice' (meaning privatization) and the promotion of voucher programmes, which use tax dollars to pay for private tuition instead of public tuition. After DeVos pioneered Detroit's charter school system, she was widely criticised by education specialists as laying the basis for disaster. Low scores in reading and maths and record levels of under-performance followed. DeVos raised money for Bush II's campaign and opposed high wages and high taxes in her state, Michigan, which she blamed for economic under-performance. Under Bush, she was finance chair for the National Republican Senatorial Committee.

Trump's Economic Plan

Tax reform. Trump says he will reduce federal income by cutting taxes. He will slash public services to balance the budget. But perhaps more importantly, he will restructure public services in such a way that financial institutions will use savings and bonds to blow more toxic bubbles. According to various tax experts, of the left and centre, Trump's proposals will financialize public services and benefit asset companies and hedge funds. Trump's tax reforms will encourage businesses to save in order to avoid paying taxes. The savings will be used as financial instruments in new derivatives markets.

In C corporations, owners and the corporation itself are taxed separately. Lawyer Robert W. Wood points out that registering as a C corporation, 'makes no sense for small businesses due to double tax on income and on proceeds of sale'. The Tax Foundation reckons that to qualify for Trump's 15% flat tax, S corporations (where owners are taxed as part of their corporation) would have to become C corporations. Under such a scheme, 'retained earnings' could be 'invested into financial assets' to delay taxes, such as into a 401(k) pension fund. The Tax Foundation estimates that Trump's plan will reduce federal revenue by a minimum $4.4 trillion. The plan may boost jobs by between 1.8m and 2.2m, but employers might offer benefits instead of wages.[15]

Americans in the fourth quintile earnings bracket earn between approximately $57–$98,000 a year. These are members of the middle class, the kind of people who were more likely to vote Trump. According to the Tax Policy Center, Trump's tax plan might actually *increase* the fourth quintile's tax burden by 1.2 percentage points. Under Trump's plan, businesses could write off equipment, inventories and structures as business expenses instead of depreciating those purchases over time as they usually do. This means that they will not be able to deduct interest expenses.[16]

Trump's plan will hurt many working people. So-called pass-through businesses avoid federal taxes by encouraging worker ownership. One of the drawbacks of this kind of scheme is that bosses are less inclined to pay fair wages because workers' pay is tied to company stock. According to the Tax Policy Center analysis, Trump's tax cuts will cause an '18 percentage point differential between the top rate [of tax] on pass-through business income and wages'. This might 'create a strong incentive for many wage earners to form a pass-through entity that provides labor services to their current employer instead of taking compensation in the form of wages'.[17]

Trump's plan, 'would cut taxes at all income levels, although the largest benefits, in dollar and percentage terms, would go to the highest-income households', the study continues. The average earner may save $2,940 on their tax bill (or 4.1%) but the average member of the richest 0.1% might save over $1m (or 14%). The poorest will enjoy a mere 0.8% cut. 'Repealing personal exemptions and the head of household filing status ... would cause many large families and single parents to face tax increases', the study continues. 'Although the tax policy might 'boost [GDP] in the short run, the authors find that federal revenues would decline in the first decade by $6.2 trillion and debt would rise to $20.7 trillion by 2036. This is due in part to the 'crowd[ing] out' of investment and the rise in interest rates.[18]

Despite his anti-hedge fund rhetoric, the analysis also finds that 'hedge funds and private equity partnerships, which earn a substantial portion of income in the form of carried interest, would qualify for the special 15-percent business tax rate and thus would retain a substantial tax advantage on their income compared with wage earners'.[19]

Americans for Tax Fairness estimate that 8.7 million families will see an increased tax burden. The burden would 'mostly' fall on 'low- and middle-income families with children, including more than half of single parents'. But Trump will be immune. 'Trump is the sole or principal owner of 500 pass-through entities. He would personally benefit from this massive tax giveaway that's been appropriately dubbed the "Trump Loophole".'[20]

Healthcare and the free market. Obama's Affordable Care Act resulted in 'less competition and fewer choices', says Trump, who sees everything as a business opportunity. After his Trump Mortgage venture tanked following the housing crisis of 2007, Ideal Health and the Trump Network literally took the piss out of their customers by charging hundreds of dollars for urine samples and individually-tailored multivitamins. Some investors filed a complaint with the Federal Trade Commission about the validity of the product's claims.[21]

In *The America We Deserve* (2000), Trump writes: 'The healthcare bureaucrats are depriving Americans of care in order to keep costs down. Medical care is so expensive, in fact, that millions of Americans have no health insurance at all' (p. 206). Britain and Canada will be 'the prototype' (p. 208) for 'universal healthcare' (p. 207), but universal healthcare of a particular kind: one in which employers are no longer responsible for paying into health insurance. This means that workers will be subject to price manipulation by insurers. Notice that Trump doesn't call for legislation to prevent insurers from hiking up prices. Under the guise of 'choice', deregulated insurance companies will provide the worst options for the poor.

In his chapter on healthcare in (2015's) *Great Again*, Trump writes: 'To succeed in business, you have to be flexible and you have to change with the realities of the world ... I don't think a single-payer system makes sense anymore' (p. 72). According to the book and his campaign website, Trump advocates allowing insurance providers to monopolize the market (he calls this competition) by eliminating state-by-state procedures. 'I'd like to see a private insurance system ... The government should get out of the way and let insurance companies compete for your business' (p. 75). But when all your money goes on rent, mortgage, food and childcare, you have nothing left for health.

'We need to fix [America's healthcare] problem by creating competition in the private sector between insurance companies, and by allowing patients to choose the family doctors they want'. In other words, take away subsidies and force poor people to get low quality care (p. xii). Although he said in his *60 Minutes* interview that he was planning to keep the core elements of the ACA, Trump's general position is pro-privatization. For all his anti-free market rhetoric, his website says: 'a Republican congress [will] lead the effort to bring much-needed free market reforms to the healthcare industry'.

In *Time to Get Tough* (2016), Trump makes clear where his priorities lie. According to him, '[b]usinesses like Boeing, Caterpillar, and Deere & Company are already tallying up the job-killing costs of Obamacare', which makes them insure their staff (p. 126).

Privatize schools. In *Great Again* (2015), Trump explicitly supports school choice. This means leaving poorer parents with the worst options and eliminating class mobility. Trump advocates 'charter schools, voucher programs, magnet schools, and opportunity scholarships' (p. 53), all of which amount to privatization. Like healthcare, Trump sees education as an opportunity to make money. 'When teacher unions fight against school choice the unions are saying that their product isn't good enough to compete in a free marketplace' (p. 56).

For the poor, Trump's ethos is survival of the fittest: '[i]nstead of creating high standards and demanding more, we're expecting less. We have to get tougher. Forget that self-esteem stuff; we need to start challenging kids. We need to allow them to fail when they don't work hard' (p. 52). But poorer children tend to do less well at school due to lack of opportunities and stresses at home.

On the campaign trail, Trump talked about eliminating 'special interests'. By that, he means unions. 'One huge obstacle [to reform] is the strength of the teacher unions ... [I]t's become almost impossible to dismiss a teacher, much less fire one' (p. 55). Trump's privatization plan also involves devolution, i.e., reducing federal funding and getting business involved in local funding. But local funding is largely reliant on federal funding. So, in the absence of a big social sector, devolution is code for privatization. Trump writes: 'We should return the basic control and responsibility for our schools to the states and local communities' (p. 59).

One can find the same sort of statements 15 years earlier in *The America We Deserve*.

Chapter 8

Trade deals and tax reform

'I'm for free and fair trade. After all, I do business all over the world.'

Donald J. Trump, *Time to Get Tough* (2016), p. 5

Let's continue debunking the Trump myths.

Donald Trump portrays himself as an outsider actively opposing globalization by erecting protectionist barriers and bringing jobs back to America. These policies will benefit ordinary Americans, says Trump; like the miners who supposedly voted for him. 'You were very good to me, and I'm going to be even better to you', Trump told them, as he repealed a law to prevent mining companies from contaminating streams.[1]

But the evidence shows that Trump is doing exactly what the big companies — Apple, Ford, Goldman Sachs, Microsoft, etc. — have lobbied for: cutting taxes and environmental regulations to repatriate US businesses and pulling out of multilateral trade deals in favour of bilateral ones. Take the 'border tax' example. By threatening companies with a heavy tax if they shift production to, say, Mexico, Trump looks like he's standing up to the greedy CEOs who have hurt so many American workers. But as we shall now see, those greedy CEOs lobbied Congress for years to cut corporation tax (as Trump is doing) so they can return home (to the US) and boost their stock value.[2]

It's easy to understand why some Trump voters actually supported Bernie Sanders before he was destroyed by Clinton's DNC: both he and Trump claimed to speak for domestic over foreign business and both he and Trump opposed NAFTA and TPP (more below) — but for opposite reasons. Sanders saw TPP as the selling out of America to human rights- and environment-abusing corporations. Trump saw it as a weak deal that didn't do enough to favour US business. Trump could hardly admit this on the campaign trail, so he crafted his opposition to TPP as the Republican answer to Sanders-esque populism, all the while pushing to get even better foreign trade deals for US business.[3]

Military Technology & 'Uncle Sucker'

Before getting into the details, it is important to understand how the military sector benefits the private technology sector.

In his book *Great Again* (2016), Trump expounds his opposition to public healthcare, universal welfare and free education. He also discusses the alleged exploitation of America by foreign powers, to whose rescue America gallantly and unselfishly comes. By letting others, including lazy welfare claimants, rip it off, America is 'Uncle Sucker' (p. 35). But the real suckers are the taxpayers. They put unprecedented revenues into the Department of Defense (Pentagon) which spends years, sometimes decades, developing technologies, often in secret, including: drones, GPS, jet engines, microwaves, wireless telephones and the internet. When these products become commercially viable, they are acquired by big business and sold to the public for profit as commercial leisure drones, SATNAV, passenger jets, microwave ovens, cell phones and of course the civilian internet.[4]

The latest developments in medicine, genetic manipulation and nanotechnology are also getting significant military support. The government then initiates huge procurements to help these companies along, buying advanced computers and software for civil service use, rescuing companies when they fail and providing huge tax breaks. When Trump talks about beefing up the military, it is only in part to do with maintaining US global hegemony. Another objective is maintaining and expanding public investment in what will become private tech ventures.[5]

Take education: by providing computers and e-learning programmes, Google and Microsoft (both of which have close ties to the military) can benefit from a government-subsidized private education system, which the Trump team is planning. Trump's tax reforms are benefitting the hi-tech sector, much of which wanted to bring jobs back to America because offshoring to India, for instance, was no longer as profitable (more below). But the high corporation tax maintained by the Democrats was stopping repatriation.[6]

Tax Inversions

A tax inversion is where an American company (e.g., Medtronic) merges with or acquires a foreign company (e.g., Covidien) and bases its headquarters in a foreign country (e.g., Ireland) in order to avoid US taxes. This is a problem for US business because 1) the ex-US company has to follow foreign rules; 2) to pay re-importation duties (hence keeps much of its money in the bank); 3) lobby to get the merger approved; 4) lose stock value; and 5) lose long-term capital value. Despite these obstacles, companies would rather go abroad than pay high domestic taxes. Ideally, they'd like it all ways: to retain their high stock values while paying low taxes. Trump is giving them what they want.[7]

The Obama years saw an explosion in the number of tax-inversions and a mass exodus of US companies. In response to losing tax revenue, the Obama Treasury adopted rules to curb the practice. The *Financial Times* reports that business lobbies immediately leaned on Congress to repeal the regulations. The US Chamber of Commerce even filed a lawsuit against the Treasury. A longitudinal study of 20 years' worth of tax inversions finds that losses from the practice are deferred to shareholders. Although CEOs prefer short-term profits, longer-term investments make companies stronger. Tax inversions prevent this. The study also finds that 25-year shares in the pharmaceutical company Pfizer, for instance, grew six times compared to shorter-term investments, which less than doubled. Tax inversions, according to the study, wipe up to 20% off the value of shares.[8]

According to *Forbes*, the 'net effect' of tax inversions 'is that the stock prices of US corporations are lower than they would be in the absence of such rules'. Corporations find it harder to raise capital. Consequently, 'future US growth will be lower than it could be'.[9]

Carl Icahn made his money in hostile takeovers and real estate investments. The billionaire owner of Icahn Enterprises is special advisor to Trump on regulatory reform. In 2015, Icahn spent $150 million 'lobby[ing] Congress to pass a repatriation tax holiday and other corporate tax reforms', says *TIME* magazine. Icahn himself writes about 'the current gridlock in Congress that prevents important legislation from being passed ... Many individuals are asking me to take action'. He goes on to note that more than 50 US companies engaged in inversions in just the last few years. This translates to 'over half a trillion dollars in market value, hundreds of millions in tax dollars, and tens of thousands of jobs'.[10]

Ergo, Trump is bringing business back to America, but for all the wrong reasons.

Bringing Jobs Back?

For the last 20 years or more, and as a core component of neoliberal practices and money-saving techniques, US corporations have outsourced and offshored production to other countries in order to get cheap labour. Car plants have relocated to Mexico, cell phone factories have opened in China and computer programming developers found higher-skilled workers at competitive prices in India.[11]

But there were problems. America's corporate tax code meant that when a company reimported its assembled goods, it often had to pay taxes. Also, US firms were subject to value-added taxes when selling in foreign countries; a clause which they regard as unfair competition. Tax inversions save US companies tax revenues but ultimately devalue their shares. The final nail in the coffin, however, has been the recent developments in automation, both physical and especially software-based. It has become less profitable to outsource production and development to countries with a large, impoverished labour force. Another factor has been the growth of competitive foreign assembly and development companies, like Tata in India.

As *Forbes* puts it, citing an industry report on the future of off-shoring, '[t]he low cost arbitrage that allowed such countries as India and China to become the world's outsourcers is no match for higher-level automation and robotic processes'. So, when Trump talks about defying the elites and the corporate fat cats by bringing jobs back to America and putting 'those beautiful, beautiful words, "Made in the USA"' back on the labels, that is what many tech companies wanted to do. Here's the evidence:[12]

By 2013, *The New York Times* was reporting that IBM employed more Indian workers than Americans. However, the cost of offshoring was starting to rise as new technologies took hold. In the same year, *The Economist* reported that offshoring had gone as far as it could, with American and European banks and financial institutions (which hold and/or invest the tech companies' money) having offshored 80% of what was possible. 'A second reason is that a lot of the jobs that might have been offshored by Western firms in the coming years have already been wiped out by productivity improvements. New jobs in Western economies tend to be of a more demanding, higher-level kind and are less likely to be sent abroad'.[13]

By late 2015, *Computer Weekly* was giving some examples: 'new technologies, such as automation software — including IBM's very own Watson — and cloud computing, are reducing the need for high numbers of offshore staff to carry out business processes and software development'. In what the article calls 'the holy grail', non-linear growth means 'adding business without needing to add to the workforce to support it — reducing the proportional increase in the cost of providing an additional service'. Where non-IT is concerned, however, IBM still finds it profitable to offshore. If a growing percentage of work doesn't need to be offshored and if tax can be avoided, it's win-win for the tech industry.[14]

In Trump's vernacular, cutting corporate taxes is called bringing jobs back to America. Despite its reputation for funding 'liberal' candidates like Clinton, many companies in the hi-tech industry (which broadly includes Apple, Amazon, Facebook, Google, IBM, Intel, Twitter, Yahoo!) lobbied Obama's Congress together with Republicans and Tea Partiers, as well as Grover Norquist's Americans for Tax Reform.[15]

Obama's 2011 deficit reduction plan excluded tax breaks for the tech sector. Bret Wincup of the Information Technology Industry Council said that tech companies get unfairly 'lumped into the rhetoric of shipping jobs overseas'. Apple is a prime example: It contracts its assembly operations to Taiwan's Foxconn, which uses Chinese labour. But they can't help it, argue people like Wincup; if only the government would entice them home by slashing taxes. Treasury Secretary Geithner confirmed that the Obama administration would not be offering repatriation because it needs to raise tax revenue. The US Chamber of Commerce argued that economic growth could reach 4% and create 2.9 million jobs if companies were allowed to avoid domestic taxes.[16]

In 2014, *Greentech Media* reported on the 'incentives at secret meetings' among business and Republican representatives to cut taxes for billionaire Elon Musk's Tesla company, which produces parts for electric cars. The aim was to coax Musk to open a battery-making plant in Arizona. This would follow the model 'offered to Apple's new plant in Mesa', Arizona, namely the elimination of energy taxes on large manufacturers. There was also talk of Panasonic, which provides parts to the Tesla company, joining the project.[17]

In 2015, Amazon, Apple, Google and Facebook stepped up their lobbying efforts to reform 'taxation and trade policies', says *Wired* magazine in an article assessing lobbying documents acquired through freedom of information filings. Facebook wanted to extend the government's R&D tax credit. Amazon sought to weaken the internet sales tax brought in via the Remote Transactions Parity Act 2015, which allows competitors to avoid taxes.[18]

In December 2016, *The New York Times* reported a top-level meeting between President-elect Trump and top executives from the hi-tech sector. The meeting included, 'Jeff Bezos of Amazon; Elon Musk of Tesla; Timothy D. Cook of Apple; Sheryl Sandberg of Facebook; Larry Page and Eric Schmidt of Alphabet, Google's parent company; and Satya Nadella of Microsoft, among others'. Trump immediately signalled his enthusiasm for the industry. '[N]owhere to be seen' was the Trump 'who warned during the presidential campaign that Amazon was going to have antitrust problems, that Apple needed to build its iPhones in the United States instead of China'. The billionaire Trump told the meeting of fellow (multi)billionaires: 'Anything we can do to help this go along ... we're going to be there for you ... [W]e're going to make it a lot easier for you to trade'.[19]

Bill Gates, who supported Clinton, also expressed his enthusiasm for Trump: 'there can be a very upbeat message that [Trump's] administration [is] going to organize things, get rid of regulatory barriers, and have American leadership through innovation'. This includes the education and health sectors, says Gates.[20]

Trade as a Weapon

'[B]usiness, especially trade, is like war', says Trump (*The America We Deserve*, 2000, p. 146). But Trump is not opposed to neoliberal globalization, also known as 'free trade'. He is opposed to the *current model* of free trade established under the 'liberal' Clinton government in the 1990s and expanded by the Obama government. In the current order, American trade and investment is diluted through multilateral arrangements. These are politically easier to manage than what Goldman Sachs-sponsored intelligence projections call the 'noodle bowl' of state-on-state (or bilateral) deals. By dismantling multilateral trade institutions like the European Union, Trump will make America even more dominant when it comes to protecting corporate privilege.[21]

In previous chapters, we note that neoliberalism, and especially neoliberal globalization, alienated large numbers of American workers, particularly by exporting jobs to Mexico and China. It was therefore easy for candidate Trump to run on a platform of opposition to globalization. Rhetoric based on bringing jobs home was bound to be a winner. Indeed, his credentials are impressive. He not only ran on a platform of opposition to the big NAFTA and TPP deals (explained below), but as soon as he took office Trump instructed his trade representative to start formal withdrawal from TPP. His voters breathed a sigh of relief, and even the few people in the alternative media critical of Trump cited this move as a testament to his anti-establishment credentials.[22]

Both Trump's victory and Brexit appear to herald a new age of domestic investment, protectionism and nationalism. But the truth is that the 'free marketeers' who have sponsored both events want to dismantle political alliances and make the US the dominant partner in every trade deal. At present, trade and investment deals are facilitated through the World Trade Organization (WTO). Since joining the WTO, the rising economies, particularly China and India, have challenged America on a number of issues – and people like Trump won't tolerate it.

India challenged America's imposition of countervailing duties on imports of certain hot rolled carbon steel flat products. India brought the challenge under General Agreement on Tariffs and Trade (GATT) rules, claiming that America's protectionist measures contravened the US Tariff Act on customs duties. Also citing GATT, India complained that the US violates agreements on non-immigrant temporary working visas. China challenged the US at the WTO, citing the US Department of Commerce's claim that majority government ownership makes any given enterprise a public body. In other words, America was unfairly subsidizing its industries. In the same complaint, China alleged that the US was levying heavy import duties on Chinese products including solar panels, steel sinks and drill pipes.[23]

Despite these protectionist measures erected by Presidents Bush and Obama, Trump screams that China has been 'raping' America's economy. In an effort to put China at a disadvantage, US and mostly East Asian countries worked out a trade and investment deal – without the participation of the publics of either region – called the Trans-Pacific Partnership (TPP). Hidden within hundreds of pages of text are provisions to privatize public services, including transport, telecoms and intellectual property.[24]

Favouring Bilateralism

A TPP-esque free trade deal was signed in 1994 between the US, Mexico and Canada. This was NAFTA, the North American Free Trade Agreement, from which Trump has promised to withdraw or renegotiate. NAFTA put hundreds of thousands of Americans out of work, destroyed Mexican peasant farming, led to Canada getting sued repeatedly for trying to protect its environment and made a load of money for US corporations.[25]

If these deals are so good for big business, why would billionaire businessman Trump and his team want to dismantle them? As we shall see, value-added taxes and currency manipulations are two problems for US businesses, which the Democrats who brought us both TPP and NAFTA failed to address. It turns out that Trump is not actually opposed to free trade. In his book *Great Again* (2016), Trump writes: '[t]he free market works – it just needs leadership' (p. 80). 'Leadership' is code for absolute American dominance. In *The America We Deserve* (2000), Trump writes: '[w]e need tougher negotiations, not protectionist walls around America' (p. 145).

When Trump talks about his opposition to trade deals, he means his opposition to *multilateral* trade deals, i.e., agreements where other countries have some power through supranational institutions, norms and regulations; or where they can work as a bloc to restrain exploitation by the US. Such deals have too many loopholes, says Trump, through which competitors take advantage. Examples of politically powerful trading blocs where the US feels hampered include the EU and Mercosur in South America. 'I am not an isolationist', says Trump, 'but neither am I one of those giddy globalists who thinks that we should leave everything to the IMF [International Monetary Fund] and the UN' (ibid.).[26]

A report by the US Council on Foreign Relations (CFR) makes the same point as Trump about the failure of US-led 'globalist' institutions to safeguard American businesses against currency manipulation, hence Trump's supposedly 'nationalistic' rhetoric. The CFR report notes: 'The international economic system has been totally ineffective at responding to such manipulation. The International Monetary Fund has clear rules against competitive devaluations. But it has no enforcement mechanism and its decision-making process is highly politicized' – remember Trump's comment that, 'nonpoliticians represent the wave of the future'? The CFR report concludes: '[WTO] rules on exchange rates are vague and have never been tested'.[27]

In other words, unless America's business class has total control over every aspect of trade and investment, America is 'getting screwed' by its trading partners, in Trump's view. For example: according to an academic study of NAFTA and the WTO, 'Mexico won in several trade dispute cases with the United States'. The authors note that Mexico challenged America's protectionist measures on tuna and bovine labelling. This led to challenges by Mexico through the WTO over tomatoes and shrimp, with Mexico emerging triumphant. Even tiny defeats over tuna are intolerable for a superpower committed to a doctrine of 'Full Spectrum Dominance' designed to 'protect U.S. interests and investment'.[28]

In the Bush years, America fought a mini trade war with the EU because the EU blocked imports of American beef, GMOs and toxic chemicals. The US retaliated by slapping huge tariffs on EU products with geographical indicators, such as Roquefort cheese and Scotch whisky. Corporate Europe Observatory discovered that TTIP – the secret, TPP-esque deal negotiated between European and American businesses – was heavily lobbied for by the US agricultural sector which has been badly hurt by Brussels' decision to ban several U.S. agricultural products and require labelling for others.[29]

By disintegrating Brussels, American businesses think they have a better chance of ramming through their products, including private insurance and energy, via bilateral trade deals. To date the US has free trade agreements with 20 countries, including Honduras, Israel, and Panama. Nations weaker than America, like South Korea, find safety in numbers. A scholarly study finds that '[a] region-wide FTA [free trade agreement] is more profitable than subregional or bilateral FTAs'. However, Chris Dent of the Evian Group points out that '[i]n bilateral FTAs, the stronger partner' – i.e., the US – 'can have the power to influence the terms of FTA[s] more in its own favour'. Pascal Lamy, then Director-general of the WTO, described bilateral deals as 'an instrument to get "brownie points" and gain an advantage over other WTO Members'.[30]

Trump has spoken publicly about his preference for bilateralism over multilateralism. In addition, a trade strategy memo obtained by CNN reveals the Trump team's plan to 'pursue bilateral trade agreements with Canada and Mexico', as well as with China.[31]

Doing Better

A report by the Congressional Research Service gives us some insight into the ideological battle being waged at the top. Generally, agribusiness was happy with the TPP arrangement, but cautioned about the lack of provisions against currency manipulation. On the issue of market access, the sugar and dairy industries are less enthusiastic about giving other countries access to US markets.[32]

'The Ford Motor Company quickly condemned the [TPP] agreement', says *The New York Times*. TPP will 'not meaningfully address currency manipulation by American trading partners, like Japan', the article continues. Ford itself is said to have written the following to the US government: 'To ensure the future competitiveness of American manufacturing, we recommend Congress not approve T.P.P. in its current form'. Indeed, Obama's majority-Republican Congress also pressed the ruling Democratic Party to include anti-currency manipulation provisions, which it failed to do.[33]

On the issue of big pharma, the article also notes that the USA sought a 12 year gap for drug makers to withhold data in order to protect their biology-based (or 'biosimilar') products. TPP negotiators from other countries succeeded in getting the US to agree to a five-year period. This has all sorts of negative implications for US drug firms which can hold back drugs until a competitor places one on the market, at which point the highly-subsidized US drug company can flood the market and kill off the competition. Peru is a TPP signatory. Its trade minister, Magali Silva, said in response to the compromise: 'We do think we have a balanced result'. In response, Senate Finance Committee chair, Orrin Hatch (a Republican from Utah), who had held fast to the 12 year demand, said: 'I think most people, once the [2016 election] is over [...] will rethink this thing'.[34]

But Trump's rhetorical opposition to TPP follows the wishes of a certain sector of the US business class which argues for better trade deals. Long before Candidate Trump, businesses and commentators opposed at least two elements of TPP: valued-added tax (VAT) and currency manipulation.

On VAT: MarketWatch notes that many members of Congress urged Obama to compensate for America's VAT disadvantage. Ten of the twelve TPP signatory countries impose VAT on their products. Congress points out that domestic VAT in, say, Australia on US imports amounts to a hidden tariff. Seven of the ten impose import VAT duties equivalent to double-digit tariffs. Even America's closest ally in the TPP bloc, Japan, raised VAT from 5% to 10% in less than a year. In a single year, US production can be hurt by as much as $440bn due to foreign VAT, hence Trump's pursuit of bilateral trade to deal with such issues.[35]

One sticking point for Trump and the far-right Republicans is that TPP includes too many opt-outs and special treatment clauses for foreign countries. According to Trump's mouthpiece *Breitbart* (run by Trump's ex-chief strategist Steve Bannon), TPP is a bad deal partly because it 'cannot be re-negotiated, particularly over the lax rules on importing foreign-made autos and auto parts into the United States', says author Kevin Kearns. Japan's Toyota, for instance, has hurt domestic US auto companies. TPP would permit Toyota to retain its global supply chains, which include outsourcing to China, the way America does. 'The TPP has, in addition to 30 main chapters, a total of 58 side agreements (called "side letters"). And Japan alone possesses 14 of these side letters, with each one laying out special conditions for Japanese participation and special deals for Japanese economic sectors'.[36]

Currency Wars: The Dollar is 'Too Strong'

TPP focused on eliminating already weak tariffs to trade and non-tariff barriers, which include public ownership. So if, for example, roads in country x are owned by the government, TPP gave US companies the right to privatize them or at least challenge government x over the alleged unfair competition of keeping roads public. If country y was keeping drug prices low to save its population from, say, tropical diseases, US pharmaceutical companies could sue government y, citing violation of the agreement over non-tariff barriers. TPP therefore seemed like a dream come true for US-based multinational corporations. But it wasn't good enough. The failure of TPP to include provisions against currency manipulation are more serious for US corporations than non-tariff barriers.

The Council on Foreign Relations is exactly the kind of organization that Trump voters, particularly in the alternative media, despise. It is based in New York (the 'liberal east coast' as they see it) and amounts to a network of 'globalist' businesses and politicians. Its journal *Foreign Affairs* reveals that as early as January 2015, '[t]he U.S. auto industry ... has indicated that it will oppose the TPP unless the issue [of currency manipulation] is effectively addressed'. Crucially, it also makes the point that 'critics of the TPP are correct to link currency and trade. Changes in exchange rates can affect trade flows and trade balances far more than any of the border, or even behind-the-border, barriers', says the report. The report concludes that 'it is just as economically distorting to artificially depress currency values', *à la* China and others, 'as it is to impose high import tariffs and subsidize exports directly'. Ergo the US 'suffered much larger trade deficits and sizable job losses than it otherwise would have'.[37]

In economic propaganda, the assumption is that a strong dollar is good for 'America'. But in the real world, neoliberalism has such distorting effects on currency and speculation that exporters want a weak dollar as a proxy to fiscal stimulus, i.e., they want people all over the world to buy American products (even if those products are assembled elsewhere, like China). Trump has repeatedly said that he will label China a currency manipulator. It makes him seem like a tough negotiator, looking out for working people and bucking the liberal trend of letting foreign countries get the better of the USA.

This is not the behaviour of a rebel President, despite how he's being portrayed. The president of New York's Federal Reserve central bank, which is hated by the Trump supporters, agrees that the US dollar is too strong: 'The recent strengthening of the dollar will put downward pressure on import prices and limit the ability of domestic producers to raise their prices'. Trump himself has said 'our currency is too strong. And it's killing us'. So it's okay for

America to manipulate its currency, but not for China to manipulate its own.[38]

Like most things in life, these are complicated issues. Trump favours business over people, but the right kind of business. A weak dollar is good for exports, but a very weak dollar can lead to inflation. So Trump's team are trying to strike a balance. All of this complexity is lost in campaign and presidential rhetoric about bringing jobs home, and making America great again, etc. Businessmen like Trump despise too much currency depreciation in other countries because it hurts the value of their products and forces the US to bring down the value of the dollar to compete.

When a small majority of Britons voted to leave the EU in 2016, the value of the pound sank. This made British products more affordable on the international market, and many British exporters benefitted. This, in theory, hurt European countries because instead of buying their products, consumers were taking advantage of the cheaper British ones. For the last half decade, China has been accused by the US of initiating a trade war by keeping its currency artificially low. This has the effect of boosting Chinese exports thanks to low prices, all at the expense of American exports. This is an affront to a country dedicated to being the global superpower. As a result of financialization outlined in the previous chapters, national economies are particularly affected by global currency and short-term stock, asset and bond valuations.[39]

In this sense, economic protection for a select few businesses and stock market players is conflated with patriotism and looking out for the average American worker. As the TPP was being negotiated, several corporate lawyers lobbied the trade rep. and Treasury Secretary (Michael Froman and later Jacob Lew) to include a chapter or at least provisions to prevent currency manipulation. They were ignored, as the Obama administration steamed ahead with the deal.[40]

This is what Trump really means when he says such deals are a disaster for America.

Chapter 9

Foreign policy: 'Carry a big stick'

'Because we are such a kind nation, it's hard for us to believe that some people around the world don't actually like us – that we have enemies dead set against us.'

– Donald J. Trump (with Dave Shiflett), *The America We Deserve* (2000), p. 113

Trump's foreign policy may appear to be a mixed bag. On one hand, Trump initially made peace overtures to Russia, which were welcomed by certain peace campaigners (those who actually believe them), because reaching out to Russia may constrain the race towards nuclear Armageddon. On the other hand, Trump has hinted that his China policy will be a continuation or expansion of Obama's 'pivot to Asia', namely the encirclement of China by US bases, destroyers and nuclear weapons. By courting Russia, Trump might have divided it from China.

But the reality is that Presidents have little influence over military matters. War is the realm of the CIA and related agencies working in concert with the multibillion dollar Pentagon. Multinational corporations rely on America's ability to dominate the world, force markets wide open and keep them open. In 1997, the US Space Command published its *Vision for 2020*, which commits America to global military domination by weaponizing land, sea, air, space and information, 'to protect U.S. interests and investment'. The doctrine is called Full Spectrum Dominance and was expanded in 2000 by all the heads of the major armed forces, the Joint Chiefs of Staff.[1]

A year before 9/11, a neocon think-tank called The Project for a New American Century published an almost 100-page document entitled, *Rebuilding America's Defenses*. In it, military-linked policy planners discuss: expanding drones to 'project US power' across the world, backing out of the Antiballistic Missile Treaty with Russia in order to build a missile system, using Europe as a global police force, expanding operations into Asia, particularly against China, and funding a new generation of drug-enhanced soldiers. A 'catastrophic and catalyzing event' would be required to speed up the process. After 9/11, the Bush administration was able to do all of the above.[2]

Since committing America to Full Spectrum Dominance, the Pentagon has attacked Iraq (several times), Serbia, Afghanistan, Yemen (with drones), Pakistan (with drones), Somalia, Libya, Syria, and has supported Israel's attacks on Lebanon and Palestine by supplying most of the weapons and blocking UN resolutions to end the violence. It has also supported the coup which ousted Ukraine's pro-Russian president and replaced him with a US ally. Despite his campaign rhetoric, Trump once told 'shock jock' Howard Stern that he supported the invasion of Iraq in 2003.[3]

In *Time to Get Tough* (2016), he writes: '[when the US] sacrifices thousands of lives of its own young servicemen and women and more than a trillion dollars to bring freedom to the people of Iraq, the least – the absolute *least* – the Iraqis should do is pick up the tab for their own liberation' (emphasis in the original). This tab would be paid for by Iraq's oil, which the US should control, says Trump in his chapter, 'Take the Oil' (p. 9).

Declaring a 'war on terror' was an attempt to give many of the above atrocities a veneer of legitimacy, as was the pretence of 'humanitarian intervention' in Serbia and Libya. But as Thomas Friedman of the *New York Times* once put it, the real reasons for war are different: 'The hidden hand of the market will never work without a hidden fist – McDonald's cannot flourish without McDonnell Douglas, the builder of the F-15 [fighter jet]. And the hidden fist that keeps the world safe for Silicon Valley's technologies is called the United States Army, Air Force, Navy and Marine Corps'. Similarly, ex-Center for Naval Warfare Studies professor, Thomas P.M. Barnett, explains: 'Any time American troops show up ... it tends to be in a place that is relatively disconnected from the world, where globalization hasn't taken root'.[4]

Donald Trump believes in Full Spectrum Dominance. According

to its website, the Center for National Interest, 'seeks to stimulate debate, promote public understanding of U.S. foreign policy and international affairs, and define principled yet pragmatic policies to advance America's national interest'. Trump spoke to the Center in April 2016. He said: 'Our military dominance must be unquestioned, and I mean unquestioned, by anybody and everybody'. Sixteen years before that, he quoted Theodore Roosevelt's maxim: 'Speak softly and carry a big stick', which he describes as 'a good MO'. (*The America We Deserve*, p. 148.)

In *Time to Get Tough* (2016), Trump acknowledges that Obama's invasion of Libya was a violation of US domestic law. He also acknowledges that NATO was led by the US and was used as the anti-Gaddafi terrorists' air support. However, he writes: 'we should have said, "Sure, we don't like the guy [Gaddafi] either. We will help you take out [Gaddafi]. But in exchange, you give us 50 percent of your oil for the next twenty-five years…" … Our policy should be: no oil, no military support. No exceptions' (pp. 102–03).[5]

China: 'Our Enemy'

Trump's view of China, and the world in general, is that different cultures are a market for US goods. When they are held captive by corrupt dictatorships, they are often too poor to buy American products. Likewise, if the given regime is socialist and sponsors domestic industry, it pushes American producers out. Ergo, America must promote a certain kind of democracy which makes people around the world free to buy American goods.

In *The America We Deserve* (2000), Trump has a subchapter called 'How to take on China' (p. 117) and calls China 'our biggest long-term challenge' (p. 125). Trump writes: 'We want to trade with China because of the size of its consumer market. But if the regime continues to oppress individual freedoms, how many consumers will there really be?' (p. 119). Trump was screaming about China's alleged theft of American technologies and secrets as far back as 2000. He writes: 'under no circumstances will we keep our markets open to countries that steal from us' (p. 123).

Trump continues China-bashing in *Great Again* (2015). 'There are people who wish I wouldn't refer to China as our enemy. But that's exactly what they are. They have destroyed entire industries by utilizing low-wage workers, cost us tens of thousands of jobs, spied on our businesses, stolen our technology, and have manipulated and devalued their currency' (p. 43). Though you wouldn't know it from his rhetoric, Trump understands that China's economy is largely a false one as it depends on foreign investments, as we shall see below. Quoting Steve Forbes: 'Beijing is becoming more dependent on the US and the rest of the world for its strength and prosperity' (pp. 44–45).

But Trump is part of the problem. He goes on to write: 'The Chinese are very savvy businesspeople, and they have great advantages over our manufacturers. I've had several Trump-brand products made there' (p. 43). He also writes: 'I'm actually landlord to China's largest bank, which has its offices in Trump Tower' (p. 45).

MYTH: China has been 'raping' America, as Trump claims.
FACT: China's huge GDP is largely a false economy because it is highly dependent on foreign investors, mainly the US. If anyone has been harming the American worker, it's been the system of globalization which has outsourced jobs to China.

The share of China's state-owned enterprises in the processing and assembly sectors has declined from 40% in 1995 to 6% in 2015. China's private corporations have increased their share of the sector from 0.01% to 11.65%. Globally, China has 38% of the world's export market in telecoms (mainly cell phones), but only 6% of the profits go to Chinese firms. US exports account for 7.4% of telecoms exports, but US firms make 59% of the profits. This pattern generalizes across telecoms, electronic data processing, office equipment, clothing, chemicals, pharmaceuticals and integrated circuits/components. Because the other sectors – banking, construction, forestry, mining, real estate and energy – are largely controlled by a state-sector at the low-end of the global value chain, it is unlikely that Chinese firms can compete globally.[6]

The materials for an iPhone 6 cost an estimated $211.10.

Assembly costs just $4.50. The phone retails for $749 in the USA. Apple subcontracts the Taiwanese firms Hon Hai Precision Industry (Foxconn) and Pegatron. 'So it is not even a Chinese firm that assembles and exports the iPhone', says Assistant Professor Sean Starrs. Starrs also points out that 'Foxconn's profit in 2014 was $4.3 billion while Apple's alone was ten times larger, at $44.5 billion'. 60% of China's assembly economy is controlled by foreign corporations (80% when we include joint China-foreign ventures).[7]

MYTH: China is a military threat to America.
FACT: America's military budget at the close of Obama's administration was $598.5bn. China's budget for 2016 was $120bn. In 2012, America spent more on its military than ten other countries combined (China, Russia, the UK, Japan, France, Saudi Arabia, India, Germany, Italy and Brazil). The question about China's threat to America is answered by the US Defense Department in its report to Congress 2016. It says that, despite regional expansion, 'China still seeks to avoid direct and explicit conflict with the United States'. China's military strategy is defensive, not offensive. Its leaders are 'developing the capabilities they deem necessary to deter or defeat adversary power projection and counter third-party – including U.S. – intervention during a crisis or conflict'.[8]

China has zero overseas military bases, except one under construction in Djibouti in the resource-rich Horn of Africa. America has at least 662 military bases in at least 38 countries. Unlike the US, China has a no-first-use policy for nuclear weapons. As early as 2008, Russia and China formally proposed banning space-based weapons via a United Nations treaty. The US rejected it and continues to do so.[9]

MYTH: China is a communist economy.
FACT: China liberalized its economy in the 1980s to the benefit of America.

The origins of China's rapid GDP growth can be traced to 1978. Between 1985 and 2005, China borrowed $3bn from the US-led World Bank and subsidiaries for privatization projects. In the

1980s, state banks extended credit beyond levels authorized by the national credit plan. Foreign direct investment 'poured in' to China 'like never before', writes Pieter Bottelier, Chief of the World Bank's Resident Mission in China from 1993 to 1997. 'China became the World Bank's largest borrower and one of the largest recipients of technical assistance in the early 1990s before the program began to shrink towards the end of the decade'. Bottelier also notes that 'the World Bank withdrew from sectors where the private sector could take over (e.g. telecommunications, commercial ports, conventional thermal power plants and highways)'.[10]

A paper by the International Monetary Fund cites three reasons for China's economic growth: 1) foreign direct investment; 2) labour mobility (farmers moving to cities to become manufacturers); and 3) privatization. '[W]hile capital investment is crucial to growth, it becomes even more potent when accompanied by market-oriented reforms that introduce profit incentives to rural enterprises and small private businesses'.[11]

A paper by Wing and Sachs notes that private interests successfully lobbied the Chinese Communist Party. During the 1980s, the liberalization of State-owned enterprise (SOE) regulation meant that the managerial class siphoned off profits. SOEs rapidly paid fewer taxes (just 1.7 percent of GDP by 1993) and made substantial losses (19.1 per cent profit in 1978 compared to 0.1 per cent in 1993). Chinese banks lent to SOEs, getting them into debt. In late-1995, the Bureau for the Administration of State Property issued a report suggesting that privatization equalled 50 billion yuan per annum, by which time the one thousand largest SOEs had been privatized (smaller ones were sold to workers). The process was accelerated by the existence of privatized town–village enterprises (TVE), whose private owners merely registered their TVE as a 'collective' for formal purposes.[12]

MYTH: China has power over the US because it owns US debt.
FACT: This myth makes it easy for politicians like Trump to sound off about China and scare the living daylights out of American voters. But the reality is that renminbi (a.k.a. yuan) is tied to the US

dollar. One yuan is worth just 14 cents. Although America owes China $1.15 trillion, China owes America $750 billion, which is more in real terms because the renminbi is so weak. America's debt to China is actually half of its debt to its own central bank, the Federal Reserve.[13]

Iran: More Myths & Facts

There's been a Pentagon plan to attack Iran as early as 2001, when NATO General Wesley Clark saw a Pentagon memo outlining a plan to 'take out seven countries in five years': Iraq, Lebanon, Libya, Somalia, Sudan, Syria and Iran.[14]

Trump is very pro-Israel, hence very anti-Iran. In 2016 he said: 'Iran cannot be allowed to have a nuclear weapon, cannot be allowed. Remember that, cannot be allowed to have a nuclear weapon. And under a Trump administration, will never, ever be allowed to have that nuclear weapon'. This presupposes that Iran actually wants a nuclear weapon, when all the evidence (below) shows that it doesn't want one and hasn't the means of acquiring one. Trump is so anti-Iran that he sees Iranian influence in its neighbour Iraq (which destroyed Iran in the 1980s) as evidence of Iran's status as a regional power. This is factually incorrect, by any measure.[15]

Under Bush and Obama, Britain, America and Israel subjected Iran to warfare on at least four fronts: 1) using terrorist proxies (the Shia Mujahideen-e Khalq, MeK and the Sunni Jundallah near Pakistan) to weaken Iran's government; 2) murdering Iranian civilian nuclear engineers; 3) launching cyber-attacks and; 4) imposing devastating economic sanctions. But this wasn't enough for Trump, who says: '[Obama] has treated Iran with tender love and care and made it a great power. Iran has, indeed, become a great, great power in just a very short period of time, because of what we've done. All of the expense and all at the expense of Israel, our allies in the region and very importantly, the United States itself'.[16]

MYTH: Iran is trying to develop a nuclear weapon.
FACT: Under Article IV of the Nuclear Non-Proliferation Treaty

1970 all signatory states, including Iran, have a right to develop nuclear energy for civilian purposes. After Britain and America invaded Iraq in 2003, Iran attempted to negotiate with the US over a host of issues, including its support for Hezbollah in Lebanon and of course the nuclear issue. The George W. Bush administration rejected the offers, as former CIA analyst Flynt Leverett revealed. In 2015, the UN International Atomic Energy Agency confirmed that Iran was not secretly developing a nuclear weapon. Director-general Yukiya Amano confirmed: 'The agency has no credible indications of activities in Iran relevant to the development of a nuclear explosive device after 2009 ... Nor has the agency found any credible indications of the diversion of nuclear material in connection with the possible military dimensions to Iran's nuclear programme'.[17]

MYTH: The Anglo–American–Israeli torture of Iran is necessary to stop it developing a nuclear weapon.
FACT: The real reason for America et al.'s pathological pursuit of Iran has to do with the price of oil. A Presidential Task Force report from 2009 explains that if Iran switches to nuclear power, America's oil-dependent allies in the region will follow suit and America could lose control of the vast Middle East oil economy and thus global prices. 'So long as the United States firmly opposed Iran's [civilian nuclear] Bushehr facility, no friendly Arab state actively pursued civil nuclear power', says the report. 'But once Washington accepted that Iran could have a nuclear power plant, the United States was in no position to press its friends not to pursue a capability it had agreed Iran could have'. It goes on to say that, 'if an agreement is reached legitimizing even limited enrichment on Iranian soil, other countries may well be interested in having the same capabilities, and it could be difficult diplomatically to dissuade them from this pursuit ... Demonstrating how seriously the international community is concerned about Iran's actions might discourage imitators'.[18]

So, when we hear 'Iran mustn't get a nuclear weapon', we should interpret it to mean Iran mustn't develop significant independent civilian nuclear power.

MYTH: Sanctions are necessary to make Iran comply.

FACT: On the basis of unfounded claims made in 2002 by the US-backed terrorist organization, MeK, the International Atomic Energy Agency adopted a resolution in 2003 calling on Iran to halt its nuclear activities, to which Iran agreed. After talks with France, Germany and the UK (Paris Agreement 2004), Iran agreed to suspend uranium enrichment, even though it is entitled to enrich uranium for civilian purposes under the NPT Treaty. (Two of the three countries – France and Britain – themselves have nuclear weapons, not just civilian reactors, and continue to violate international law by retaining them. Who will hold them accountable?)[19]

After working out a deal to acquire Russian uranium, Iran was placed under scrutiny by the UN in 2006. In 2007, the P5+1 states (the UN Security Council permanent members, plus Germany) negotiated a framework for compelling Iran to halt enrichment. But the US's own National Intelligence Estimate 'judg[ed] with high confidence' that Iran stopped its nuclear weapons programme in 2003 and would be unable to acquire nuclear weapons until at least 2010. Still, the Western powers made Iran jump through hoops. In 2009, Brazil and Turkey intervened to negotiate a fuel swap, in which Iran would export its enriched uranium to Turkey in exchange for fuels from France and Russia. America rejected the move.[20]

In 2010, the US-led United Nations imposed sanctions on Iran, which greatly hurt the country. Two years later, UN Secretary-general Ban Ki-moon said: 'The sanctions … have had significant effects on the general population, including an escalation in inflation, a rise in commodities and energy costs, an increase in the rate of unemployment and a shortage of necessary items, including medicine'. Britain's Defence Secretary (now Chancellor) Philip Hammond violated the Fourth Geneva Convention, which forbids collective punishments. He explained that the goal of the sanctions was to compel the civilian population to put pressure on the government. 'We can definitely make the pain much greater', said Hammond.[21]

In 2015, Iran agreed to the Joint Comprehensive Plan of Action which allows Iran to enrich uranium at a very low level whilst giving up 98% of its existing enriched uranium. The sanctions were lifted in exchange for the deal, which will limit Iran's civilian nuclear energy programmes and force its continued reliance on fossil fuels.[22]

Trump writes: 'The deal President Obama negotiated with Iran was the worst I have ever seen ... Iran was boxed in and the sanctions were hurting them ... Instead of removing the sanctions that forced the Iranians to negotiate, we should have doubled or tripled the sanctions ... I would have increased the sanctions until the conditions there were so terrible that the Iranian leaders were begging for a deal' (*Great Again*, pp. 39–40).

Russia: Friend or Foe, or Both?

As soon as Trump was announced winner of the 2016 popular presidential election, numerous Western commentators expressed concern that Trump might demilitarize in Syria and Ukraine, thereby placating Putin. Their reaction to Trump's victory suggests that many European and American political commentators are so pathologically anti-Russian that they are willing to increase the likelihood of nuclear Armageddon rather than compromise with Russia and de-escalate tensions.

The Bulletin of the Atomic Scientists recently moved the hand of its Doomsday clock from five to two-and-a-half minutes to Midnight – Midnight meaning the end – citing tensions over Ukraine and the shooting down of a Russian jet by the US–British-backed Turkish military in 2015. This kind of cat-and-mouse tactic is very danger-ous, and not by accident. Trump has pledged to expand America's military, including its nuclear weapons programme. '[W]e have to rebuild our military and our economy', says Trump, ignoring the fact that America has by far the biggest military in the world. 'The Russians and Chinese have rapidly expanded their military capa-bility, but look at what's happened to us. Our nuclear weapons arsenal, our ultimate deterrent, has been allowed to atrophy and is desperately in need of modernization and renewal. And it has to happen immediately'.[23]

Trump is referring to the $348bn programme to upgrade America's current 1,750 strategic warheads out to the year 2024.[24]

In the late-1960s and '70s, President Nixon used what he called the madman theory of politics in dealing with China. The aim was to simply make the United States seem irrational and dangerous. In the 1990s, the Strategic Command published a now-declassified document called *Essentials of Post-Cold War Deterrence*. In it, the authors recommend that, '[b]ecause of the value that comes from the ambiguity of what the US may do to an adversary ... it hurts to portray ourselves as too fully rational and cool-headed'. It goes on to recommend that 'some elements may appear to be potentially "out of control"'. Trump continues this madman policy. He has said: 'we must as a nation be more unpredictable'.[25]

In *The America We Deserve*, Trump has a subchapter called 'Rehabilitating Russia'. Trump's view is that the smashed-up Soviet Union was, 'like an old business or professional adversary who falls on hard times'. But America can impose 'free market' economics on Russia, as it attempted to do in the 1990s, and 'get the guy back on his feet, clean him up, give him a few bucks, and hope for the best' (p. 133). But this kind of charity comes at a price, says Trump. 'We need to tell Russia and other recipients that if they want our dime they had better do our dance, at least in matters regarding our national security' (p. 134).

Russia was put at a strategic disadvantage. As part of the Lisbon Protocol to the 1991 Strategic Arms Reduction Treaty, ex-Soviet states Belarus, Kazakhstan and Ukraine gave up their nuclear weapons. America's allies in Europe and elsewhere – Britain, France, India and Israel – retained theirs.

Trump has little to say about Russia in *Great Again*, except to express his bafflement as to 'why Germany and other countries watched impassively as Putin marched into Ukraine' (p. 48). The reality of Ukraine is that since its independence from the Soviet Union in 1991, Ukraine has been a proxy battleground for US–Russian influence. After independence, Ukraine immediately announced training exercises with the US-led North Atlantic Treaty Organization (NATO). Think how America would have reacted if

Canada had started exercises with the former Warsaw Pact countries, or how Britain would have reacted if Russia had started large-scale exercises with Ireland.[26]

The US and Ukraine had been working on a bilateral trade deal to allow US companies to penetrate Ukrainian banks, agriculture and energy. Various energy journals and specialists – civilian and military – consider Ukraine as Russia's energy corridor to Europe. Controlling Ukrainian politics gives Europe and America the edge over Russia in terms of oil and gas. In the Orange Revolution of 2004, Russia's favourite Viktor Yanukovych was ousted and replaced by America's favourite, Viktor Yushchenko. But by 2010, Yanukovych was back in office. After protests erupted by mainly pro-EU demonstrators in 2014, the government was shut down in a coup, backed by the neo-Nazi Azov Battalion.[27]

The other serious issue facing Russia is America's commitment to a missile system in Eastern Europe. At present, it includes Patriot missiles based in Poland (which is currently under the leadership of a far-right government linked to neo-Nazis, as Chapter 4 documents). In response in 2010, Russia moved its mobile nuclear weapons up to the Polish border in Kaliningrad. The system also consists of: the RAF Menwith Hill listening base, Flyingdales early warning radar and secret nuclear weapons installations in the UK; SM-3 missiles stationed in Poland and Romania; sea-based radars and interceptors in the Mediterranean sea; and a radar system in Turkey.[28]

In the real world, Obama continued America's commitment to the missile system, stationing Patriot missiles in Poland. However, Trump has signalled his intention to expand the system and has criticized Obama for not going far enough. 'President Obama gutted our missile defense program', says Trump, 'and then abandoned our missile defense plans with Poland and the Czech Republic'. In reality, Obama repositioned the missiles in Romania.[29]

What about hacking? Russia has formally denied the allegations, but on the basis of no evidence whatsoever, and on the claims of anonymous sources in the US intelligence community (a group not known for its honesty), the US media reported that Russia was trying to influence the 2016 election in Trump's favour by hacking the Democratic National Committee.

The Democrats claimed that Trump knew about the hacking before the election. This fed the false narrative that Trump might be a friend of Russia. What is missing in media discourse is that Russia has made several attempts to negotiate a treaty with America on protocols to cyber wars and information standards. In 2009, the *New York Times* reported that Russia had proposed an international treaty to ban cyber warfare. The US rejected the proposal. In 2011, the Arms Control Association reported that China and Russia submitted a proposal to the UN General Assembly on an International Code of Conduct for Information Security. Again, the US rejected the proposal.[30]

Conclusion

Coup d'Trump

President Trump is what happens when business replaces politics. Trump is the wealthiest President in US history (even when adjusted for inflation) and with a combined worth of $11bn, his administration is also the wealthiest in history. Billionaires make up 0.00016% of America's population (as entrepreneur and near-billionaire Palmer Luckey likes to boast). Not only is his administration stacked with billionaires, it — and its alt-right media — is largely financed by billionaires.[1]

Deep State: 'The FBI is Trumpland'

Trump's deep state connections go way back. He was tipped to become President as early as 1987. Richard Nixon's wife, Pat, saw Trump on *The Phil Donahue Show* and told her ex-President husband that Trump could be the next big thing. Nixon wrote to Trump: '[Pat] is an expert on politics and she predicts that whenever you decide to run for office, you will be a winner!' Shortly after, Trump started speaking with quiet confidence to Oprah Winfrey about making a bid for the White House. Since then, Trump has donated to both Democrats and Republicans, even joining the ephemeral Reform Party headed by billionaire independent, Ross Perot.[2]

Trump is connected to America's political police force, the Federal Bureau of Investigation (FBI) and very likely to America's foreign spy and subversion unit, the Central Intelligence Agency (CIA).

In the 1970s Trump and his father Fred, together with the late lawyer Roy Cohn, were under investigation by the Department of Justice (DoJ) for alleged discrimination against prospective black tenants. The DoJ asked the FBI to put a couple of agents on the case.

Cohn famously accused the FBI of conducting 'gestapo' style investigations into their alleged misconduct. But by the 1980s, Trump's associates were providing the FBI with valuable information on organized crime and union activity. Trump sought to develop property on land owned by Kenny Shapiro, who was connected to the Scarfo crime family which disrupted Atlantic City's 20,000-strong construction unions. Shapiro's associate at the Teamsters' union was Daniel Sullivan, an FBI informant. The FBI was in touch with Trump as early as 1981 with questions about alleged mob involvement in the construction industry. By the 1990s, another of Trump's associates was engaged in 'extraordinary cooperation' with the FBI over its secret operations. That associate was Felix Sater, a violent Russian émigré with connections to organized crime. Sater went on to lead New York's development firm, the Bayrock Group.[3]

It is also very likely that Trump's extra-American activities stoked the interest of the CIA. Since 1987, he had planned to build in the Soviet Union/Russia. Until the fall in oil prices in 2015, Trump had building projects lined up in ex-Soviet Azerbaijan. He has business connections with an Azerbaijan-born mogul, Aras Agalarov, whom Russian President Vladimir Putin awarded the national Order of Honour. Agalarov's son, Emin, married the daughter of Azerbaijan's human rights-abusing President, Ilham Aliyev. Quite apart from this, Trump has or had building projects lined up in countries as diverse as Indonesia, Turkey and the United Arab Emirates.[4]

The FBI was eager to ensure a Trump victory. '[M]ultiple bureau sources' informed the *Guardian* newspaper that '[d]eep antipathy to Hillary Clinton exists within the FBI ... spurring a rapid series of leaks damaging to her campaign'. WikiLeaks aided the anti-Clinton campaign with its targeted leaking of Democratic Party-related material. One FBI agent told the *Guardian*: 'The FBI is Trumpland'. The agent said that to many in the FBI, Clinton is 'the antichrist personified'.[5]

From the 1950s to the 1970s, the FBI ran COINTELPRO (counterintelligence program). It targeted unions, left-wing political groups, the New Left, students, women's groups, Native American organizers, the Black Panthers and Civil Rights groups and leaders, sending letters to Martin Luther King, for example, urging him to commit suicide. The overall objective was to stop social progress. Today, the FBI – in conjunction with other agencies – is running a similar campaign against Black Lives Matter. In 2014, mass demonstrations erupted in Ferguson, Missouri. It was the first major response in years by black people to police victimization and the underlying racist socioeconomic conditions. Obama's Department of Homeland Security (DHS) and FBI gathered files on the protestors, including data location, planned events and social media feeds. The scale of the spying stretched from Ferguson to Baltimore to Washington, DC, to New York. A law suit filed against the FBI and DHS by the Center for Constitutional Rights claims that activists are identified as 'threat actors'.[6]

Trump, who has taken a pro-policing, pro-military, anti-immigration and social justice position, will be expected to crack down on Black Lives Matter. Trump expressed his contempt for the movement by announcing a new campaign to strengthen the police, called Blue Lives Matter.[7]

After the 'PussyGate' scandal (the leaked audio of Trump talking about molesting women), it looked all over for The Donald. His approval rating was at record lows. Then the FBI under director James Comey (whom Trump later fired) did what the FBI often does and interfered politically; this time in violation of the Hatch Act which forbids government employees from interfering in elections. Comey wrote a letter to Congress, which was quickly brought to public attention by the media, announcing the FBI's intention to relaunch an investigation into Clinton's alleged email server misconducts. At that point, Clinton's approval rating plummeted to about the level of Trump's.[8]

Comey's father J. Brien Comey worked in real estate. Comey himself was Acting Attorney General during the NSA wiretapping scandals which culminated years later in the Edward Snowden revelations. Comey became senior Vice President of Lockheed Martin weapons manufacturer, General Counsel at Bridgewater

Associates hedge fund and served on the board of directors of HSBC bank in London, whose American branch had previously been found guilty of laundering money for al-Qaeda and Mexican drug gangs.[9]

On election night 2016, the Associated Press (which in its own words has been 'declar[ing] winners since 1848') called Pennsylvania before the ballots had been counted. As usual, the mainstream media — BBC, CNN, C-SPAN, Sky — failed to wait until the results were officially in and simply quoted the AP. This gave Trump the Electoral College lead over Clinton. For her part, Clinton effectively conceded defeat by going to bed before all the states were called. It later emerged that President Obama had advised Clinton to officially concede. Clinton was so dedicated to losing that she even tried to block Green Party leader Jill Stein's efforts to force a recount to stop Trump. In his *60 Minutes* interview Trump immediately flip-flopped on his promise to put his friends the Clintons under a criminal investigation for alleged email misconduct. ('I don't wanna hurt them. They're good people'.) If it wasn't a set-up for Trump's victory, it sure smelled like one.[10]

In 2015, ex-CIA director and Democrat-voter Leon Panetta joked that a Trump administration 'scares the hell out of me'. But the 'biggest national security threat in this country [is] the dysfunction in [Obama's] Washington ... They can't even come up with War Authority for the President of the United States' — referring to giving Obama a blank cheque to bomb Syria and Libya — 'and I worry about that'. The hope was that a hard-line Trump would give the CIA a free pass to kill more foreigners on behalf of its big business backers. After Trump compared the CIA to Nazis because of their ludicrous allegations that Russia had hacked the US election campaign in favour of Trump, outgoing head John Brennan said it is 'outrageous ... equating the intelligence community with Nazi Germany'.[11]

Trump seemed nervous a week later during his address to the CIA at its headquarters in Langley Virginia. He fawned over the CIA: 'I am so behind you. And I know maybe sometimes you haven't gotten the backing that you've wanted, and you're going to get so much backing. Maybe you're going to say, please don't give us so much backing ... Mr. President, please, we don't need that much backing'.[12]

Trump's advisor, the billionaire Peter Thiel, has connections with the CIA and other agencies. Palantir is a big data analysis company chaired by Thiel. It has won $1.2bn in federal contracts 'from the Marine Corps, Defense Intelligence Agency, Department of Justice, FBI, State Department, CIA, Internal Revenue Service, Immigration and Customs Enforcement, Department of Homeland Security and the National Center for Missing and Exploited Children', says *Politico*. Its offshoots specialize in counterterrorism and are allegedly hired by hedge funds to help them bet on world events. Thiel convinced the CIA to invest $2m in the company through its In-Q-Tel venture capital firm.[13]

By 2016, 40% of Palantir's profits came from the federal sector. Palantir lobbied congressmen, including John McCain and Tom Cotton, to help it compete against established contractors, including Raytheon and Northrop Grumman. Former senators John Breaux and Trent Lott lobbied for Palantir military-intelligence contracts via the Patton–Boggs firm, as did Alexander Silbey (of ATS Communications) and Marine Corps Brig. Gen. Terry Paul (of Cassidy & Associates).[14]

Donald the Dictator

Trump has no mandate to be president – if democracy matters. He was the least popular candidate in history, lost the popular vote and attained a record-low approval rating in his first month. For the first time since 1928, Trump's illegitimate victory (again, illegitimate if democracy matters,) gave the Republicans majority-control of the White House, Congress (both House and Senate), Majority of Governors and the Supreme Court. Trump stacked his cabinet with more Generals than any President since World War II: James Mattis (Defense Sec.), John Kelly (Homeland Security, responsible for rounding up immigrants during Trump's travel ban and immigration crackdown) and Michael Flynn

(National Security Adviser, who was subsequently fired or quit. Or both).[15]

But it's not just Generals in the cabinet. Trump's ephemeral advisor Bannon is an ex-Naval Officer with a degree in national security studies. Dr Sebastian Gorka is a British-born deputy assistant to Trump. Gorka has held numerous positions, including Major General Horner Distinguished Chair of Military Theory at the Marine Corps University Foundation. Gorka was employed by Bannon at *Breitbart*. Education Secretary Betsy DeVos's brother is Erik Prince, founder of the Blackwater (now Academi) mercenary group, whose employees killed Iraqi civilians during the occupation which began in 2003. Blackwater expert Jeremy Scahill alleges that Prince is advising Trump from the shadows. One of Trump's mega-rich hedge fund backers, Robert Mercer, has invested in the UK-based SCL Group, which influences public opinion in foreign countries (including Afghanistan) on behalf of the British Ministry of Defence and US Pentagon.[16]

With his military-heavy cabinet, Trump behaves like a dictator. In his first week in office Trump signed 13 Congress-bypassing executive orders (EOs), one of which banned everybody from five Muslim-majority countries from entering the USA for 90 days: people from the sixth country, Syria, were indefinitely banned. This affected more than 30,000 individuals, leaving many stranded at airports. Earlier, we noted a Pentagon plan from 2001, 'to take out seven countries in five years'. All but one of those countries (Lebanon) are on Trump's 90-day/permanent travel-ban list: Iraq, Iran, Libya, Somalia, Sudan, Syria and Yemen. (The EO is called Protecting the Nation From Terrorist Attacks by Foreign Nationals.)[17]

America and Britain have directly attacked all of those countries with war or sanctions, and attacked Sudan and Iran by proxy. Trump is violating international law (the UN Refugee Convention) by imposing the ban. Former New York Mayor and close Trump supporter, Rudolph Giuliani, acknowledged that although the executive order does not mention Islam or Muslims it is designed to target Muslims. It is therefore a violation of America's constitutional commitments to religious tolerance and equality (specifically the Fourteenth Amendment's Equal Protection Clause). Trump wanted a 'Muslim ban', says Giuliani. 'He called me up, he said, "Put a commission together, show me the right way to do it legally"' – hence the avoidance of the terms Islam and Muslim in the EO.[18] Citing its unconstitutionality, Acting Attorney General Sally Yates refused to enforce the order. Trump fired her. Trump also personally insulted Seattle District Judge James Robart, who blocked Trump's ban, calling him a 'so-called judge'.[19]

The Syria ban has affected ailing people including Mohammad al-Khaled (7 years old), whose parents hoped to send him to the US for cancer treatment. An Iraq boy called Dilbreen (18 months) was burned in a Jordanian refugee camp when a heater exploded (as they are prone to do in poor countries). It was only thanks to the activist group Road to Peace that Dilbreen and his father were able to fly to Michigan, stay with the House of Peace organization and receive surgery. Dilbreen was left in the care of Adlay Kejjin, director of the Yazidi American Women Organization which is affiliated with Road to Peace. The ban means that Dilbreen's surgery is jeopardized because his parents cannot return to the US and be with him. Arina Yaghoubi (21 years old) has battled leukaemia since she was 14. She's currently receiving treatment in St. Jude Hospital, Memphis. 'When you are going through treatment for something so serious, the last thing you want to think about is your [immigration] status', says Yaghoubi. 'It's heartbreaking'.[20]

The truth about terrorism in the US is as follows:

A leaked Department of Homeland Security memo reveals that 'most foreign-born, U.S.-based violent extremists are only radicalized after living in the U.S. for a number of years, and are unlikely to pose a threat upon arrival' (cited by *Democracy Now!*). Alex Nowrasteh of the Cato Institute notes that '[n]ationals of the seven countries singled out by Trump have killed zero people in terrorist attacks on U.S. soil between 1975 and 2015' (cited by *The Atlantic*). A report by New America says: '[e]very jihadist who conducted a lethal attack inside the United States since 9/11 was a citizen or legal resident'. Of those convicted of attempted terrorism in the US, many have been provoked into terrorism by the FBI. Michael German, a former undercover agent, says of the FBI: 'They're manufacturing terrorism cases'. According to the *New York Times*, about two-thirds of the 90 terrorism convictions up to the end of the year 2015 resulted from FBI sting operations and provocateurs. Cases include handlers and informants actually buying weapons in Walmart to give to entrapped 'terrorists' who didn't even have the money to shop. As Michael B. Steinbach of the FBI's national security branch puts it: 'We're not going to wait for the person to mobilize in his own time'.[21]

Liberals Behind the Fascism

The Associated Press obtained a draft memo written by Secretary of Homeland Security, Gen. John Kelly. The memo was addressed to US Immigration and Customs Enforcement and US Customs and Border Protection. The plan was to use up to 100,000 National Guards to further militarize law enforcement and immigration enforcement over seven states, including four on the US–Mexico border. The ultimate aim was mass deportation of alleged foreign criminals. At the time of writing, the plan has not been implemented. In early February, DHS rounded up 680 immigrants.[22]

Another one of the many Trump myths is that his migrant roundup policy is unique to the far-right. The reality is that supposed liberals, particularly in the hi-tech sector, had been lobbying for years to close and militarize the border. Their plan was to stop low-skilled migrants from coming in (whom they allege are a drain on social security) and to replace them with high-skilled workers. Because the US education system is one of the worst in the developed world, there is a skills shortage, particularly in the hi-tech sector. This is a problem for the US, which wants to lead the world in hi-technology. Their solution to this problem is to grant long-term working visas to high-skilled foreign workers and to fast-track citizenship for high-skilled foreigners living in the US.[23]

In 2011, Obama attended a dinner with Steve Jobs (Apple) and Mark Zuckerberg (Facebook). Jobs told Obama that Apple 'employs

700,000 factory workers in China because he cannot recruit 30,000 engineers in the United States'. In 2013, the Information Technology Industry Council and the US Chamber of Commerce wrote a report advocating immigration reform. The report notes that, 'skills gaps are found at companies large and small all over the US economy'.[24]

Of particular concern for the tech sector is the absence of American students who qualify in Science, Technology, Engineering and Math(s) (STEM). 'Foreign-born students make up 41 percent of masters and 45 percent of PhDs in STEM at US universities', the report continues. 'At the top 10 patent-producing US Universities ... more than 3 out of every 4 patents (76 percent) the schools received in 2011 had an immigrant inventor'. The report laments that 'under current immigration laws, many of these students have to leave after they graduate because there is no clear path for them to stay in the US'. The report recommends that, '[t]o spur innovation, meet labor force needs and help the economy grow, Congress should reform immigration laws to recruit and retain more foreign-born STEM workers trained in US universities'.[25]

In the same year, left-leaning multibillionaires pushed for migration reform via their newly-founded FWD.us group. Contrary to the myth that Trump and Trump alone is a hardliner on migration, the FWD.us website makes clear that Gates et al. wanted to shut the borders to poor, low-skilled migrants and streamline citizenship and visas for high-skilled ones – long before Trump ran for President. To quote the website's 'Secure Our Borders' section: 'Providing law enforcement the tools necessary to secure the border will allow them to focus resources on enforcement priorities such as violent criminals and terror threats'.[26]

Politico reports that FWD.us was formed by 'tech giants', such as Facebook's Mark Zuckerberg, Microsoft's Bill Gates, LinkedIn's Reid Hoffman and Google's Eric Schmidt. Between 2013 and 2014, FWD.us 'accounted for 75 percent of all paid media spent ... to support immigration reform and had field operations in 29 states and 149 target House districts at the peak of the debate'. Many of these organizations and the individuals associated with them wanted Hillary Clinton to win and financed the Clinton presidential campaign. But, crucially, the organization doesn't work in isolation. It finances both Republicans and Democrats.[27]

Reuters says: 'FWD.us's political operation is managed by a group of Washington insiders with leadership roles in both Republican and Democratic organizations. It joins other technology groups and alliances lobbying Congress for more H-1B visas for high-skilled workers and easier hiring of foreign math, science and engineering experts'. The multibillionaires preferred Clinton, but they were happy to work with Trump. The Republican and FWD.us campaign manager Rob Jesmer said of the 2016 presidential campaign: 'If we have a pro-reform Democrat and Republican, then this is great news ... What the project looks like somewhat depends on who the candidate is'.[28]

In 2015, Amazon, Apple, Facebook and Google stepped up their lobbying efforts to reform immigration laws. Astonishingly, the anti-immigration policy (which favours a small number of high-skilled migrants over the larger number of low-skilled ones) is portrayed in the media as a pro-immigration policy. The media succeeds in its false portrayal by ignoring FWD.us's pro-border militarization statements on its own website. (It would seem that Trump went too far. In February 2017, Apple et al. drafted a letter to Trump: 'We share your goal of ensuring that our immigration system meets today's security needs and keeps our country safe ... We are concerned, however, that your recent Executive Order will affect many visa holders who work hard here in the United States and contribute to our country's success'.)[29]

Trump: More of the Same

For all his bravado and arrogance, Trump is merely following the precedent set by other presidents. Obama personally authorized the murder of many of the 2,500 individuals in the Middle East, North Africa and Central Asia killed in America's military and CIA drone programme since the war on terror was re-declared in 2001 (Reagan actually declared one in the 1980s). At home,

Obama prosecuted a record number of whistleblowers (11 individuals by 2014) and introduced more anti-whistleblower legislation. The figures are disputed, but everyone agrees that Obama deported a record number of immigrants (2.5m is the lowest estimate).[30]

Or take Trump's relationship with the media. In 2015, over 50 individuals representing as many media organizations wrote to President Obama. Their letter complained that the administration was 'prohibiting staff from communicating with journalists unless they maneuver through public affairs offices or through political appointees'. The administration was, the signatories allege, 'refusing to allow reporters to speak to staff at all, or delaying interviews past the point they would be useful'. Obama and his team were also guilty of 'monitoring interviews; and ... speaking only on the condition that the official not be identified even when he or she has title of spokesperson'.[31]

Take the issue of Trump using Twitter to bypass the distorting media lens and speak 'directly' to the people. Obama was doing the same, to the chagrin of the mainstream: 'Obama may be the least newspaper-friendly president in a generation', says the *Washington Post*. 'TV interviews enable the president to take his message directly to a wide number of viewers, largely free of the "filter" that a print interview may entail. On TV, after all', the report continues, 'the president rarely contends with contradictory comments from opponents or the shades-of-gray context about an issue that newspaper and online stories often offer'.[32]

The state-funded PBS also notes that Obama took only 107 unprompted press questions after photo ops compared to his predecessor George W. Bush's 355. PBS cites the observations of other news organizations that 'Obama gives [interviews] to local and national TV anchors rather than White House beat reporters'. They also lament 'the copious official administration photos compared to scant opportunities for photojournalists; weekend document releases that take advantage of slow news cycles; and the White House press team's method of using Twitter and social media to control the release of information'. Mike Allen and Jim Vandehei of

Politico noted at the time: 'the balance of power between the White House and press has tipped unmistakably toward the government'.[33]

Consider Trump's executive orders. Between 20 January and 15 February, Trump issued 12 executive orders, 'the third-most issued by a President since 1829 in the first month of a new administration', says the Constitution Center. 'With a week left in President Trump's first month in office, he could tie Harry Truman at 13 orders if Trump issues a revised immigration order this week' – as indeed he did. But, the Center continues, 'Barack Obama issued 16 executive orders by the end of his first month in office back in 2009, the most issued by a President during his first month in office'.[34]

Also consider the alleged liberal status quo shock over Trump's supposed protectionism. As it happens, countries had been raising barriers to trade and investment in the years running up to Trump's presidency. A World Bank report from 2012 noted that '[a] troubling phenomenon is occurring in large, emerging economies: the gates are closing ... India, China, Indonesia, Argentina, Russia, and Brazil together accounted for almost half of all the new NTMs [non-tariff measures] imposed by countries worldwide'. In 2014, the World Trade Organization found that '[r]estrictive trade measures introduced by G-20 economies since 2008 continue to rise'. In 2016, the EU Trade Commissioner Cecilia Malmström said: 'Trade protectionism continues to be on the rise around the world. Open markets are proven to bring more innovation, increased productivity, economic growth and prosperity'. She went on to say that, '[d]espite this, few barriers to trade have been removed, while new ones have been introduced'. The main culprits, according to Malmström, are China ('limitations in access to public procurement and foreign direct investment'), Russia ('discriminatory subsidy programmes'), India ('an increase of duties on several products') and Argentina ('export taxes').[35]

So, despite Trump's protectionist rhetoric, the global trend was towards protectionism.

Final Thoughts

The Electoral College victory of a misogynistic, anti-Islamic xenophobe has provoked some positive responses.

For perhaps the first time in history, major universities in the US and Europe issued advice and counselling to students emotionally distressed by the election result. In November 2016, student demonstrators held banners reading 'Sanctuary Everywhere'. They walked out of classes in an effort to pressure staff to turn universities and colleges into sanctuaries for refugees and migrants, who fear that Trump will deport them. The universities included the elite ones: Brown, Columbia, Notre Dame, Tufts and Yale.[36]

Governors have defied Trump's efforts to deport millions of 'illegals' and have turned cities and counties into so-called sanctuary cities. They include Chicago and New York, as well as Sioux County (Iowa), even though 82% of its voting population supported Trump.[37]

On 5 December 2016, a group of Republican and Democratic Electoral College electors announced their intention to become so-called faithless voters and reject Trump. Several electors resigned or were forced to resign after stating their intention not to vote for The Donald. They include Texas Republican Art Sisneros and Georgia Republican Baoky Vu. These so-called Hamilton Electors were offered help by prominent lawyers, including Lawrence Lessig of Harvard. The Hamilton Electors' website explains: 'The Founding Fathers intended the Electoral College to stop an unfit man from becoming President. The Constitution they crafted gives us this tool. Conscience demands that we use it'. In reality, an 'unfit man' could be a genuine democrat brought to power on a wave of populism, but it can also include far-right figures like Trump.[38]

Teenage Electoral College member, Levi Guerra, became the seventh elector to break ranks and vote against Trump. 'I promised those who elected me that I would do everything I could to keep Donald Trump out of office'.[39]

In addition to this spurt of direct, progressive activism, millions of young Americans are behind Bernie Sanders, whom, as we saw, may very well have beaten Trump. As noted, Sanders has voted for illegal wars and shown no interest in supporting socialists (like Hugo Chávez)* abroad. But Sanders is the only left-wing candidate anywhere near the mainstream who has a chance of winning.

At present, Sanders leads a campaign called Our Revolution. It openly advocates a 'political revolution' by 'the working people of our country'. The movement is committed to ending international trade deals like TPP, stopping big money from influencing politics, making America deal with climate change, legislating for a minimum wage, fighting for racial justice, making housing affordable and more. It also seeks to repeal the death penalty and repeal Citizens United (which, passed under Obama, allows corporations and rich people to indirectly buy elections by directly influencing media).[40]

These and other reactions to Trump have created an opportunity for progressive individuals to get involved in local politics and compel their representatives, including people like Sanders, to hold firm to their pledges. Most politicians are liars, deceivers and manipulators. Even if they are not that way inclined as human beings, the system in its current form virtually demands that they act that way because of the compromises they make and the different interests within their parties. For that reason, masses of people who have the same interest – social justice – have historically spoken as one voice and forced them to keep their promises or have gone on to change the system entirely.

Another issue that requires addressing is the formation of a voters' rights movement. Take Michigan, a state with a population of 9.9 million. Trump won by just 10,704 votes. However, as award-winning investigator Greg Palast notes, 'a record 75,335 votes were never counted'. Most of those votes were in cities with large numbers of black, i.e., probably anti-Trump, voters: Detroit and Flint. The voting machines in Michigan and Wisconsin cannot read ballots properly. Green Party candidate, Jill Stein, raised the money to hire human readers for a recount. Pro-Trump Attorney General of

---

* Sanders called Chávez 'a dead communist dictator' (*Venezuela Today*).

Michigan, Bill Schuette, ordered 59% of voting precincts in Detroit barred from scrutiny. In Detroit alone, 87 machines disappeared. According to Carlos Garcia of Michigan State University, the replacement machines simply failed to count some of the older ballots.[41]

Perhaps even worse is the racist system imposed by pro-Trump Kris Kobach, Secretary of State for Kansas and counsel with the Immigration Law Reform Institute. Kobach initiated the anti-voter fraud Interstate Registration Crosscheck Program which checks the eligibility of voters. But an analysis by Palast of secretly obtained records suggests that Crosscheck 'disproportionately threatens solid Democratic constituencies: young, Black, Hispanic and Asian–American voters — with some of the biggest possible purges underway in Ohio and North Carolina, two crucial swing states with tight Senate races'.[42]

In Michigan alone, there are nearly half a million names on the Crosscheck list. 'Statistical experts who have looked at this list say it's heavily overweighted against minorities, because it's .... just basically a list of common names', i.e., it mixes innocent voters with allegedly guilty voters and prevents the innocent voters from voting. We don't hear them in the media because they are poor, isolated and have no access to the media or the justice system. This is why a major voters' rights reform organization could empower millions of voters across the US to get far-right candidates out and bring pro-gressives to the fore.[43]

Although Trump is cosmetically less pleasant than Obama, Clinton and even many Republicans in terms of his vulgarity, America's political and business institutions — like those in much of the world — are inherently anti-human and in major need of reform. If we are to survive climate change and the threat of nuclear war or accident, we need to get active in local politics. Even more than this, we need to democratize politics.

Notes

Preface

1. On neoliberalism and law-making, Professor David Miller of SpinWatch writes: 'corporate lobbying has been at the centre of efforts to expand and globalise corporate power, to introduce and develop the "doctrine" of neoliberalism'. Establishing politically-connected think tanks is one such method. ('How Neoliberalism Got Where It Is: Elite Planning, Corporate Lobbying and the Release of the Free Market', Strathclyde University, https://pure.strath.ac.uk/portal/files/543408/Final_Ch2_Miller_Neoliberalism_(2).doc+&cd=2&hl=en&ct=clnk&gl=uk.)

   On inequality and mega-wealth generation, a paper published by the International Monetary Fund notes that politicians have 'allow[ed] lobbyists to push for financial deregulation' and that '[f]inancial deregulation and globalization have also been cited as factors underlying the increase in financial wealth, relative skill intensity, and wages in the finance industry'. (Era Dabla-Norris, Kalpana Kochhar, Nujin Suphaphiphat, Frantisek Ricka and Evridiki Tsounta, 'Causes and Consequences of Income Inequality: A Global Perspective', IMF, SDN/15/13, June 2015, https://www.imf.org/external/pubs/ft/sdn/2015/sdn1513.pdf.)

   On the similarity of left and right governments' policymaking, Imbeau et al. studied 693 policies across members of the Organization for Economic Cooperation and Development. They found that 71% of policy implementations are bipartisan. Interestingly, their data are drawn from the post-1971, i.e., neoliberal, to the pre-housing bubble 2001 period. They write: 'We find that 154 (22%) estimates support the left–right partisan theory hypothesis, 48 (7%) estimates contradict the hypothesis, and 491 (71%) estimates fail to support the hypothesis'. (Louis M. Imbeau, François Pétry and Moktar Lamari, 'Left-Right Party Ideology and Government Policies: A Meta-Analysis', *European Journal of Political Research*, 40(1), August 2001, pp. 1–29.)

   On Trump and neoliberalism vs. reform and protectionism: Marie Currie Fellow of Sociology at Goldsmiths College (UK), Catherine Rottenberg, writes: 'under neoliberalism, we increasingly relate to ourselves as a resource in which we must invest in order to increase our value over time. In such a regime, only capital-enhancing subjects are worthy and only human capital that enhances the credit of the nation, now construed as a business enterprise, will thrive. This is precisely Trump's dream for America'. ('Trumping it up:

Neoliberalism on steroids', *Al-Jazeera*, 18 December 2016,
http://www.aljazeera.com/indepth/opinion/2016/12/trumping-
neoliberalism-steroids-161215144834626.html.) Environmentalist and
Guardian commentator George Monbiot says that neoliberalism has alienated
voters from the political system. Monbiot's analysis also includes an astute
observation on the neoliberal understanding of Constitutional liberty (See
Propaganda Translator, Libertarian): 'liberty depends on preventing the
majority from exercising choice over the direction that politics and society
might take'. This is the neoliberalism advanced by Hayek in *The Constitution of
Liberty* (1960). Monbiot concludes: 'The paradoxical result is that the backlash
against neoliberalism's crushing of political choice has elevated just the kind
of man that Hayek worshipped', i.e., Donald Trump. (George Monbiot, 'Neoliberalism: the deep story that lies beneath Donald Trump's triumph', *Guardian*, 14 November 2016, https://www.theguardian.com/commentisfree/
2016/nov/14/neoliberalsim-donald-trump-george-monbiot.)

2. Donald Trump, 'Trump pledges to drain the swamp and impose Congressional term limits', 18 October 2016, https://www.donaldjtrump.com/press-
releases/trump-pledges-to-drain-the-swamp.

3. Kashyap et al. describe Dodd–Frank and other moves made by the Obama
administration as 'a banking reform agenda not seen since the New Deal
response to the Great Depression'. But the authors caution that, 'unlike the
New Deal bank reforms that were aimed at the bank runs on retail deposits
that characterized the Great Depression, the financial crisis of 2007 and 2008
has produced reform aimed at institutional bank runs on repurchase agreement (repo) markets, prime brokerage, collateral, and prime money market
mutual funds'. This means that questions arise over the long-term effective-
ness of Dodd–Frank: a point that Tea Party and other ultra- and far-righters
twisted as an excuse to repeal the Act. (Anil K. Kashyap, James Overdahl,
Anjan Thakor and John Walsh, 'Panel discussion on banking reform' in Paul
H. Schultz (ed.), 2014, *Perspectives on Dodd-Frank and Finance*, MIT Press,
p. 56.)

4. Kathrina Maramba, 'The Dodd–Frank Act: Framing Financial Reform', Faculty
of the Public Communication Graduate Program, School of Communication,
American University, Washington, DC, April 2012,
https://www.american.edu/soc/communication/upload/Capstone-
Maramba.pdf and Bruce Drake, 'Public has mixed views about government
regulation of banks', Pew Research Center, 20 November 2013,
http://www.pewresearch.org/fact-tank/2013/11/20/public-has-mixed-views-
about-government-regulation-of-banks/.

5. Arlie Russell Hochschild, 2016, *Strangers in Their Own Land: Anger and
Mourning on the American Right*, The New Press. Gallup reports that 52% of

Americans own stocks. The number of young, middle class Americans who invest is at a record low. (Justin McCarthy, 'Just Over Half of Americans Own Stocks, Matching Record Low', Gallup, 20 April 2016, http://www.gallup.com/poll/190883/half-americans-own-stocks-matching-record-low.aspx.)

6. McCarthy, op. cit.

7. Jonathan Weisman and Eric Lipton, 'In new Congress, Wall St. pushes to undermine Dodd–Frank reform', New York Times, 13 January 2015.

8. Steve Denning, 'With Dodd–Frank Rollback, The Big Bad Banks Are Back', Forbes, 12 December 2014, www.forbes.com%2Fsites%2Fstevedenning%2F2014%2F12%2F12%2Fwith-dodd-frank-rollback-the-big-bad-banks-are-back%2F%20&cd=2&hl=en&ct=clnk&gl=uk#3bbd38c02834 and Weisman and Lipton, op. cit.

9. Roger Yu, 'Trump signs legislation to scrap Dodd–Frank rule on oil extraction', USA Today, 15 February 2017, http://www.usatoday.com/story/money/2017/02/14/trump-scraps-dodd-frank-rule-resource-extraction-disclosure/97912600/.

10. On the effect of power and inequality on democracy in the USA alone, Gilens and Page studied 1,799 policy issue. They conclude that 'economic elites and organized groups representing business interests have substantial independent impacts on U.S. government policy, while average citizens and mass-based interest groups have little or no independent influence'. (Martin Gilens and Benjamin I. Page, 'Testing Theories of American Politics: Elites, Interest Groups, and Average Citizens', Perspectives on Politics, 12(3), September 2014, p. 564.)

A report by the European Parliament concludes that 'voter turnout has been on a consistently downward path at elections, both within the European Union and in the United States. Indeed, these trends are consistent with a general decline in turnout at elections in most G20 [Group of 20] democracies since 1945 – from around 80% in the immediate post war period to just over 60% today'. (European Parliamentary Research Service, 'Turnout in European elections', Briefing Paper, 7 March 2014, http://www.europarl.europa.eu/RegData/bibliotheque/briefing/2014/140739/LDM_BRI(2014)140739_REV1_EN.pdf.)

Neoliberalism has hurt Latin America worse than the USA and Europe because the region has been trying to unhook itself from colonialism. Therefore the best studies on the effects of neoliberalism have focused on that region. See, for instance, R. Ryan Younger and Jeffrey J. Ryan, 'The Electoral Consequence of Neoliberal Reform', Inquiry, Vol. 6, 2005, pp. 44–55. See also Ryan's '"Painful Exit": Electoral Abstention and Neoliberal Reform in Latin

America', Latin American Studies Association, September 2001, http://lasa.international.pitt.edu/Lasa2001/RyanJeffrey.pdf.

On the rise of the far-right, Audrey Sheehy cites the 'broken economy' as an underlying factor in the 'success' of far-right parties in Europe and Trump's hijacking of the Republican Party. '[S]uccess of this magnitude across Europe has not occurred since before World War II'. Sheehy also notes that, 'While coverage of right–populist movements has mainly focused on Brexit and the rise of Donald Trump, the far right has been strengthening throughout the West. Austria almost saw the Austrian Freedom Party gain the presidency, the National Front is making great political strides in France, and the Party for Freedom is ahead in the Netherland's presidential polls. Additionally, the Golden Dawn has been a strong force in Greece, while in Germany, the Alternative for Deutschland party is expected to gain seats in its state's parliaments'. ('The Rise of the Far Right', *Harvard Political Review*, February 2017, http://harvardpolitics.com/world/rise-of-far-right/.)

11. On the connections between neoliberalism and Brexit, see my *The Great Brexit Swindle*, 2016, Clairview Books. See also, Paul Mason, who writes that Brexit is a 'fake revolt' led by elites and that 'people have fallen for the scam'. Mason concludes: 'a Brexit led by Ukip and the Tory right will not make any of these things better: it will make them worse. Take a look at the people leading the Brexit movement. Nigel Farage, Neil Hamilton, Boris Johnson, Michael Gove. They have fought all their lives for one objective: to give more power to employers and less to workers'. ('Brexit is a fake revolt — working-class culture is being hijacked to help the elite', *Guardian*, 20 June 2016, https://www.theguardian.com/commentisfree/2016/jun/20/brexit-fake-revolt-eu-working-class-culture-hijacked-help-elite.)

Trump's racism, misogyny, xenophobia and Islamophobia can hardly be in doubt. On racism and xenophobia, Trump has denied being racist but promised to deport three million alleged Mexican criminals. He said that Mexican immigrants are 'rapists' and 'bad hombres', though 'some, I assume, are good people'. On misogyny, leaked footage revealed Trump bragging about sexually assaulting women by forcing kisses on them: 'I'm automatically attracted to beautiful [women]. I just start kissing them'. It was alleged by writer Marie Brenner that Trump once said, 'You have to treat women like shit'. Trump responded to the allegation: 'I didn't say that. The woman's a liar, extremely unattractive, lots of problems because of her looks'. When told that women think Trump is a chauvinist, he replied: 'They're right — and not. People say, "How can you say such a thing?" but there's a truth in it, in a modified form. Psychologists will tell you that some women want to be treated with respect, others differently. I tell friends who treat their wives magnificently, get treated like crap in return, "Be rougher and you'll see a different relationship." Unfortunately, with people in general, you get more with vinegar than honey'. On Islam, Trump's website said in 2015: 'Trump is calling for a total and complete shutdown of Muslims entering the United States until our country's representatives can figure out what is going on' with terrorism.

Sources: *Washington Post*, 'Full text: Donald Trump announces a presidential bid', 16 June 2015, https://www.washingtonpost.com/news/post-politics/wp/2015/06/16/full-text-donald-trump-announces-a-presidential-bid/?utm_term=.ef95a18d5d1f. Kapitol, 'Donald Trump – "Grab Her By the Pussy" ', YouTube, 7 October 2016, https://www.youtube.com/watch?v=8wM248Wo54U. Claire Landsbaum, 'Donald Trump Said Only Some Women Want to Be Treated With Respect in ABC Interview', *The Cut* (*New York Magazine*), 14 October 2016, http://nymag.com/thecut/2016/10/trump-only-some-women-want-to-be-treated-with-respect.html. Donald J. Trump, 'Trump statement on preventing Muslim immigration', 7 December 2015, https://www.donaldjtrump.com/press-releases/donald-j.-trump-statement-on-preventing-muslim-immigration.

On Le Pen, she was seen at Trump Tower but is not reported to have met with Trump. However, she was on a fund-raising mission, supposedly not connected with Trump. But Le Pen hoped to get money from Trump supporters. Reuters, 'French far right leader Le Pen visits Trump Tower but no Trump talks', 12 January 2017, http://www.reuters.com/article/us-usa-trump-lepen-idUSKBN14W2EO.

Introduction

1. Thomas I. Palley traces neoliberalism in Europe back even further, to the 1980s. It resulted in 'wage stagnation and widened income inequality'. Low interest rates (like today) and fiscal stimuli were tools to prevent total collapse. '[F]ictitious prosperity' was created by a decade long asset and price bubble in the Eurozone, which ultimately led to a public loss of faith in the European Union, not in neoliberalism: a policy which has been carefully hidden from the public by the privately-owned mass media. ('Europe's Crisis without End: The Consequences of Neoliberalism', *Contributions to Political Economy*, 32(1), pp. 29–50.)

With regards to financialization, i.e., making money out of money as opposed to making money out of real things, Professor Gerald Epstein of the University of Massachusetts, Amherst, writes that compared to the volumes written about globalization and neoliberalism, by 2005 relatively little had been written about financialization, yet it had become a global phenomenon starting in the 1970s. Definitions and meanings include: 'the ascendancy of "shareholder value" as a mode of corporate governance; ... growing dominance of capital market financial systems over bank-based financial systems; ... [and] the increasing political and economic power of a particular class grouping: the rentier class; for some financialization represents the explosion of financial trading with a myriad of new financial instruments'. (*Financialization and the World Economy*, 2005, Edward Elgar Publishing, p. 3.)

Nobel Prize-winner Milton Friedman is widely regarded by scholars as one of the fathers of modern neoliberalism. Friedman favoured economic deregulation, i.e., the dismantling of rules to restrain the actions of financial institutions. Friedman writes that 'destabilizing speculation ... may in [some circumstances] confer economic benefit', regardless of the mass destruction caused by bursting bubbles. In Chapter 1, we quote Trump's comment about the casino economy. Friedman writes that the desire for regulation is the result of a 'bias of the academic student against gambling and in favor of insurance'. (*The Optimum Quality of Money*, 2009 [1969], AldineTransaction, pp. 285–86.)

Another architect of what became neoliberalism was Nobel Prize-winner F.A. Hayek, who writes of the need for a strong state to support 'individual' freedoms, meaning corporations, not social spending: 'when a fall of demand threatens [sales] ... the monetary authorities of the participating countries will be offered any commodity units which cannot be disposed in the market at the fixed price'. But the public won't see the benefits: 'the actual storing of the commodities could be safely left to private initiative. Specialist brokers would soon take care of the collecting and tendering of warrants as soon as their aggregate market price fell'. (*Individualism and Economic Order*, 1948, University of Chicago Press, pp. 214, 216.)

2. Bob Jessop, 'Neoliberalism' in George Ritzer (ed.), *The Wiley-Blackwell Encyclopedia of Globalization: Volume 3*, 2012, Wiley, pp. 1513–21.

3. Viviane Reding, 'Why we need a United States of Europe now', European Commission, 8 November 2012,
http://europa.eu/rapid/press-release_SPEECH-12-796_en.htm.

4. Grzegorz W. Kolodko, 'New pragmatism versus failing neoliberalism', World Bank, 25 February 2011, http://blogs.worldbank.org/developmenttalk/new-pragmatism-versus-failing-neoliberalism.

5. John Williams, 'From reform agenda to Damaged Brand Name', *Finance & Development*, September 2003,
http://www.imf.org/external/pubs/ft/fandd/2003/09/pdf/williams.pdf.

6. Ricardo Hausmann, 'Ricardo Hausmann on the changing political narratives in Latin America', WEF, 6 May 2016, https://www.weforum.org/agenda/2016/05/ricardo-hausmann-on-the-changing-political-narratives-in-latin-america.

7. Peter Middlebrook, 'Building a "fragile consensus": Liberalisation and state fragility', OECD, WP 6/2012, December 2012,

http://www.oecd.org/dac/governance-peace/conflictfragilityandresilience/docs/WP6%20Liberalisation%202012.pdf.

8. UN News Centre, 'In hard-hitting speech, UN human rights chief warns against populists and demagogues', 6 September 2016, http://www.un.org/apps/news/story.asp?NewsID=54862#.WNzNFFUrLIU.

9. Ronald F. Inglehart and Pippa Norris, 'Trump, Brexit, and the Rise of Populism: Economic Have-Nots and Cultural Backlash', Harvard Kennedy School, RWP16-026, August 2016, https://research.hks.harvard.edu/publications/getFile.aspx?Id=1401.

10. European Humanist Federation, 'The European Union and the Challenge of Extremism and Populism', October 2013, http://ec.europa.eu/justice/events/assises-justice-2013/files/contributions/24.europeanhumanistfederationtheeuandthechallengeofextremismandpopulism_ehf_en.pdf.

On doctors and dentists, under Chávez, '[t]he younger Cuban doctors, who graduated from medical school ... and were able to complete their residencies in comprehensive general medicine in Venezuela, were able to expand their medical expertise ... They encountered a range of experiences with diseases and maladies that they never would have encountered in Cuba ... There was a similar experience for another group of young Cuban graduates, those who had finished their dentistry programs at Cuban universities'. (Stever Brouwer, 2011, *Revolutionary Doctors: How Venezuela and Cuba Are Changing the World's Conception of Health Care*, Monthly Review Press, pp. 126–27.)

On free heating to the US, see Rebekah Kebede, 'Venezuela brings free heating oil to poor in NY', Reuters, 14 December 2007, http://www.reuters.com/article/citgo-energy-bronx-assistance-idUSN1425588920071214.

11. In response to crushing neoliberal reforms imposed on the people of Venezuela by President Carlos Andrés Pérez, the young revolutionary Hugo Chávez led the Revolutionary Bolivarian Movement-200 in a 1992 coup attempt. After his release from prison, Chávez founded the Fifth Republic Movement and was elected President of Venezuela in 1998. Chávez was re-elected several times until his death from cancer in 2013. Ethridge and Handelman criticize Chávez's crackdowns on press freedoms as well as corruption and the enrichment of political allies via oil revenues. However, despite these practices, under Chávez, 'the Venezuelan government spent billions on education, health care, and other social programs. The data show that poverty declined significantly, and that life expectancy and education improved as a result ... [I]ncome is now more equally distributed in Venezuela [than the USA]'. (Marcus E. Ethridge and Howard Handelman, 2015, *Politics in a Changing World*, 7th, Cengage Learning, p. 206.)

In terms of his authoritarian practices, Chávez added 12 seats to the 20 seat

Supreme Court to fill it with 'government supporters'. The justices 'openly rejected the principle of separation of powers', pledging allegiance to Chávez's brand of politics. The government barred Human Rights Watch from the country. The then Foreign Minister and chosen successor Nicolás Maduro said: 'Any foreigner who comes to criticize our country will be immediately expelled'. (HRW, 'Venezuela: Chávez's Authoritarian Legacy', 5 March 2013, https://www.hrw.org/news/2013/03/05/venezuela-chavezs-authoritarian-legacy.)

12. Matthew Goodwin, 'Right Response: Understanding and Countering Populist Extremism in Europe', Chatham House, September 2011, https://www.chathamhouse.org/sites/files/chathamhouse/r0911_goodwin.pdf.

13. Thomas Greven, 'The Rise of Right-wing Populism in Europe and the United States: A Comparative Perspective', http://www.fesdc.org/fileadmin/user_upload/publications/RightwingPopulism.pdf.

14. Ibid.

15. On infiltrating the Republican Party: Professor Alan Ware of University College London writes that when Trump was a candidate, he built momentum as an independent with his own source of campaign funding (a move that alarmed many Republican politicians) and built on his fame as a TV personality. ('Donald Trump's Hijacking of the Republican Party in Historical Perspective', *The Political Quarterly*, 87(3), July–September 2016, pp. 406–414.) After his comments about women in a secret recording were revealed, dozens of Republicans formally denounced Trump. See Eugene Scott, 'List', CNN, 10 October 2016, www.cnn.com/2016/10/08/politics/donald-trump-video-women-remarks-republicans/+&cd=3&hl=en&ct=clnk&gl=uk.

On media not reflecting people's interests, Gallup reports that by 2016, Americans' trust in mass media was at all-time low, with just 32% trusting the media. Among Republicans, trust was 14%. Trust has been consistently falling since 1997. Over a longer period, it peaked in 1976 at 72%. (Art Swift, 'Americans' Trust in Mass Media Sinks to New Low', Gallup, 14 September 2016, http://www.gallup.com/poll/195542/americans-trust-mass-media-sinks-new-low.aspx.)

On low voter turnout, see Chapter 6.

16. Although most Americans have not heard of the 'alt-right' (see Chapter 5), its appeal is broad. According to Norton and Samuels, most white Americans now feel that anti-white discrimination has increased, particularly over the last 30 years (a time-frame correlation with neoliberalism). They write: 'decreases in perceived bias against Blacks over the past six decades are associated with increases in perceived bias against Whites'. What makes the survey particularly fascinating is that both black and white respondents agree that anti-black

discrimination was more of a problem than anti-white discrimination. The authors attribute this to 'different reference points for racism'. (Michael I. Norton and Samuel R. Sommers, 'Whites See Racism as a Zero-Sum Game That They Are Now Losing', *Perspectives on Psychological Science*, 6(3), 2011, pp. 215–218.)

17. See Chapter 5 for details.

18. See Chapter 6.

19. Ibid.

20. A longitudinal analysis by Arendt and Northup finds that racial media stereotyping affects viewers on an emotional, irrational level: 'Long-term exposure to local television news, wherein African Americans are depicted stereotypically as criminals, predicted implicit [racist] attitudes. Thus, heavy viewers show more negative automatic affective reactions toward African Americans. Implicit attitudes, in turn, were used as a basis for explicit attitudes. Although media exposure had an indirect effect on explicit attitudes through implicit attitudes, there was no direct exposure effect on explicit attitudes. Furthermore, media exposure did not have a total effect on explicit attitudes. The findings indicate that stereotypical news content can influence implicit attitudes – our automatically activated gut reactions – even when there is no (total) effect on explicit attitudes – controllable overtly expressed judgments'. (Florian Arendt and Temple Northup, 'Effects of Long-Term Exposure to News Stereotypes on Implicit and Explicit Attitudes', *International Journal of Communication*, Vol. 9, 2015, pp. 2370–2390.)

21. On Islamophobia and the mainstream, Fairness and Accuracy in Reporting (FAIR, a US organization), wrote that its report *Smearcasting: How Islamophobes Spread Fear, Bigotry and Misinformation* (2008) finds 'violent and dangerous portrayals of Muslims alive and well in centrist and liberal media habitats'. FAIR's 2013 analysis concludes that Islamophobia remains rampant in left and right media. (Steve Rendall and Sara McCloskey, 'A Media Microscope on Islam-Linked Violence', FAIR, 1 August 2013, http://fair.org/extra/a-media-microscope-on-islam-linked-violence/.)

22. M. Taylors, 2016, *What is the Alt-Right?*, M. Taylors and Matthew N. Lyons, 2017, *Ctrl-Alt-Delete: An Antifascist Report on the Alternative Right*, Kersplebedeb Publishing.

23. See Chapter 6.

24. See note 3 above. On Trump's prejudice towards people with disabilities, journalist Serge Kovaleski has a condition called arthrogryposis, which causes a joint contracture in his right arm and hand. In a co-authored article, Kovaleski claimed that people were celebrating the 9/11 attacks on the morning of the atrocities. Trump spun this to claim that thousands of Muslims were celebrating. When Kovaleski was asked about it, he repudiated the claim that

'thousands' celebrated. At a campaign rally, Trump said of Kovaleski: 'You gotta see this guy'. Trump then contorted his body (particularly his arm) and shook, mimicking Kovaleski's gesticulations and speech.

25. Emanuele et al. write: 'extreme Left-wing parties and Right-wing parties are more Eurosceptic than parties tending towards the centre of the political continuum'. (Vincenzo Emanuele, Nicola Maggini and Bruno Marino, 'Gaining votes in Europe against Europe?', European Consortium for Political Research, no date, https://ecpr.eu/Filestore/PaperProposal/98df836d-abef-4799-bc8a-3a560ecacd2f.pdf.)

26. A study published by Keele University highlights the complexities of European extreme politics and the role of religion. 'There is no obvious explanation for the moderate negative direct effect of religiosity on the likelihood of a radical right vote in Italy, or its clearly stronger positive effect in Switzerland', the report states. 'By contrast, however, the positive effect of religiosity on the likelihood of a vote for the radical right in France is more easily accounted for. Not only has the Front National always taken a tough stand on issues such as abortion, homosexuality and the role of the church, but the party also has links with ultra- Catholic groups opposed to the church's alleged "liberalism" '. The study concludes: 'While studies of the Front National's electorate demonstrate that most of its voters are overwhelmingly attracted by the party's ethnocentrism and do not care about issues related to the church and its traditional teachings, and while the official church has become a leading critic of the FN's anti-minority policies, it is quite possible that these elements of the party's appeal are attractive to a small segment of Catholic fundamentalists'. (Kai Arzheimer and Elisabeth Carter, 'Religiosity and Voting for the Radical Right', Keele European Parties Research Unit, Working Paper 28, 2009, https://www.keele.ac.uk/media/keeleuniversity/group/kepru/KEPRU%20WP%2028.pdf.)

27. Goodwin, note 11.

28. In 2001, Alesina et al. wrote: 'European countries are much more generous to the poor relative to the US level of generosity'. They suggest that, 'the differences appear to be the result of racial heterogeneity in the US and American political institutions. Racial animosity in the US makes redistribution to the poor, who are disproportionately black, unappealing to many voters'. (Alberto Alesina, Edward Glaeser and Bruce Sacerdote, 'Why doesn't the US have a European-style welfare state?', Harvard Institute of Economic Research, Discussion Paper No. 1933, September 2001, http://scholar.harvard.edu/files/glaeser/files/why_doesnt_the_u.s._have_a_european-style_welfare_state.pdf.)

29. Baker Institute, 'How does the Tea Party compare with European far right movements?', January 2012, http://www.bakerinstitute.org/media/files/files/f6f08c52/IFRI-pub-SirkesTeaParty-2012-1-.pdf.

30. Julia Arciga (George Washington University), 'Who and what is the alt-right? Here's a helpful explainer', *USA Today College*, 5 September 2016, http://college.usatoday.com/2016/09/05/who-and-what-is-the-alt-right-heres-a-helpful-explainer/.

31. See Chapter 1.

32. Ibid.

33. See Chapter 2.

34. See Chapter 4.

35. Ibid.

36. See Chapter 5.

37. Donald Trump, 'Read the Full Transcript of Donald Trump's Jobs Speech', *Fortune*, 29 June 2016, http://fortune.com/2016/06/28/transcript-donald-trump-speech-jobs/.

38. Ibid.

39. Nigel Farage, 'Nigel Farage's speech at the UKIP conference – full text and audio', *Spectator*, 20 September 2013, http://blogs.spectator.co.uk/2013/09/nigel-farages-speech-full-text-and-audio/.

40. Nigel Farage, 'Debates', European Parliament, 28 June 2016, http://www.europarl.europa.eu/sides/getDoc.do?type=CRE&reference=20160628&secondRef=ITEM-004&format=XML&language=EN.

41. Susannah Savage, 'Marine Le Pen and post-colonial overseas departments', *Al-Jazeera*, 5 February 2017, http://www.aljazeera.com/indepth/features/2017/02/marine-le-pen-post-colonial-overseas-departments-170205075558399.html.

42. CNBC, 'CNBC Transcript: French Presidential Candidate & National Front Party Leader Marine Le Pen Speaks with CNBC's Michelle Caruso-Cabrera Today', 21 November 2016, http://www.cnbc.com/2016/11/21/cnbc-transcript-french-presidential-candidate-national-front-party-leader-marine-le-pen-speaks-with-cnbcs-michelle-caruso-cabrera-today.html.

43. Geert Wilders, Manifesto, 13 March 2005, https://www.pvv.nl/index.php/component/content/article/30-publicaties/684-onafhankelijkheidsverklaring.

44. Ibid.

Chapter 1

1. David R. Henderson, 'The U.S. postwar miracle', working paper no. 10–67, Mercatus Center, George Mason University, November 2010, https://www.mercatus.org/system/files/U.S.%20Postwar%20Miracle.Henderson.11.4.10.pdf.

2. Ibid.

3. Ibid.

4. Ibid.

5. Ibid.

6. Ibid.

7. Bureau of Labor Statistics (US), '1950' in *100 Years of U.S. Consumer Spending: Data for the Nation, New York City, and Boston*, August 2006, Office of Special Publications and Special Studies, http://www.bls.gov/opub/uscs/.

8. Ronald E. Kutscher, 'The American work force, 1992–2005: Historical trends, 1950–92, and current uncertainties', *Monthly Labor Review*, November 1993, http://www.bls.gov/mlr/1993/11/art1full.pdf.

9. Bureau of Labor Statistics, '1984–85' in *100 Years of U.S. Consumer Spending: Data for the Nation, New York City, and Boston*, August 2006, Office of Special Publications and Special Studies, http://www.bls.gov/opub/uscs/.

10. Kutscher, op. cit.

11. Ibid.

12. Al Campbell and Erdogan Bakir, 'The Pre-1980 Roots of Neoliberal Financial Deregulation', *Journal of Economic Issues*, 66(2), June 2012, pp. 531–539.

13. Ibid. and Douglas W. Diamond and Philip H. Dybvig, 'Banking Theory, Deposit Insurance, and Bank Regulation', *The Journal of Business*, 59(1), January 1986, pp. 55–68.

14. Campbell and Bakir, op. cit.

15. Ibid.

16. Ibid.

17. Ibid.

18. Matthew Sherman, 'A Short History of Financial Deregulation in the United States', Center for Economic and Policy Research, July 2009, http://cepr.net/documents/publications/dereg-timeline-2009-07.pdf.

19. Campbell and Bakir, op. cit.

20. Ibid.

21. Ibid.

22. Ibid

23. Ibid.

24. David Corn, 'SiCKO is Boffo', *The Nation*, 21 June 2007, https://www.thenation.com/article/sicko-boffo/.

25. Gary L. Free and Anup Bas, 'Nixon or Obama: Who is the real radical liberal on health care?', *Pediatrics Perspectives*, 136(2), August 2015, http://pediatrics.aappublications.org/content/pediatrics/early/2015/07/08/peds.2015-1122.full.pdf.

26. Evan M. Melhado, 'Health Planning in the United States and the Decline of Public-interest Policymaking', *Milbank Quarterly*, June, 2006, 84(2), pp. 359–440.

27. Karen Davis and Kristof Stremikis, 'The Costs of Failure: Economic Con-

sequences of Failure to Enact Nixon, Carter, and Clinton Health Reforms', The Commonwealth Fund, 21 December 2009, http://www.commonwealthfund.org/publications/blog/the-costs-of-failure.

28. Lawrence Mishel, Elise Gould and Josh Bivens, 'Wage Stagnation in Nine Charts', Economic Policy Institute, 6 January 2015, http://www.epi.org/publication/charting-wage-stagnation/.

29. Diamond and Dybvig, op. cit.

30. Matthew Sherman, 'A Short History of Financial Deregulation in the United States', Center for Economic and Policy Research, July 2009, http://cepr.net/documents/publications/dereg-timeline-2009-07.pdf.

31. Ibid.

32. Ibid.

33. Ibid.

34. For details and sources, see: James R. Barth S. Trimbath and Glenn Yago (eds.), 2004, *The Savings and Loan Crisis: Lessons from a Regulatory Failure*, Springer. Kitty Calavita, Henry N. Pontell and Robert Tillman, 1997, *Big Money, Big Crime: Fraud and Politics in the Savings and Loan Crisis*, University of California Press. Kathleen Day, 1993, *S&L Hell: The People and the Politics Behind the $1 Trillion Savings and Loan Scandal*, W.W. Norton & Co. Stephen Pizzo, Mary Fricker and Paul Muolo, 1991, *Inside Job: The Looting of America's Savings and Loans*, HarperPerennial.

35. Ibid.

36. Otis L. Graham, 1992, *Losing Time: The Industrial Policy Debate*, Harvard University Press.

37. Ibid.

38. Ibid.

39. Ibid.

40. Daniel Griswold, 'Reagan embraced free trade and immigration', CATO Institute, 24 June 2004, https://www.cato.org/publications/commentary/reagan-embraced-free-trade-immigration.

41. Ibid.

Chapter 2

1. Lawrence Mishel, Elise Gould and Josh Bivens, 'Wage Stagnation in Nine Charts', Economic Policy Institute, 6 January 2015, http://www.epi.org/publication/charting-wage-stagnation/.

2. *Wall Street Journal*, 'U.S. has record number of millionaires', 22 June 2011, http://blogs.wsj.com/wealth/2011/06/22/u-s-has-record-number-of-millionaires/. *Forbes*, 'Here are the states with the most billionaires', 3 May 2016, www.forbes.com/sites/katiesola/2016/03/05/here-are-the-states-with-the-most-billionaires/+&cd=5&hl=en&ct=clnk&gl=uk. Robert Frank, 'Record

number of millionaires living in the US', CNBC, 7 March 2016, http://www.cnbc.com/2016/03/07/record-number-of-millionaires-living-in-the-us.html.

3. Mishel et al., op. cit.

4. Ibid.

5. Ibid.

6. Ibid.

7. David Jacobs, 'Rising income inequality in the U.S. was fuelled by Ronald Reagan's attacks on union strength, and continued by Bill Clinton's financial deregulation', London School of Economics, 12 August 2014, http://eprints.lse.ac.uk/59386/1/blogs.lse.ac.uk-Rising_income_inequality_ in_the_US_was_fuelled_by_Ronald_Reagans_attacks_on_union_strength_ and_contin.pdf.

8. Pew Research Center, 'The American Middle Class Is Losing Ground', 9 December 2015, http://www.pewsocialtrends.org/2015/12/09/the-american-middle-class-is-losing-ground/ and Richard Fry and Rakesh Kochhar, 'Are you in the American middle class? Find out with our income calculator', Pew Research Center, 11 May 2016, http://www.pewresearch.org/fact-tank/2016/05/11/are-you-in-the-american-middle-class/.

9. Kathleen Elkins, 'Here's how much you have to earn to be considered middle class in the US', CNBC, 14 October 2016, http://www.cnbc.com/2016/10/14/heres-how-much-you-have-to-earn-to-be-considered-middle-class-in-the-us.html and Libby Kane, 'How much you have to earn to be considered middle class in every US state', *Business Insider*, 2 April 2015, http://uk.businessinsider.com/middle-class-in-every-us-state-2015-4?r=US&IR=T.

10. Sabrina Tavernise, 'Middle-Class Areas Shrink as Income Gap Grows, New Report Finds', *New York Times*, 15 November 2011, http://www.nytimes.com/2011/11/16/us/middle-class-areas-shrink-as-income-gap-grows-report-finds.html and Pew Research Center, 'The Lost Decade of the Middle Class', 22 August 2012, http://www.pewsocialtrends.org/2012/08/22/the-lost-decade-of-the-middle-class/.

11. Sean F. Reardon and Kendra Bischoff, 'Growth in the Residential Segregation of Families by Income, 1970-2009', Stanford University, November 2011, https://s4.ad.brown.edu/Projects/Diversity/Data/Report/report111111.pdf.

12. Statista, 'Household income distribution in the United States in 2015', https://www.statista.com/statistics/203183/percentage-distribution-of-household-income-in-the-us/.

13. Black Demographics, 'The African American Middle Class', no date, http://blackdemographics.com/households/middle-class/.

14. Bruce D. Meyer and James X. Sullivan, 'Five decades of consumption and

income poverty', National Bureau of Economic Research, March 2009, http://www.nber.org/papers/w14827.pdf.

15. Ibid.

16. Drew DeSilver, 'Who's poor in America? 50 years into the "War on Poverty," a data portrait', Pew Research Center, 13 January 2014, http://www.pewresearch.org/fact-tank/2014/01/13/whos-poor-in-america-50-years-into-the-war-on-poverty-a-data-portrait/.

17. Ibid.

18. Ibid.

19. Maude Barlow, 'Canada is the most sued country in the "developed" world, and that should sound alarm bells in the EU', Global Justice Now, 30 October 2015, http://www.globaljustice.org.uk/blog/2015/oct/30/canada-most-sued-country-developed-world-and-should-sound-alarm-bells-eu.

20. Jeff Faux, 'NAFTA's Impact on U.S. Workers', 9 December 2013, http://www.epi.org/blog/naftas-impact-workers/.

21. Lance Compa, 'American Trade Unions and NAFTA', Cornell University ILR School, April 1994, http://digitalcommons.ilr.cornell.edu/cgi/viewcontent.cgi?article=1009&context=conference.

22. Faux, op. cit.

23. Sherman, op. cit.

24. Ibid.

25. Ibid.

26. For example, Robert Scheer, 2010, *The Great American Stickup*, Nation Books.

Chapter 3

1. For instance: Robert J. Allison, 2007, *The Boston Tea Party*, Applewood Books.

2. Kevin Eckstrom, 'Tea Party More Religious Than U.S., Less Than Conservative Christians', *Huffington Post*, 10 June 2010, http://www.huffingtonpost.com/2010/10/06/tea-party-more-religious-_n_753468.html and PRRI, 'Alignment of Evangelical and Tea Party Values', November 2011, http://www.prri.org/wp-content/uploads/2011/11/Fact-Sheet-Teavangelicals.pdf.

3. Theda Skocpol and Vanessa Williamson, 2012, *The Tea Party and the Remaking of Republican Conservatism*, Oxford University Press.

4. SourceWatch, 'FreedomWorks', no date, http://www.sourcewatch.org/index.php/FreedomWorks and SourceWatch, 'Americans for Prosperity', no date, http://www.sourcewatch.org/index.php/Americans_for_Prosperity.

5. Ibid.

6. Ibid.

7. Ibid.

8. Ibid.

9. Samuel J. Wurzelbacher, 2008, *Joe the Plumber: Fighting for the American Dream*, Pearlgate.

10. Seth Cline, 'Tea Party House members even wealthier than other GOP lawmakers', Center for Responsive Politics, 4 January 2012, https://www.opensecrets.org/news/2012/01/tea-party-house-members-wealthy-gop/.

11. *New York Times*, 'Polling the Tea Party', 14 April 2010, http://www.nytimes.com/interactive/2010/04/14/us/politics/20100414-tea-party-poll-graphic.html?ref=politics.

12. Ibid.

13. PRRI, op. cit.

14. Ibid.

15. Paul Street and Anthony R. Dimaggio, 2011, *Crashing the Tea Party: Mass Media and the Campaign to Remake American Politics*, Paradigm Publishers and Vanessa Williamson, Theda Skocpol, and John Coggin, 'The Tea Party and the Remaking of Republican Conservatism', *Perspectives on Politics*, March 2011, 9(1), pp. 25–43.

16. Heather Boushey, 'Are the Tea Party Backers Really Wealthy and Highly Educated?', *Slate*, 28 April 2015, http://www.slate.com/articles/double_x/doublex/2010/04/are_the_tea_party_backers_really_wealthy_and_highly_educated.html.

17. Ibid.

18. Harry J. Enten, 'The Tea Party is losing support, even among Republicans', *Guardian*, 12 November 2013, https://www.theguardian.com/commentisfree/2013/nov/12/tea-party-losing-support-new-jersey-virginia.

Chapter 4

1. Robert E. Bohrer, Lauren A. Krohn and Alexander C. Tan, 'Taking Advantage: Far-Right Parties in Post-Maastricht Europe', 2001, Annual Meeting of the Midwest Political Science Association, Palmer House Hilton, http://www.academia.edu/15783285/Taking_Advantage_Far-Right_Parties_in_Post-Maastricht_Europe.

2. Ibid.

3. Ibid.

4. Nicky Woolf and Jessica Elgot, 'Nigel Farage would be great UK ambassador to US, says Donald Trump', *Guardian*, 22 November 2016, https://www.theguardian.com/politics/2016/nov/22/nigel-farage-uk-ambassador-us-donald-trump.

5. For example: Matthew Goodwin and Caitlin Milazzo, 2015, *UKIP: Inside the Campaign to Redraw the Map of British Politics*, Oxford University Press. Bill Etheridge, 2014, *The Rise of UKIP*, Bretwalda Books. Robert Ford and Matthew J. Goodwin, 2014, *Revolt on the Right: Explaining Support for the Radical Right in*

Britain, Routledge. Mark Daniel, 2005, *Cranks and Gadflies: The Story of UKIP*, Timewell Press.

6. Ibid.

7. Ibid.

8. Ben Glaze, 'Nigel Farage's UKIP General Election campaign to be funded by City fatcats', *Mirror*, 1 January 2015, http://www.mirror.co.uk/news/uk-news/nigel-farages-ukip-general-election-4906652 and Anna Leach, 'Meet UKIP's 5 biggest donors', *Mirror*, 2 January, 2015, http://www.mirror.co.uk/news/ampp3d/meet-ukips-5-biggest-donors-4909075.

9. Eric Kaufmann and Gareth Harris, 'Changing Places', 2014, Demos, https://www.demos.co.uk/files/Changing_places_-_web.pdf.

10. Ibid.

11. Ibid.

12. Ibid.

13. Ibid.

14. Ibid.

15. Ibid.

16. Laurence Dodds and Raziye Akkoc, 'Mapped: where is Ukip's support strongest? Where there are no immigrants', *Telegraph*, 17 April 2015, http://www.telegraph.co.uk/news/politics/ukip/11539388/Mapped-where-is-Ukips-support-strongest-Where-there-are-no-immigrants.html.

17. J.G. Shields, 2007, *The Extreme Right in France*, Routledge.

18. Ibid and Abderahmen Moumen, 'The National Front and the Harkis. From French Algeria to Marine Le Pen', *Fragments sur les Temps Présents*, 28 November 2011.

19. Shields, op. cit.

20. Ibid.

21. Ibid.

22. Ibid.

23. BBC News Online, 'Austria presidential poll result overturned', 1 July 2016, http://www.bbc.co.uk/news/world-europe-36681475.

24. The Democratic Society, 'The Greens – The Green Alternative', Democratic Society, 2 March 2014, http://www.demsoc.org/2014/02/03/the-greens-the-green-alternative/.

25. US Library of Congress, 'The Green Parties', Country Studies, no date, http://countrystudies.us/austria/121.htm and Democratic Society, op. cit.

26. Democratic Society, 'Freedom Party of Austria', 2 March 2014, http://www.demsoc.org/2014/02/03/freedom-party-of-austria/.

27. Euronews, 'Norbert Hofer the "friendly face" of Austria's far-right Freedom Party', 20 May 2016, http://www.euronews.com/2016/05/20/norbert-hofer-the-friendly-face-of-austria-s-far-right-freedom-party.

28. Bernhard Clemm von Hohenberg, 'Men voted for Hofer, women for Van der Bellen', *Franfurter Allgemeine*, 23 May 2016, http://www.faz.net/aktuell/politik/oesterreich-waehler-von-norbert-hofer-alexander-van-der-bellen-14248319.html.

29. Ibid.

30. Roland Verwiebe, Tobias Troger, Laura Wiesböck, Roland Teitzer and Nina-Sophie Fritsch, 'Growing inequalities and their impacts in Austria', *GINI: Growing Inequalities' Impacts*, http://gini-research.org/system/uploads/436/original/Austria.pdf?1370077182.

31. Ibid.

32. Ibid.

33. Ibid.

34. OECD, 'OECD Economic Surveys: Austria', 2013.

Chapter 5

1. Stulz writes: 'At the end of 1993, assets under management of hedge funds were less than 4 percent of the assets managed by mutual funds; by 2005, this percentage had grown to more than 10 percent. In 1990, less than $50 billion was invested in hedge funds; in 2006, more than $1 trillion was invested in hedge funds'. (René M. Stulz, 'Hedge Funds: Past, Present, and Future', *Journal of Economic Perspectives*, 21(2), Spring 2007, pp. 175–194.) Eechoud et al. point out that it was as late as 2009 at the Group of 20 meeting that world leaders decided 'for the first time ever' to regulate hedge funds. (Wouter van Eechoud, Wybe Hamersma, Arnd Sieling and David Young, 'Future Regulation of Hedge Funds – A Systemic Risk Perspective', *Financial Markets, Institutions and Instruments*, 19(4), November 2010, pp. 269–353.)

2. *Bloomberg* reports: '[Anthony] Scaramucci, founder of SkyBridge Capital and impresario of an annual industry conference in Las Vegas, says over-regulation was the "root cause" of the 2008 financial crisis'. (Simone Foxman, 'Hedge funds that backed Trump enter Washington, demands in hand', *Bloomberg*, 17 November 2016, https://www.bloomberg.com/news/articles/2016-11-17/mr-hedge-fund-goes-to-washington-looking-for-ally-in-trump+&cd=1&hl=en&ct=clnk&gl=uk.)

3. Jeff Cox, 'Hedge fund managers bullish about a Trump presidency . . . so far', CNBC, 17 November 2016, www.cnbc.com/2016/11/17/here-is-what-hedge-funds-think-about-a-donald-trump-presidency.html+&cd=7&hl=en&ct=clnk&gl=uk.

4. Dominic Rushe, ' "I'm really rich": Donald Trump claims $9bn fortune during campaign launch', *Guardian*, 16 June 2016, https://www.theguardian.com/us-news/2015/jun/16/donald-trump-reveals-net-worth-presidential-campaign-launch.

5. Lucinda Shen and Stephen Gandel, 'Nope, Clinton Is Not Completely Annihilating Trump Among Hedge Fund Donors', *Fortune*, 2 August 2016, http://fortune.com/2016/08/02/hillary-clinton-donald-trump-campaign-fundraising-wall-street-donors/.

6. Ibid.

7. Reuters, 'Here's Who Top Hedge Fund Managers Are Backing for President', 10 March 2016, http://fortune.com/2016/03/10/heres-who-top-hedge-fund-managers-are-backing-for-president/.

8. Robert Hackett, 'Here are all the billionaires backing Donald Trump', *Fortune*, 3 August 2016, http://fortune.com/2016/08/03/trump-billionaire-backers-list/.

9. Simone Foxman, 'Hedge Funds That Backed Trump Enter Washington, Demands in Hand', *Bloomberg*, 17 November 2016, https://www.bloomberg.com/news/articles/2016-11-17/mr-hedge-fund-goes-to-washington-looking-for-ally-in-trump+&cd=2&hl=en&ct=clnk&gl=uk and Dominic O'Connell, 'Hedge fund boss Ray Dalio says Trump will boost growth', BBC News Online, 20 January 2017, http://www.bbc.co.uk/news/business-38688559.

10. Stephen Gandel, 'Bill Ackman says he's bullish on Donald Trump', *Fortune*, 10 November 2016, http://fortune.com/2016/11/10/bill-ackman-donald-trump/ and Lawrence Delevingne, 'Dan Loeb: Trump will make hedge funds great again', Reuters, 2 February 2017, http://www.reuters.com/article/us-hedgefunds-thirdpoint-idUSKBN15H0EU.

11. On the rich and taxes, Pew Research says: 'In 2014, people with adjusted gross income, or AGI, above $250,000 paid just over half (51.6%) of all individual income taxes, though they accounted for only 2.7% of all returns filed, according to our analysis of preliminary IRS data. Their average tax rate (total taxes paid divided by cumulative AGI) was 25.7%. By contrast, people with incomes of less than $50,000 accounted for 62.3% of all individual returns filed, but they paid just 5.7% of total taxes. Their average tax rate was 4.3%'. (Drew DeSilver, 'High-income Americans pay most income taxes, but enough to be "fair"?', Pew Research Center, 13 April 2016, http://www.pewresearch.org/fact-tank/2016/04/13/high-income-americans-pay-most-income-taxes-but-enough-to-be-fair/.)

12. Josh Harkinson, 'The Dark History of the White House Aides Who Crafted Trump's "Muslim Ban" ', *Mother Jones*, 30 January 2017, www.motherjones.com/politics/2017/01/stephen-bannon-miller-trump-refugee-ban-islamophobia-white-nationalist+&cd=8&hl=en&ct=clnk&gl=uk.

13. Milo Yiannopoulos, for instance, is a gay ethnic Greek-Irish-Jew. See his forthcoming book, *Dangerous* (circa 2017, publisher to be certified).

14. Andrew Breitbart, 2012, *Righteous Indignation: Excuse Me While I Save the World*, Hachette.

15. Ibid.
16. Eagle Bites, 'Steve Bannon Lays Out his AMAZING Political Philosophy', YouTube, 18 November 2016,
https://www.youtube.com/watch?v=7nTd2ZAX_tc.
17. Ibid.
18. Ibid.
19. Mitchell Sunderland, 'Ann Coulter is a human being', *Vice*, 13 August 2015,
https://broadly.vice.com/en_us/article/ann-coulter-is-a-human-being
and Ann Coulter, 2016, *In Trump We Trust*, Biteback.
20. Ibid.
21. Ibid.
22. Lauren Southern, 2016, *Barbarians: How Baby Boomers, Immigrants, and Islam Screwed My Generation*, Creative Space Independent Publishing.
23. Ibid.
24. Ibid.
25. Ibid.
26. Emily Jane Fox, 'The billionaire father–daughter team behind Trump's apocalyptic turn to the alt-right', *Vanity Fair*, 18 August 2016,
http://www.vanityfair.com/news/2016/08/donald-trump-mercers-stephen-bannon and Zachary Mider, 'What Kind of Man Spends Millions to Elect Ted Cruz?', *Bloomberg*, 20 January 2016, https://www.bloomberg.com/politics/features/2016-01-20/what-kind-of-man-spends-millions-to-elect-ted-cruz-+&cd=1&hl=en&ct=clnk&gl=uk.
27. Peter A. Thiel and Blake Masters, 2014, *Zero to One: Notes on Startups, Or How to Build the Future*, Crown Business.
28. Don, '/r/The_Donald', KnowYourMeme.com, September 2016,
http://knowyourmeme.com/memes/sites/r-the_donald.
29. Ryan Mac and Matt Drange, 'A Troll Outside Trump Tower Is Helping To Pick Your Next Government', *Forbes*, 9 January 2017,
www.forbes.com%2Fsites%2Fmattdrange%2F2017%2F01%2F09%2Fchuck-johnson-troll-trump-transition-team%2F%20&cd=1&hl=en&ct=clnk&gl=uk#1b80bff02834.
30. Joel Hruska, 'Oculus founder Palmer Luckey confirmed as anonymous backer behind pro-Trump memes', *ExtremeTech*, 23 September 2016,
https://www.extremetech.com/gaming/236198-oculus-founder-palmer-luckey-confirmed-as-anonymous-backer-behind-pro-trump-memes.
31. Don, op. cit.
32. David Stannard, 1992, *American Holocaust: The Conquest of the New World*, Oxford University Press and Scott Tighe, ' "Of Course We Are Crazy": Discrimination of Native American Indians Through Criminal Justice', *Justice Policy Journal*, 11(1), pp. 1–38. Tighe concludes: 'The loss of tribal core

cultural competencies, U.S. Government policies including forced assimilation and self-determination policies, the reservation system, forced attendance at boarding schools, and a number of other issues that are a part of Native American life have resulted in social disparity for many Native Americans. Native Americans will never have their traditional lands returned to them. They will never get to live the lives of their ancestors. This is the reality of the modern world. What can be done is to bring power back to oneself'.

33. On the USA prison population: Adam Liptak, 'U.S. prison population dwarfs that of other nations', *New York Times*, 23 April 2008, http://www.nytimes.com/2008/04/23/world/americas/23iht-23prison.12253738.html. On prison labour, see National Institute of Justice, 'Work in American Prisons: Joint Ventures with the Private Sector', no date, https://www.ncjrs.gov/pdffiles/workampr.pdf. On killings by police, see Miller et al., 'Perils of police action: a cautionary tale from US data sets', *BMJ*, 23(1), 2016, http://injuryprevention.bmj.com/content/23/1/27.

34. Namir Shabibi and Nasser al Sane, 'Nine young children killed: The full details of botched US raid in Yemen', Bureau of Investigative Journalism, 8 February 2017, https://www.thebureauinvestigates.com/2017/02/08/nine-young-children-killed-full-details-botched-us-raid-yemen/. The murdered children are: Asma Fahad Ali al-Ameri (3 months), Aisha Mohammed Abdallah al-Ameri (4 years), Halima Hussein al Aifa al-Ameri (5), Hussein Mohammed Abdallah Mabkhout al-Ameri (5), Mursil Abedraboh Masad al-Ameri (6), Khadija Abdallah Mabkhout al-Ameri (7), Nawar Anwar al-Awlaqi (8), Ahmed Abdelilah Ahmed al-Dahab (11) and Nasser Abdallah Ahmed al-Dahab (12).

35. David Horowitz, 2017, *Big Agenda: President Trump's Plan to Save America*, Humanix Books and Andrew McGill, 'The Missing Black Students at Elite American Universities', *The Atlantic*, 23 November 2015, https://www.theatlantic.com/politics/archive/2015/11/black-college-student-body/417189/.

36. Horowitz, op. cit. and Arlie Russell Hochschild, 2016, *Strangers in Their Own Land: Anger and Mourning on the American Right*, The New Press.

37. John Gramlich, 'Most Americans haven't heard of the "alt-right"', Pew Research Center, 12 December 2016, http://www.pewresearch.org/fact-tank/2016/12/12/most-americans-havent-heard-of-the-alt-right/.

Chapter 6

1. Alyssa Davis, 'Record One in Five in Bad Mood on Day After Election', Gallup, 23 November 2016, http://www.gallup.com/poll/198161/record-one-five-bad-mood-day-election.aspx.

2. David Wasserman, 'Overall Votes', 2016 National Popular Vote Tracker,

https://docs.google.com/spreadsheets/d/
133Eb4qQmOxNvtesw2hdVns073R68EZx4SfCnP4IGQf8/htmlview?sle=
true#gid=19.

3. National Archives and Records Administration, 'Presidential Election Laws',
   US Electoral College,
   https://www.archives.gov/federal-register/electoral-college/provisions.html.

4. Ibid.

5. National Archives and Records Administration, 'What is the Electoral
   College?',
   https://www.archives.gov/federal-register/electoral-college/about.html.

6. National Archives and Records Administration, 'About the Electors', US
   Electoral College,
   https://www.archives.gov/federal-register/electoral-college/electors.html.

7. National Archives and Records Administration, 'Frequently asked questions',
   US Electoral College,
   https://www.archives.gov/federal-register/electoral-college/faq.html
   and George C. Edwards, 2004, *Why the Electoral College Is Bad for America*, Yale
   University Press.

8. Todd Estes, 'The Connecticut Effect', *The Historian*, Vol. 73(2), Summer 2011,
   pp. 255–83.

9. Tim Meko, Denise Lu and Lazaro Gamio, 'How Trump won the presidency
   with razor-thin margins in swing states', *Washington Post*, 11 November 2016,
   https://www.washingtonpost.com/graphics/politics/2016-election/swing-
   state-margins/ and Andrea Cerrato, Francesco Ruggieri and Federico Maria
   Ferrara, 'Trump won in counties that lost jobs to China and Mexico',
   Washington Post, 2 December 2016, https://www.washingtonpost.com/pb/
   news/monkey-cage/wp/2016/12/02/trump-won-where-import-shocks-from-
   china-and-mexico-were-strongest/?outputType=accessibility&nid=menu_
   nav_accessibilityforscreenreader.

10. Ibid.

11. Ibid.

12. Gabriel Sherman, 'Why Rupert Murdoch Decided to Back Donald Trump',
    New York Magazine, May 2016, http://nymag.com/daily/intelligencer/2016/
    05/why-rupert-murdoch-decided-to-support-trump.html.
    Fortune, 'Donald Trump Has Spent $0 on TV Advertising', 9 August 2016,
    www.fortune.com/2016/08/09/donald-trump-tv-ads-clinton/
    +&cd=5&hl=en&ct=clnk&gl=uk. Tyndall Report, '2015 Year in Review: Top
    Twenty Stories of 2015', http://tyndallreport.com/yearinreview2015/.

13. Doug Mataconis, 'How Saturday debates protect Hillary Clinton', *Christian
    Science Monitor*, 22 December 2015, http://www.csmonitor.com/USA/
    Politics/Politics-Voices/2015/1222/How-Saturday-debates-protect-Hillary-

Clinton and Robert Schroder, 'Trump has gotten nearly $3 billion in "free" advertising', MarketWatch, 6 May 2016, http://www.marketwatch.com/story/trump-has-gotten-nearly-3-billion-in-free-advertising-2016-05-06.

14. Quantcast, 'Infowars.com', https://www.quantcast.com/infowars.com.

15. John K. Wilson, 2011, *The Most Dangerous Man in America: Rush Limbaugh's Assault on Reason*, St. Martin's Press and Kathleen Hall Jamieson and Joseph N. Cappella, 2008, *Echo Chamber: Rush Limbaugh and the Conservative Media Establishment*, Oxford University Press.

16. Quantcast, 'Rushlimbaugh.com', https://www.quantcast.com/rushlimbaugh.com.

17. Quantcast, 'Foxnews.com', https://www.quantcast.com/foxnews.com and Derek Thompson, 'The twilight of Fox News', *Atlantic*, 29 August 2016, http://www.theatlantic.com/business/archive/2016/08/the-twilight-of-fox-news/497684/.

18. Jennifer Agiesta, 'Poll: Most oppose Trump's wall, split on who is best on immigration', CNN Politics, 7 September 2016, http://edition.cnn.com/2016/09/07/politics/2016-election-presidential-poll-immigration-donald-trump-hillary-clinton/.

19. Frank Newport, 'Majority in U.S. Support Idea of Fed-Funded Healthcare System', Gallup, 16 May 2016, http://www.gallup.com/poll/191504/majority-support-idea-fed-funded-healthcare-system.aspx.

20. Associated Press-NORC Center for Public Affairs Research, 'Inequality: Trends in Americans' Attitudes', 2016, http://www.apnorc.org/projects/Pages/HTML%20Reports/inequality-trends-in-americans-attitudes0317-6562.aspx.

21. Vote Smart, 'Bernie Sanders' Voting Records', https://votesmart.org/candidate/key-votes/27110/bernie-sanders.

22. Andrew Buncombe, 'Donald Trump would have lost US election if Bernie Sanders had been the candidate', *Independent*, 9 November 2016, http://www.independent.co.uk/news/people/presidential-election-donald-trump-would-have-lost-if-bernie-sanders-had-been-the-candidate-a7406346.html and RealClearPolitics, 'General Election: Trump vs. Sanders', http://www.realclearpolitics.com/epolls/2016/president/us/general_election_trump_vs_sanders-5565.html.

23. Garvis Marketing, 'Current National Polling', 6 November 2016, http://big.assets.huffingtonpost.com/Gravis_Sanders_Election_Poll.pdf.

24. Ibid.

25. Ibid.

26. Jesse Yomtov, 'Would Bernie Sanders have defeated Donald Trump?', *USA Today*, 9 November 2016, http://www.usatoday.com/story/news/politics/onpolitics/2016/11/09/bernie-sanders-donald-trump/93530352/.

27. Mataconis, op. cit.

28. Dan Merica and Brian Stelter, 'Clinton declines to debate Sanders in California', CNN Politics, 24 May 2016, http://edition.cnn.com/2016/05/23/politics/hillary-clinton-bernie-sanders-fox-debate-california/.

29. Michael Sainato, 'Class Action Lawsuit Against Debbie Wasserman Schultz Moves Forward', *Observer* (US), 18 August 2016, http://observer.com/2016/08/class-action-lawsuit-against-debbie-wasserman-schultz-moves-forward/.

30. Lee Fang, 'Atlanta Mayor's Column Ripping Bernie Sanders Drafted by Lobbyist, Emails Show', *The Intercept*, 6 May 2016, https://theintercept.com/2016/05/06/hillary-super-pac-draft-oped/ and Abigail Abrams, 'Bernie Sanders Voter Data Controversy: Supporters See DNC Punishment As Unfairly Helping Hillary Clinton', *International Business Times*, 18 December 2015, http://www.ibtimes.com/bernie-sanders-voter-data-controversy-supporters-see-dnc-punishment-unfairly-helping-2232497.

Chapter 7

1. Susan Page and Brad Heath, 'How anti-establishment outsider Donald Trump was elected the 45th president of the United States', *USA Today*, 9 November 2016, http://www.usatoday.com/story/news/politics/elections/2016/11/09/election-analysis-hillary-clinton-donald-trump/93198882/.

2. Justin McCarthy, 'U.S. Approval of Congress Improves, but Still Low at 18%', Gallup, 18 August 2016, http://www.gallup.com/poll/194684/approval-congress-improves-low.aspx?g_source=Politics&g_medium=newsfeed&g_campaign=tiles.

3. Gregory Wallace, 'Voter turnout at 20-year low in 2016', CNN Politics, 30 November 2016, http://edition.cnn.com/2016/11/11/politics/popular-vote-turnout-2016/.

4. Ibid.

5. John Hudak, 'A reality check on 2016's economically marginalized', Brookings, 16 November 2016, https://www.brookings.edu/blog/fixgov/2016/11/16/economic-marginalization-reality-check/.

6. Gregory A. Smith and Jessica Martínez, 'How the faithful voted: A preliminary 2016 analysis', Pew Research Center, 9 November 2016, http://www.pewresearch.org/fact-tank/2016/11/09/how-the-faithful-voted-a-preliminary-2016-analysis/.

7. Ibid.

8. Ibid.

9. Shiva Maniam and Alec Tyson, 'Behind Trump's victory: Divisions by race, gender, education', Pew Research Center, 9 November 2016, http://www.pewresearch.org/fact-tank/2016/11/09/behind-trumps-victory-divisions-by-race-gender-education/.

10. Ibid.

11. Ibid.

12. Jens Manuel Krogstad and Mark Hugo Lopez, 'Hillary Clinton won Latino vote but fell below 2012 support for Obama', Pew Research Center, 29 November 2016, http://www.pewresearch.org/fact-tank/2016/11/29/hillary-clinton-wins-latino-vote-but-falls-below-2012-support-for-obama/.

13. Kerry A. Dolan and Luisa Kroll, 'Forbes 2016 World's Billionaires: Meet The Richest People On The Planet', *Forbes*, 3 January 2016, www.forbes.com/sites/luisakroll/2016/03/01/forbes-2016-worlds-billionaires-meet-the-richest-people-on-the-planet/+&cd=1&hl=en&ct=clnk&gl=uk.

14. Jennifer Wang, 'Trump's Stock Portfolio: Big Oil, Big Banks And More Foreign Connections', *Forbes*, 29 November 2016, www.forbes.com/sites/jenniferwang/2016/11/29/trumps-stock-portfolio-big-oil-big-banks-and-more-foreign-connections/+&cd=1&hl=en&ct=clnk&gl=uk.

15. Robert W. Woods, 'C or S Corporation Choice is Critical for Small Business', *Forbes*, 3 May 2012, www.forbes.com/sites/robertwood/2012/05/03/c-or-s-corporation-choice-is-critical-for-small-business/+&cd=19&hl=en&ct=clnk&gl=uk and Alan Cole, 'Details and analysis of the Donald Trump tax reform plan, September 2016', Tax Foundation, No. 528, September 2016, http://taxfoundation.org/sites/taxfoundation.org/files/docs/TaxFoundation_FF528_FINAL3.pdf.

16. Jim Nunns, Len Burman, Ben Page, Jeff Rohaly and Joe Rosenberg, 'An analysis of Donald Trump's Revised Tax Plan', Tax Policy Center, 18 October 2016.

17. Ibid.

18. Ibid.

19. Ibid.

20. Americans for Tax Fairness, 'The six worst features of Donald Trump's tax plan', http://americansfortaxfairness.org/wp-content/uploads/ATF-Six-Worst-Features-of-Donald-Trumps-Tax-Plan-FINAL-.pdf.

21. Trump, 'Healthcare reform to make America great again', https://www.donaldjtrump.com/positions/healthcare-reform and Michael Kranish and Marc Fisher, 2016, *Trump Revealed*, Simon and Schuster, p. 237.

Chapter 8

1. Donald Trump, 'Remarks by President Trump at Signing of H.J. Resolution 38', White House, 16 February 2016, https://www.whitehouse.gov/the-press-office/2017/02/16/remarks-president-trump-signing-hj-resolution-38.
   HJ Res. 38 repealed the Stream Protection Rule of Office of Surface Mining Reclamation and Enforcement of the Department of the Interior (81 Fed. Reg. 93066 (December 20, 2016). (United States Congress, 'H.J.Res.38 – 115th

Congress (2017-2018)', https://www.congress.gov/bill/115th-congress/house-joint-resolution/38/text.)

One of the disagreements between the Republicans and the Democrats has been over coal. The Hillary Clinton-led State Department was pushing fracking for gas on other countries at the expense of domestic coal mines and production. These deals were to be established through Trump-like bilateral trade deals for the benefit of Chevron, Exxon and other big players. (See Mariah Blake, 'How Hillary Clinton's State Department Sold Fracking to the World', *Mother Jones*, September-October 2014, http://www.motherjones.com/environment/2014/09/hillary-clinton-fracking-shale-state-department-chevron.) Whether or not it would have really happened is another matter, but Clinton promised during her Presidential campaign to invest in coal mining towns and convert them into hubs of renewable energy production: 'Clinton has a $30 billion plan to reinvest in the coal communities so they can continue to be an engine of economic growth in the 21st century. This includes guaranteeing coal miners and their families get the benefits they have earned and deserve, expanding broadband and other infrastructure in coalfield communities, repurposing abandoned mine lands and power plant sites for new economic activity, providing tax credits to attract new jobs and investment, and creating a new Coal Communities Challenge Fund to support locally-driven economic development strategies'. (Hillary Clinton, 'Hillary Clinton's Plan for Combatting Climate Change and Making America the Clean Energy Superpower of the 21st Century', The Briefing, 10 October 2016, https://www.hillaryclinton.com/briefing/factsheets/2016/10/10/hillary-clintons-plan-for-combatting-climate-change-and-making-america-the-clean-energy-superpower-of-the-21st-century/.) Via carefully edited video which removed the context, this was reported in sectors of the Trump-supporting alternative media as Clinton's plan to destroy coal mining communities.

2. Jeremy Diamond, 'Donald Trump threatens business leaders with border tax', CNN, 23 January 2017, http://edition.cnn.com/2017/01/23/politics/trump-business-leaders-border-tax/.

3. Metadata of various polls suggest that one in ten Sanders's supporters voted Trump instead of Clinton after Sanders was knocked out of the race. To give some anecdotal evidence as to why, one male Sanders's supporter explained why he'd be voting Trump: 'Trump is an obnoxious vulgar blowhard who says foolish things. However, unlike Clinton – but like Sanders – at least he is an outsider who understands that the government and the economy are broken'. (Ed Pilkington and Mona Chalabi, 'The Bernie Sanders' voters who would choose Trump over Clinton', *Guardian*, 13 March 2016, https://www.theguardian.com/us-news/2016/mar/13/bernie-sanders-supporters-consider-donald-trump-no-hillary-clinton.)

4. Philip Russell, 2013, *100 Military Inventions that Changed the World*, Little, Brown Book Group.

5. It is not just the military that helps tech firms monopolize innovation. Hourihan and Parkes write: 'there is no overall "R&D budget" and no special treatment for R&D within most agency budgets. R&D is folded into the budgets of more than two dozen federal departments and independent agencies, and there may be little or no distinction made between activities'. (Matt Hourihan and David Parkes, 'Federal R&D in the FY 2016 Budget: An Overview' in *The President's FY 2016 Budget*, American Association for the Advancement of Science, https://www.aaas.org/fy16budget/federal-rd-fy-2016-budget-overview.)

6. Microsoft has a webpage explaining its military connections: http://military.microsoft.com/. Nafeez Ahmed connects the Google–NSA dots and concludes, citing plenty of evidence, that Google's development was 'seeded' with help from the deep state and intelligence community. ('How the CIA made Google', *Insurgence Intelligence*, in two parts, no date, https://medium.com/insurge-intelligence/how-the-cia-made-google-e836451a959e#.73n19y6f6.)

7. For example: Medtronic, 'Medtronic completes acquisition of Covidien', Press Release, 26 January 2016, http://newsroom.medtronic.com/phoenix.zhtml?c=251324&p=irol-newsArticle&ID=2010595.

8. Barney Jopson, 'Corporate America lobbies Trump for tax reversal', *Financial Times*, 28 November 2016, https://www.ft.com/content/8bac949e-b45c-11e6-ba85-95d1533d9a62 and Anton Babkin, Brent Glover and Oliver Levine, 'Are Corporate Inversions Good for Shareholders?', *Journal of Financial Economics*, October 2016, https://papers.ssrn.com/sol3/papers2.cfm?abstract_id=2700987.

9. Tim Worstall, 'Pfizer-Allergan: If Corporate Taxes Cause Inversions Maybe We Should Change Taxes?', *Forbes*, 26 November 2016, www.forbes.com%2Fsites%2Ftimworstall%2F2015%2F11%2F26%2Fpfizer-allergan-if-corporate-taxes-cause-inversions-maybe-we-should-change-taxes%2F%20&cd=1&hl=fr&ct=clnk&gl=uk#59d2b9902834.

10. Ryan Teague Beckwith, 'Carl Icahn to Spend $150 Million on Corporate Tax Reform', *TIME*, 21 October 2015, www.time.com/4081335/carl-icahn-corporate-tax-reform and Carl Icahn, 'Letter Discussing Desperately Needed Legislation', 21 October 2015, http://carlicahn.com/needed-legislation-letter/.

11. John Urry, 2014, *Offshoring*, Polity Press.

12. Erika Morphy, 'A.T. Kearney Predicts The End Of Offshoring As We Know It', *Forbes*, 11 January 2016, www.forbes.com%2Fsites%2Ferikamorphy%2F2016%2F01%2F11%2Fa-t-

kearney-predicts-the-end-of-offshoring-as-we-know-it%2F%20&cd= 2&hl=en&ct=clnk&gl=uk#52eb51a82834 and Donald Trump, 'Transcript: President Donald Trump's rally in Melbourne, Florida', *Vox*, 18 February 2017, http://www.vox.com/2017/2/18/14659952/trump-transcript-rally-melbourne-florida.

13. *The Economist*, 'On the turn', 19 January 2013, http://www.economist.com/news/special-report/21569571-india-no-longer-automatic-choice-it-services-and-back-office-work-turn.

14. Karl Flinders, 'IBM India staff reductions are sign of shift in outsourcing sector', *Computer Weekly*, October 2015, http://www.computerweekly.com/feature/IBM-India-staff-reductions-are-sign-of-shift-in-outsourcing-sector.

15. Simon Bowers, 'US tech giants launch fierce fightback against global tax avoidance crackdown', *Guardian*, 21 January 2015, https://www.theguardian.com/business/2015/jan/21/us-tech-tax-avoidance-google-amazon-apple and Janie Lorber, 'Tech Sector Fights for Repatriation', *Roll Call*, 19 September 2011, http://www.rollcall.com/news/Tech_Sector_Fights_for_Repatriation-208842-1.html.

16. Lorber, op. cit.

17. Eric Wesoff, 'Tesla's $5B Giga Battery Factory and Deep Politics in AZ, TX, NV and NM', *Greentech Media*, 1 March 2014, https://www.greentechmedia.com/articles/read/Teslas-5B-Giga-Battery-Factory-and-Deep-Politics-in-AZ-TX-NV-and-NM.

18. Issie Lapowsky, 'What tech giants are spending millions lobbying for', *Wired*, July 2015, https://www.wired.com/2015/07/google-facebook-amazon-lobbying/.

19. David Streitfeld, ' "I'm Here to Help," Trump Tells Tech Executives at Meeting', *New York Times*, 14 December 2016, https://www.nytimes.com/2016/12/14/technology/trump-tech-summit.html?_r=0.

20. Matthew J. Belvedere, 'Bill Gates says Trump has the opportunity to be like JFK', CNBC, 13 December 2016, http://www.cnbc.com/2016/12/13/after-talking-with-trump-bill-gates-likens-president-elect-to-jfk.html.

21. Development, Concepts and Doctrine Centre, 'Strategic Trends: Out to 2040' (2nd), 9 February 2010, Ministry of Defence, https://www.gov.uk/government/uploads/system/uploads/attachment_data/file/33717/GST4_v9_Feb10.pdf.

22. Donald Trump, 'Presidential Memorandum Regarding Withdrawal of the United States from the Trans-Pacific Partnership Negotiations and Agreement', White House, 23 January 2017, https://www.whitehouse.gov/the-press-office/2017/01/23/presidential-memorandum-regarding-withdrawal-united-states-trans-pacific.

23. WTO, 'United States countervailing measures on certain hot-rolled carbon

steel flat products from India', Report of the Panel, WT/DS436/R, 14 July 2014, https://www.wto.org/english/tratop_e/dispu_e/436r_e.pdf.

WTO, 'India files dispute against the US over non-immigrant temporary working visas', 4 March 2016, https://www.wto.org/english/news_e/news16_e/ds503rfc_04mar16_e.htm.

WTO, 'DS437: United States – Countervailing Duty Measures on Certain Products from China', 21 July 2016, https://www.wto.org/english/tratop_e/dispu_e/cases_e/ds437_e.htm.

24. Full Text of the Trans-Pacific Partnership, 2015, Office of the US Trade Rep., https://ustr.gov/trade-agreements/free-trade-agreements/trans-pacific-partnership/tpp-full-text.

25. Robert E. Scott, 'NAFTA's Legacy', Economic Policy Institute, 17 December 2017, http://www.epi.org/publication/nafta-legacy-growing-us-trade-deficits-cost-682900-jobs/. Maude Barlow, 'Canada is the most sued country in the "developed" world, and that should sound alarm bells in the EU', 30 October 2015, http://www.globaljustice.org.uk/blog/2015/oct/30/canada-most-sued-country-developed-world-and-should-sound-alarm-bells-eu.

Laura Carlsen, 'Under Nafta, Mexico Suffered, and the United States Felt Its Pain', *New York Times*, 24 November 2013, http://www.nytimes.com/roomfordebate/2013/11/24/what-weve-learned-from-nafta/under-nafta-mexico-suffered-and-the-united-states-felt-its-pain.

26. Ibid.

27. C. Fred Bergsten, 'The Truth About Currency Manipulation', *Foreign Affairs*, 18 January 2015, https://www.foreignaffairs.com/articles/united-states/2015-01-18/truth-about-currency-manipulation.

28. Jorge I. Domínguez and Rafael Fernández de Castro, 'US–Mexico Relations: Coping with Domestic and International Crises' in Domínguez and de Castro (eds.), 2016, *Contemporary U.S.–Latin American Relations: Cooperation or Conflict in the 21st Century?* (2nd), Routledge. For 'Full Spectrum Dominance', see Chapter 9 of this book.

29. Renée Johnson, 'The U.S.–EU Beef Hormone Dispute', Congressional Research Service, 14 January, 2015, https://www.fas.org/sgp/crs/row/R40449.pdf.

30. Office of the United States Trade Representative, 'Free Trade Agreements', no date, https://ustr.gov/trade-agreements/free-trade-agreements. Young Jong Choi, 'A rise of regionalist ideas in East Asia' in Jorge Dominguez and Byung Kook Kim (eds.), 2005, *Between Compliance and Conflict*, Routledge, p. 69. Chris Dent, 'Free Trade Agreements in the Asia–Pacific: A Risky Game Being Played at the Wrong Time', The Evian Group, Policy Brief, April 2006, http://www.imd.org/uupload/EvianGroup/PUBLICATIONS/1236.pdf.

Pascal Lamy, 'Regional agreements: the "pepper" in the multilateral "curry" –

Lamy', WTO, 17 January 2007,
https://www.wto.org/english/news_e/sppl_e/sppl53_e.htm.

31. Allan Smith, 'Trump's agenda on one of his signature campaign issues is starting to take shape', *Business Insider*, 23 November 2016, http://uk.businessinsider.com/donald-trump-trade-agenda-2016-11?r=US&IR=T and Tal Kopan, 'Trump transition memo: Trade reform begins Day 1', CNN, 16 November 2016, http://edition.cnn.com/2016/11/15/politics/donald-trump-trade-memo-transition/.

32. Ian F. Fergusson, Mark A. McMinimy and Brock R. Williams, 'The Trans-Pacific Partnership (TPP) Negotiations and Issues for Congress', Congressional Research Service, 20 March 2015, https://fas.org/sgp/crs/row/R42694.pdf.

33. Jackie Calmes, 'Trans-Pacific Partnership Is Reached, but Faces Scrutiny in Congress', NYT, 5 October 2015, https://www.nytimes.com/2015/10/06/business/trans-pacific-partnership-trade-deal-is-reached.html?_r=0.

34. Ibid. and Adam Behsudi, 'Hatch wants TPP and his 12 years, too', *Politico*, 28 September 2016, http://www.politico.com/tipsheets/morning-trade/2016/09/hatch-wants-tpp-and-his-12-years-too-216566.

35. Alan Tonelson, 'Opinion: Pacific trade deal won't close massive tax loophole that kills American jobs', *MarketWatch*, 31 March 2015, http://www.marketwatch.com/story/pacific-trade-deal-wont-close-massive-tax-loophole-that-kills-american-jobs-2015-03-31.

36. Kevin Kearns, 'Full TPP text reveals a very bad deal for America', *Breitbart*, 5 November 2015, http://www.breitbart.com/big-government/2015/11/05/full-tpp-text-reveals-a-very-bad-deal-for-america/.

37. Bergsten, note 26.

38. Elena Holodny, 'TRUMP: The strong dollar is "killing us" ', *Business Insider*, 17 January 2017, http://markets.businessinsider.com/currencies/news/fx-currency-market-update-january-17-2017-2017-1-1001671411.

39. See my *The Great Brexit Swindle*, 2016, Clairview Books.

40. Joseph Adinolfi, 'Why the TPP is better off without currency manipulation protection', *MarketWatch*, 6 October 2015, http://www.marketwatch.com/story/why-the-tpp-is-better-off-without-currency-manipulation-protection-2015-10-06.

Chapter 9

1. For details and sources, see my *Britain's Secret Wars*, 2016, Clairview Books.

2. Ibid.

3. Ibid. On Trump and Stern, see Michael Kranish and Marc Fisher, 2016, *Trump Revealed*, Simon and Schuster, p. 342.

4. Thomas L. Friedman, 'A manifesto for the fast world', *New York Times Magazine*,

28 March 1999,
http://www.nytimes.com/books/99/04/25/reviews/friedman-mag.html
and Thomas P. M. Barnett, 'Why the Pentagon keeps changing its maps and why
we keep going to war', *Esquire*, March 2003, http://www.esquire.com/news-
politics/a1546/thomas-barnett-iraq-war-primer/?click=main_sr.

5. Center for National Interest, 'About the Center', https://cftni.org/about/ and
   Donald Trump, 'Transcript: Donald Trump's Foreign Policy Speech', *New York
   Times*, 27 April 2016, http://www.nytimes.com/2016/04/28/us/politics/
   transcript-trump-foreign-policy.html?_r=0.

6. Sean Starrs, 'China's Rise is Designed in America, Assembled in China',
   China's World, Vol. 2(2), 2015, https://www.du.edu/korbel/media/korbel-
   internal-newsletter/szhao-china-and-globalisation-in-the-era-of-xi-jinping.pdf.

7. Ibid.

8. Mark Koba, 'U.S. Military Spending Dwarfs Rest of World', NBC News, 24
   February 2014, http://www.nbcnews.com/storyline/military-spending-cuts/
   u-s-military-spending-dwarfs-rest-world-n37461 and Department of Defense
   (US), 'Annual Report to Congress: Military and Security Developments
   Involving the People's Republic of China 2016', 26 April 2016,
   http://www.defense.gov/Portals/1/Documents/pubs/
   2016%20China%20Military%20Power%20Report.pdf

9. Ward Carroll, 'Russia and China propose space weapons ban', *Defensetech*, 15
   February 2008, http://www.defensetech.org/2008/02/15/russia-and-china-
   propose-space-weapons-ban/.

10. Pieter Bottelier, 'China and the World Bank: how a partnership was built',
    Journal of Contemporary China, Volume 16(51), 2007, pp. 239–58.

11. Zuliu Hu and Mohsin S. Khan, 'Why is China growing so fast?', *Economic
    Issues*, June 1997,
    https://www.imf.org/EXTERNAL/PUBS/FT/ISSUES8/INDEX.HTM.

12. Jeffrey D. Sachs and Wing Thye Woo, 'Understanding China's Economic
    Performance', National Bureau of Economic Research, Working Paper No.
    5935, February 1997, http://www.nber.org/papers/w5935.

13. Investopedia, 'China Owns US Debt, but How Much?', 6 August 2015,
    http://www.investopedia.com/articles/investing/080615/china-owns-us-
    debt-how-much.asp.

14. Wesley Clark, 'Gen. Wesley Clark Weighs Presidential Bid: "I Think About It
    Every Day" ', *Democracy Now!*, 2 March 2007,
    https://www.democracynow.org/2007/3/2/gen_wesley_clark_weighs_
    presidential_bid.

15. Trump, foreign policy speech, op. cit.

16. Ibid. See also my *Britain's Secret Wars*, op. cit.

17. Julian Borger, 'Yukiya Amano, head of the IAEA, at a press conference where

he announced the end of the investigation of Iran', *Guardian*, 15 December 2015, https://www.theguardian.com/world/2015/dec/15/un-atomic-iran-weapons-nuclear-deal.

18. See my 'The real reason the US opposes Iran's nuclear power', *Axis of Logic*, 13 July 2015, http://axisoflogic.com/artman/publish/Article_70960.shtml.

19. Arms Control Association, 'Timeline of nuclear diplomacy with Iran', https://www.armscontrol.org/factsheet/Timeline-of-Nuclear-Diplomacy-With-Iran.

20. Ibid.

21. Ibid.

22. Ibid.

23. Bulletin of the Atomic Scientists, 'Doomsday Clock hands remain unchanged, despite Iran deal and Paris talks', 26 January 2016, http://thebulletin.org/press-release/doomsday-clock-hands-remain-unchanged-despite-iran-deal-and-paris-talks9122 and Trump, foreign policy speech, op. cit.

24. Arms Control Association, 'U.S. nuclear modernization programs', December 2016, https://www.armscontrol.org/factsheets/USNuclearModernization.

25. US Strategic Command, 1995, *The Essentials of Post-Cold War Deterrence*, http://www.nukestrat.com/us/stratcom/SAGessentials.PDF.

26. *Britain's Secret Wars*, op. cit.

27. Ibid.

28. Ibid.

29. Trump, foreign policy speech, op. cit.

30. John Markoff and Andrew E. Kramer, 'U.S. and Russia differ on a treaty for cyberspace', *New York Times*, 27 June 2009, http://www.nytimes.com/2009/06/28/world/28cyber.html and Timothy Farnsworth, 'China and Russia submit cyber proposal', Arms Control Association, 2 November 2011, https://www.armscontrol.org/act/2011_11/China_and_Russia_Submit_Cyber_Proposal.

Conclusion

1. Julia Goldman, 'Donald Trump's Cabinet richest in U.S. history, historians say', CBS, 20 December 2016, www.cbsnews.com/news/donald-trump-cabinet-richest-in-us-history-historians-say/+&cd=4&hl=en&ct=clnk&gl=uk.

2. Nixon quoted in Michael Kranish and Marc Fisher, 2016, *Trump Revealed*, Simon and Schuster, p. 277.

3. On the DoJ racism allegations, see Michael D'Antonio, 2016, *The Truth About Trump*, Thomas Dunne Books, pp. 79–81 and Kranish and Fisher, op. cit., pp. 126–27, 232–33.

4. Kranish and Fisher, op. cit. pp. 156, 243–47.

5. Spencer Ackerman, '"The FBI is Trumpland": anti-Clinton atmosphere

spurred leaking, sources say', *Guardian*, 4 November 2016, https://www.theguardian.com/us-news/2016/nov/03/fbi-leaks-hillary-clinton-james-comey-donald-trump#top.

6. George Joseph, 'Exclusive: Feds regularly monitored Black Lives Matter since Ferguson', *The Intercept*, 24 July 2015, https://theintercept.com/2015/07/24/documents-show-department-homeland-security-monitoring-black-lives-matter-since-ferguson/ and Ben Norton, 'FBI, Homeland Security sued for records on surveillance of Black Lives Matter activists', *Salon*, 20 October 2016, www.salon.com/2016/10/20/fbi-homeland-security-sued-for-records-on-surveillance-of-black-lives-matter-activists/+&cd=1&hl=en&ct=clnk&gl=uk.

7. Ibid. and *Democracy Now!*, 'Trump Launches "Blue Lives Matter Regime" with Three New Executive Orders on Law Enforcement', 10 February 2017, https://www.democracynow.org/2017/2/10/trump_launches_blue_lives_matter_regime.

8. Steve Vladeck, 'What is the Hatch Act – and did James Comey break it?', CNN, 31 October 2016, www.cnn.com/2016/10/31/politics/what-is-the-hatch-act/+&cd=4&hl=en&ct=clnk&gl=uk.

9. HSBC, 'Former US Deputy Attorney General joins HSBC Board', 30 January 2013, http://www.hsbc.com/news-and-insight/media-resources/media-releases/2013/former-us-deputy-attorney-general-joins-hsbc-board and Shawn Boburg, 'FBI nominee Comey was held captive as a Bergen teen', *North Jersey (USA Today)*, 31 May 2013, http://archive.northjersey.com/news/fbi-nominee-comey-was-held-captive-as-a-bergen-teen-1.589446?page=all.

10. Lauren Easton, 'Calling the presidential race state by state', AP, 9 November 2016, https://blog.ap.org/behind-the-news/calling-the-presidential-race-state-by-state. 31 Mike, '2016 CSPAN Election Night Coverage 8PM to 250AM', YouTube, 27 December 2016, https://www.youtube.com/watch?v=Y6zmG5N2UNA. Scott Arthur, 'US Elections 2016 – BBC Election Night in America – Part Three', YouTube, 13 November 2016, https://www.youtube.com/watch?v=5mnrAIb-oSU and Amie Parnes, 'Obama urged Clinton to concede on election night', *The Hill*, 25 November 2016, http://thehill.com/homenews/campaign/307536-obama-urged-clinton-to-concede-on-election-night.

11. Leon Panetta, 'Leon Panetta on Trump and National Security: "It Scares the Hell Out of Me"', *Fortune Magazine*, 4 November 2015, https://www.youtube.com/watch?v=ygThr2bhmYk and BBC News Online, 'CIA head John Brennan warns Trump to watch his tongue', 15 January 2017, www.bbc.co.uk/news/world-us-canada-38630016.

12. Donald Trump, 'Trump CIA speech transcript', CBS, 23 January 2017, http://www.cbsnews.com/news/trump-cia-speech-transcript/.

13. Ellen Mitchell, 'How Silicon Valley's Palantir wired Washington', *Politico*, 14 August 2016, http://www.politico.com/story/2016/08/palantir-defense-contracts-lobbyists-226969.

14. Ibid.

15. DN!, 'Trump Has Appointed More Generals in His Cabinet Than Any President Since World War II', 16 December 2016, https://www.democracynow.org/2016/12/16/trump_has_appointed_more_generals_in+&cd=1&hl=en&ct=clnk&gl=uk.

16. Kate Storey, 'Who Is Steve Bannon? 16 Things to Know About Donald Trump's Chief Strategist', *Cosmopolitan*, 23 February 2017, www.cosmopolitan.com/politics/a8288455/who-is-steve-bannon-trump-chief-strategist/+&cd=2&hl=en&ct=clnk&gl=uk. Institute of World Politics, 'Sebastian Gorka', no date, http://www.iwp.edu/faculty/detail/sebastian-gorka. Jeremy Scahill, 'Notorious mercenary Erik Prince is advising Trump from the shadows', *The Intercept*, 17 January 2017, https://theintercept.com/2017/01/17/notorious-mercenary-erik-prince-is-advising-trump-from-the-shadows/+&cd=3&hl=en&ct=clnk&gl=uk.

17. Bart Jansen, 'Trump visa ban blocked, but sparks travel uncertainty for tens of thousands', *USA Today*, 28 January 2017, http://www.usatoday.com/story/news/2017/01/28/2-iraqis-denied-us-entry-challenge-trumps-visa-order/97183820/. The author puts the number of visas issued by the State Department as follows: '7,727 to Iranians, 3,660 to Iraqis, 383 to Libyans, 1,797 to Somalians [sic], 2,606 to Sudanese, 2,633 to Syrians and 12,998 to Yemenis'.

18. Corey Brettschneider, 'Why Trump's Immigration Rules Are Unconstitutional', *Politico*, 1 February 2017, www.politico.com/magazine/story/2017/02/why-trumps-immigration-rules-are-unconstitutional-214722+&cd=2&hl=en&ct=clnk&gl=uk and Rebecca Savransky, 'Giuliani: Trump asked me how to do a Muslim ban "legally"', *The Hill*, 29 January 2017, www.thehill.com/homenews/administration/316726-giuliani-trump-asked-me-how-to-do-a-muslim-ban-legally+&cd=1&hl=en&ct=clnk&gl=uk.

19. DW, 'Trump attacks adversaries on Twitter for revoking travel ban', 4 February 2017, www.dw.com/en/trump-attacks-adversaries-on-twitter-for-revoking-travel-ban/a-37413282+&cd=5&hl=en&ct=clnk&gl=uk.

20. Cheyenne Roundtree, '"I pray to God that Trump will have mercy on these children": Syrian father makes an emotional plea for son, 7, who has cancer to be allowed entry to US for treatment following immigration ban', *Daily Mail*, 30 January 2017, http://www.dailymail.co.uk/news/article-4172498/Syrian-boy-cancer-not-receive-treatment-US.html. Rachel Revesz, 'Donald Trump's travel ban separates badly burned Iraqi boy from family', *Independent*, 1 February 2017, www.independent.co.uk/news/world/americas/donald-trump-muslim-travel-ban-iraq-young-boy-dilbreen-road-to-peace-sick-injured-

burned-separated-a7557846.html+&cd=2&hl=en&ct=clnk&gl=uk. Tara Golshan, 'This 21-year-old Iranian woman is fighting cancer in the US. Now her father can't visit her', *Vox*, 28 January 2017, http://www.vox.com/policy-and-politics/2017/1/28/14424402/trump-visa-ban-iran-cancer.

21. Eric Lichtblau, 'F.B.I. steps up use of stings in ISIS cases', *New York Times*, 7 June 2016, https://www.nytimes.com/2016/06/08/us/fbi-isis-terrorism-stings.html?rref=collection%2Fsectioncollection%2Fus&action=click&contentCollection=us&region=rank&module=package&version=highlights&contentPlacement=2&pgtype=sectionfront&_r=1. Uri Friedman, 'Where America's Terrorists Actually Come From', *The Atlantic*, 30 January 2017, https://www.theatlantic.com/international/archive/2017/01/trump-immigration-ban-terrorism/514361/+&cd=1&hl=en&ct=clnk&gl=uk.

22. Ian Gordon, 'Trump's Deportation Raids: What We Know and Don't Know', *Mother Jones*, 17 February 2017, www.motherjones.com/politics/2017/02/deportation-raid-rumors-immigration-customs-enforcement+&cd=6&hl=en&ct=clnk&gl=uk and Associated Press, 'Trump administration denies it is considering using National Guard to round up unauthorized immigrants', 17 February 2017, www.cnbc.com/2017/02/17/trump-considers-mobilizing-100000-national-guard-troops-to-round-up-unauthorized-immigrants.html+&cd=5&hl=en&ct=clnk&gl=uk.

23. Drew DeSilver, 'U.S. students' academic achievement still lags that of their peers in many other countries', Pew Research Center, 15 February 2017, www.pewresearch.org/fact-tank/2017/02/15/u-s-students-internationally-math-science/+&cd=4&hl=en&ct=clnk&gl=uk. The report says: 'In the most recent tests, from 2015, 10 countries (out of 48 total) had statistically higher average fourth-grade math scores than the U.S., while seven countries had higher average science scores. In the eighth-grade tests, seven out of 37 countries had statistically higher average math scores than the U.S., and seven had higher science scores'.

24. Industry Technology Industry Council and US Chamber of Commerce, 'Help Wanted: The Role of Foreign Workers in the Innovation Economy', July 2013, http://www.renewoureconomy.org/wp-content/uploads/2013/07/stem-report.pdf.

25. Ibid.

26. FWD.us, 'About our cause', https://www.fwd.us/about_reform.

27. Anna Palmer, 'Zuckerberg immigration group launches 2016 reform blitz', *Politico*, 1 December 2015, www.politico.com/story/2015/12/mark-zuckerberg-facebook-immigration-donald-trump-2016-election-216327+&cd=3&hl=en&ct=clnk&gl=uk.

28. Sarah McBride and Alina Selyukh, 'Exclusive: Elon Musk quits Zuckerberg's immigration advocacy group', Reuters, 10 May 2013, uk.reuters.com/article/

net-us-usa-immigration-technology-idUSBRE94910K20130510+&cd= 14&hl=en&ct=clnk&gl=uk.

29. Issie Lapowsky, 'What tech giants are spending millions lobbying for', *Wired*, 23 July 2015, https://www.wired.com/2015/07/google-facebook-amazon-lobbying/+&cd=1&hl=en&ct=clnk&gl=uk and Andy Kroll, 'Execs at Facebook, Google, Apple, and Other Tech Giants Sign Letter Opposing Trump's Immigration Order', *Mother Jones*, 2 February 2017, www.motherjones.com/politics/2017/02/facebook-google-apple-ceos-slam-trump-immigration-order%3Ffb_comment_id%3D1395515653855628_1396081977132329+ &cd=2&hl=en&ct=clnk&gl=uk.

30. Gabe Rottman, 'On Leak Prosecutions, Obama Takes it to 11. (Or Should We Say 526?)', ACLU, 14 October 2014, https://www.aclu.org/blog/leak-prosecutions-obama-takes-it-11-or-should-we-say-526.

31. Society of Professional Journalists, Letter to President Obama, 10 August 2015, http://spj.org/pdf/news/obama-letter-final-08102015.pdf. Paul Farhi, 'Obama keeps newspaper reporters at arm's length', *Washington Post*, 10 February 2013, https://www.washingtonpost.com/lifestyle/style/obama-keeps-newspaper-reporters-at-arms-length/2013/02/10/3638c5ae-7082-11e2-ac36-d8d9dcaa2e2_story.html?utm_term=.799ebf9ff0f4 and Christina Bellantoni and Katelyn Polantz, 'White House reporters frustrated with Obama administration', PBS, 19 February 2013, http://www.pbs.org/newshour/rundown/white-house-faces-scrutiny-from-press-corps-with-little-access/.

32. Ibid.

33. Quoted in Bellantoni and Polantz, op. cit.

34. Scott Bomboy, 'Trump just trails record opening pace for executive orders', Constitution Center, 15 February 2017, http://blog.constitutioncenter.org/2017/02/trump-just-trails-record-opening-pace-for-executive-orders/.

35. Julia Oliver and Mariem Malouche, 'Rise of non-tariff protectionism amid global uncertainty', World Bank, 31 January 2012, blogs.worldbank.org/growth/rise-non-tariff-protectionism-amid-global-uncertainty+&cd=8&hl= en&ct=clnk&gl=uk. WTO, 'WTO report says restrictive trade measures continue to rise in G-20 economies', 6 November 2014, www.wto.org/english/news_e/news14_e/trdev_05nov14_e.htm+&cd=6&hl=en&ct=clnk&gl=uk. European Commission, 'Commission report Points to Rising Global Protectionism', 21 June 2016, trade.ec.europa.eu/doclib/press/index.cfm%3Fid%3D1513+&cd=3&hl=en&ct=clnk&gl=uk.

36. Michael Edison Hayden, 'Students Walk Out in Solidarity with Immigrants as Anti-Trump Protests Continue', ABC News, 16 November 2016, http://abcnews.go.com/Politics/students-walk-solidarity-immigrants-anti-trump-protests-continue/story?id=43588609.

37. Tim Henderson, 'Will Small "Sanctuary Cities" Defy a Trump Crackdown?', Pew Charitable Trust, 1 December 2016, www.pewtrusts.org/en/research-and-analysis/blogs/stateline/2016/12/1/will-small-sanctuary-cities-defy-a-trump-crackdown+&cd=3&hl=en&ct=clnk&gl=uk.
38. Hamilton Electors, http://www.hamiltonelectors.com/.
39. Ed Pilkington, 'Teen becomes seventh "faithless elector" to protest Trump as president-elect', *Guardian*, 30 November 2016, https://www.theguardian.com/us-news/2016/nov/30/faithless-electors-electoral-college-donald-trump.
40. Our Revolution, https://ourrevolution.com.
41. Greg Palast, 'Greg Palast: By Rejecting Recount, Is Michigan Covering Up 75,000 Ballots Never Counted?', *Democracy Now!*, 13 December 2016, https://www.democracynow.org/2016/12/13/greg_palast_by_rejecting_recount_is.
42. Greg Palast, 'The GOP's Stealth War Against Voters', *Rolling Stone*, 24 August 2016, http://www.rollingstone.com/politics/features/the-gops-stealth-war-against-voters-w435890.
43. Palast, *Democracy Now!*, op. cit.

Index

Books to challenge  *your perception of reality*

A message from Clairview

We are an independent publishing company with a focus on cutting-edge, non-fiction books. Our innovative list covers current affairs and politics, health, the arts, history, science and spirituality. But regardless of subject, our books have a common link: they all question conventional thinking, dogmas and received wisdom.

Despite being a small company, our list features some big names, such as Booker Prize winner Ben Okri, literary giant Gore Vidal, world leader Mikhail Gorbachev, modern artist Joseph Beuys and natural childbirth pioneer Michel Odent.

So, check out our full catalogue online at
www.clairviewbooks.com
and join our emailing list for news on new titles.

office@clairviewbooks.com

CLAIRVIEW